D0948445

BRIAN MOORE

NOVELS BY BRIAN MOORE

Judith Hearne	1955
The Feast of Lupercal	1958
The Luck of Ginger Coffey	1960
An Answer From Limbo	1963
The Emperor of Ice Cream	1966
I Am Mary Dunne	1968
Fergus	1971
The Revolution Script	1972
Catholics	1972
The Great Victorian Collection	1975
The Doctor's Wife	1976
The Mangan Inheritance	1979
The Temptation of Eileen Hughes	1981
Cold Heaven	1983
Black Robe	1985
The Colour of Blood	1987
Lies of Silence	1990
No Other Life	1993
The Statement	1995
The Magician's Wife	1997

BRIAN MOORE

A BIOGRAPHY

PATRICIA CRAIG

BLOOMSBURY

Grateful acknowledgement is made to: Faber and Faber Ltd, London for permission to reproduce 'Remembering Malibu' by Seamus Heaney, and lines from 'Clearances' by Seamus Heaney; to the Blackstaff Press, Belfast for permission to reproduce lines from 'Kites in Spring' by John Hewitt; and to the Marvell Press, England and Australia for permission to reproduce 'Going' by Philip Larkin.

First published 2002

Bloomsbury Publishing Plc, 38 Soho Square, London W1D 3HB

A CIP catalogue record for this book is available from the British Library

ISBN 0 7475 6004 8

10 9 8 7 6 5 4 3 2

Typeset by Hewer Text Ltd, Edinburgh
Printed in Great Britain by Clays Ltd, St Ives plc

ACKNOWLEDGEMENTS

I should like to thank the following for help and encouragement of various kinds: first the Authors' Foundation, the Arts Council of Northern Ireland, and An Comhairle Ealaion, whose award of small grants, including travel grants, at crucial moments proved invaluable. I am indebted to many individuals for information and other assistance, and should like in particular to express my gratitude to the following: Diana Athill, Julian Barnes, Ann Barr, Scott Bradfield, Mary Cadogan, Liz Calder, Douglas and Marie Carson, Patrick Carville, the late Dr Rory Casement, Marlys Chevrefils, Eveleen Coyle, the late Mrs N.T. Craig, Peter Crookston, Mrs Eibhlin Darbyshire, Gerald Dawe, Dr Niall Dempsey, Brice Dickson, John Wilson Foster, Philip French, Michael Paul Gallagher, Sue Gordon, John Gross, Seamus Heaney, Patrick Hicks, Mrs Clodagh Hopkirk, Georgina Howell, Mrs Peggy Igoe, Neil Johnston, Pat Kavanagh, Gerry Keenan, Jean Hanff Korelitz, Hermione Lee, Michael and Edna Longley, Roisin McAuley, John McCabe, Bernard McCloskey, Cal McCrystal, Mrs Eilis McDowell, Gareth McGrath, Gerard McNamee, Mrs Una Maguire and the late Dr Diarmuid Maguire, Derek Mahon, Patricia Mallon, D.E.S. Maxwell, Naomi and Nigel May, John Kennedy Melling, John Minihan, John Montague, Sister Anne (Eilis Moore), Jean Moore, Michael Moore, the late Dr Sean Moore and Mrs Cynthia Moore, Dr Seamus Moore, Jeffrey Morgan, Paul Muldoon, Maureen Murphy, Brian O'Hara, Paddy O'Hara, Stanley and Judy Price, Archie Reid, the late Mordecai Richler, the late Robert Rubens, Mrs Aimie Stammers, Appolonia Steele, Robert Sullivan, Mary Tomlinson, Charles Walker, William and Magda Weintraub, Mrs Peggy Weir, Robert and Marie Whiter.

for Jeffrey Morgan

CONTENTS

INTRODUCTION

The only wise prediction to make about a new Brian Moore novel is that it will be unpredictable and wise. Supremely clear-headed and clear-hearted, he is the best living novelist of conscience.

Christopher Ricks, Review of *Black Robe, Observer*

BRIAN MOORE DIED IN Malibu, California, on 11 January 1999. He was seventy-seven. His death made front-page headlines the following morning in the Belfast paper the *Irish News*. He might have taken a certain ironic pleasure in this: the *Irish News*, a Catholic nationalist paper, represented much of what he was in flight from, when he shook the dust of Belfast off his heels in 1943. Moreover, the paper was one esteemed by his father, Dr James Bernard Moore, who – according to the novelist – 'died thinking I was a wimp'.[1] This was not true, as we shall see; but Dr Moore would indeed have liked his second son to uphold the family status by going on to Queen's University to study medicine, a course unfortunately not available to him because of his failure to gain the necessary marks in his maths exam. In a family of believers and exam-passers, Brian was the odd man out, the maverick storyteller, the agnostic cuckoo in the prayerful nest. Finding himself in an awkward position, throughout his childhood, he wished he was like the rest of them, or else in a different cultural setting altogether – French for preference. All the time, though, his critical and creative faculties were being wonderfully stimulated by all the things he had to react against – religion, politics, pettiness and stupefaction on all sides, the looming presence of Victorian forebears. Unbeknownst to himself and everyone else, he was accumulating the material and evolving the outlook that would put him in the first rank of Irish novelists of the twentieth century. The apparent underachiever was destined to outstrip the conventional progress of many of his contemporaries. He was an old boy, he joked, whom his school, St Malachy's College in Belfast, 'both claimed and disclaimed', and for a long time the same was true of his native city, in which he was held in a somewhat ambivalent regard. If he reflected credit on the place, it was by way of castigating it, which made it hard for those at home to know what to make of him, whether to applaud or succumb to umbrage. ('Novelist flays his native city', etc.)

But slowly, Belfast (for the most part) was won over, as Brian Moore's novels began to make an impact internationally, as prize after prize was heaped on his head, and as it became clear that an exasperated affection, or at least a sense of an ineradicable bond, underlay his attacks on the scourges, and the dreariness, of Northern Irish society as he first knew it. It was what had set him off. ('The door closes at twenty,' he was fond of quoting, after Mauriac.) Of course – as a novelist famous for the variety of his literary concerns – he moved on and away from Belfast as a subject for fiction, to encompass new, sophisticated worlds and show himself a master of every literary mode from impassive surrealism to comic naturalism. By the time he died, he had made his mark on Belfast – and Belfast, through him, had made its mark in a branch of literature (prose fiction) not previously associated with it. There was no carping or begrudgery, in the Northern Irish press, about the responses to his death.

For quite a long time, however, a question mark had remained over the tag, Irish novelist. In the 1950s and '60s, literary Ireland was still thought of as quintessentially rural, pietistic and picturesque, despite the best efforts of satirists such as a Flann O'Brien, and the arrival of a fresh, disabused contingent of writers who included John McGahern, Aidan Higgins and Edna O'Brien: even these somehow confirmed the stereotype at the same time as dismantling it. Their novels signalled a new approach to Irish matters, but not, by and large, a new subject-matter. Among this lot, his near contemporaries, Brian Moore was the odd man out yet again. He told the story of how he'd gone into a Dublin bookshop and asked if they had any novels by the Irish writer, Brian Moore. No, he was told; but they did have one or two novels by the Canadian writer of the same name. Well, it was true that *Judith*

Hearne had won an award as a first novel by a *Canadian* novelist, its author having by that time opted for Canadian citizenship. A documentary film made about him in 1985 began portentously by intoning, 'Brian Moore: at home everywhere – and nowhere.' If Northern Ireland had shaped him, Canada freed him to become a writer, London took a chance and published him, America became his home . . . In the end, he derived a certain pleasure from the fact that he seemed to be unclassifiable by nationality, allegiance or literary practice: this is a large motif in his life story. However, 'If you began in Ireland, Ireland remains the norm,' Elizabeth Bowen said,[2] 'like it or not,' and this was indeed true for Brian Moore. For him, the process of deracination was always a partial and fraught affair. The critic Terry Eagleton[3] made the humorous (but also the serious) point, 'It's hard not to see his fiction as among other things a set of elaborate strategies for rationalising his reluctance to live [in Ireland].' But you have to add that, in his life, as in his books, he was the last person to make a fuss: an Ulster reticence and self-mockery kept him wary of dramatising any of his concerns.

Seamus Heaney, who became a friend, described him as 'sweet-natured' – but always with a novelist's vigilance and curiosity about the world around him.[4] Everyone who knew him was struck by Brian Moore's immense affability; however, lapses from this state were known to occur, especially during social occasions as the evening wore on and zestful gossip gave way to something a bit more argumentative or rebarbative. Tales were told of the odd ferocious quarrel, including one with friend and neighbour John Gregory Dunne. They were at a dinner party, when Dunne began vociferously praising some Hollywood producer of whom Brian had a low opinion. 'That schlockmeister,' he chimed in, in his most contemptuous tone. Things rapidly deteriorated. Dunne stormed out of the house, ignoring his hostess and everyone else; Brian, realising he had been a bit rude, followed after and, as Dunne got into his car, knelt down in front of it with arms outstretched, in a humorous gesture of apology. The other guests, who'd come to the front door to see what was going on, then began to shout, 'Brian, Brian – get up, get out of the way, he's got the car in gear!' (The director Tony Richardson, who was present, later declared that he hadn't had so much fun in years.) An accident was averted, the fracas blew over, the friendship was resumed (which didn't always happen whenever Brian got on bad terms with someone); and, after Brian Moore's death, John Gregory Dunne was quoted as saying, 'Brian, in every sense of the word, was a professional writer, the writer other writers loved to read, just to see how he did it.'[5] It was a well-directed tribute. Brian Moore worked – and made his novels work – by following his nose, eschewing dangerous influences and arriving at a complete understanding of the nature of his particular gift. For example – though he started off as a tremendous Joyce enthusiast, and remained one all his life, he might, as a writer, be placed at the opposite extreme from Joyce, and indeed from the whole modernist tradition with its denigration of plot-making as something a bit bourgeois and *passé*. Plot-making was his forte – and although that's not to say that he wasn't also an 'experimental' novelist, trying something new with each successive work, even his most exorbitant experiments were conducted with at least one foot on the ground.

Self-imposed exile, along with his well-known refusal to keep on writing the same book in a different guise, meant that Brian Moore did not have a fixed audience for his work, a deficiency he accepted as the price of his untrammelled unpredictability. Because his novels don't conform to a preordained pattern, each one, as it appeared, aroused strong opinions for and against. Mordecai Richler (for example) 'loved' *Catholics* but hated *The Great Victorian Collection*. The critic and broadcaster Philip French would place 'the Irish emigrant quintet' (*Judith Hearne* to *The Emperor of Ice Cream*) among the finest fiction of the twentieth century, but expressed reservations about some of the later novels, in particular *The Doctor's Wife*. The Irish critic and novelist John Banville has nominated *Judith Hearne* and *Cold Heaven* as the outstanding Moore achievements. Another critic and novelist, Colm Toíbín, disliked *Lies of Silence* but admired *Catholics*, *Black Robe* and the ubiquitous *Judith Hearne*. *Judith Hearne*, in fact, is the novel most serious readers of Brian Moore would want to enshrine. But we're all well able to argue passionately for the merits of this one or that one. For myself – I prefer the embittered vigour of *The Feast of Lupercal* to the downward spiral of *Judith Hearne*, the comedy of *Fergus* to the theology of *Catholics*, the poetic truth of *The Mangan Inheritance* to the 'holy vision' fabrication of *Cold Heaven*. And the one I read over and over is *The Emperor of Ice Cream*. And I found it impossible not to fall under the spell of the last published novel, *The Magician's Wife*, with its bedazzling evocations . . .

The collision of cultures, European and Arab, which is central to the plot of that novel, sets off reverberations going right back to colonial Ireland and its outcome in the Catholic/Protestant conflict of the author's childhood. That paradigmatic opposition surfaces every now and then in a different form – the *noirs* of *No Other Life* versus the Mulatto elite; the Quebec Liberation Front and Anglo-Canadian Montreal in *The Revolution Script*; *Black Robe*'s native Indians and French Jesuit missionaries. What adds complexity to these and other cultural clashes is the imaginative understanding extended not in one direction only, but to all factions, all those acting – as they believe – for the best. 'I find myself sympathetic to both sides of this argument (the Ecumenical and the Traditional),' Brian Moore wrote (in connection with *Catholics*) to his Jesuit friend Michael Paul Gallagher.[6] There is no repetition in Brian Moore's work but there are constants – and if this is one, you can point to others: a temperate virtuosity, for example, a tautness of style, the moment of crisis awaiting each protagonist.

His novels inevitably aroused a measure of controversy ('His best since . . .' 'Not what we expect from . . .'), but Brian Moore's literary status was assured, at least from *Catholics* on. For his hordes of admirers, the announcement of his death came as a tremendous blow; but for those closest to him, it was devastating. A week after his death in Malibu, a small group of mourners gathered at the Moore home, where Jean Moore's courage and stamina were put to the test. At one point, someone, trying to say the right thing, as one does on these occasions, observed to Michael Moore that Brian's death was a great loss to literature. Whereupon Brian's son – though he kept silent – felt a robust retort rising to his lips: 'Literature be blowed' (or words to that effect) '– he was my *father*.'[7]

Hermione Lee, a friend of Brian Moore's from the 1980s on, begins her biography of Virginia Woolf[8] by quoting Virginia Woolf: 'My God, how does one write a biography?'[9] It's a question that must exercise all would-be biographers. How do you overcome your sense of impertinence at attempting to summarise the events of anyone's life? How can you be sure the tone is right, let alone the facts? (Nothing is more irritating than the supposedly 'authoritative' work which proves to have taken no pains to guard against inaccuracy.) What do you do if your version of the subject doesn't correspond with that of others who knew him (or her) much better? If you've imposed your own *idées fixes* on top of the ascertainable information? In the end, there's nothing you can do, other than keeping these pitfalls constantly in mind, tackling your research as diligently as possible, following your instinct and hoping for the best. It's not a recipe for success, indeed, but it might reduce the likelihood of egregious failure.

I first read Brian Moore in the 1960s, beginning at the beginning with *Judith Hearne*, which was recommended to me by a friend in a spirit of comic warning about the fate of the non-marriageable in Belfast. Not knowing what to expect, I opened the book and read: 'By the holy, thought Mr Molloy (the rake), that one wouldn't be an occasion of sin for any man . . . On the wrong side of forty with a face as plain as a plank.' And: 'Royal Avenue was asleep, a wet grey belt studded with garish street lamps.' I was captivated. I then scoured libraries and second-hand bookshops for other titles by this addictive author, who – unimaginably – had started life in backward old Belfast, whatever glamorous locality he might inhabit at present. It didn't take me long to discover some mild similarities between myself and my new literary front-runner. We'd both been bored at Mass in childhood, had been ill served by our schools, and had left Northern Ireland as soon as an opportunity presented itself. (Unlike him, though, I went with some reluctance – only as far as London – and returned for good a couple of years ago.) It turned out that my mother had been friendly with one of Brian Moore's sisters, a fellow student at Queen's University in the 1930s. One or two other exiguous connections came to light much later. The Casement girls, sisters of Brian Moore's schoolfriends Rory and Enda Casement, both became teachers and taught me (French and English) at the rotten school I went to, where they were almost the only normal and enlightened members of the staff. And a writer I got to know a bit at the end of his life, Michael McLaverty, had conducted Brian Moore, as a schoolboy, round the slums of Belfast on behalf of the Catholic Charity, the St Vincent de Paul Society.

None of this would have amounted to a brass farthing, of course, if it hadn't been for the remarkable series of novels which appeared in the bookshops at tantalising intervals – novels written from, and about, all corners of the globe, it seemed, from Montreal, New York, Los Angeles, Nova Scotia – a world away from the glooms of Belfast. I'd fall on these as they came hot off the press, but I didn't actually get to meet their author until 1988, when the *Observer* sent me to interview him in London in connection with the television film of *The Temptation of Eileen Hughes*. In the same year, I'd been asked to contribute to the Brian Moore 'Special Issue' of the *Irish University Review*, for which I wrote an appraisal of his early Belfast novels under the title 'Moore's Maladies'. When he wrote to the editor, Christopher Murray, to thank him for putting the issue together, Brian Moore specified this piece, along with articles by Seamus Deane and Brian Cosgrove, as the three that had pleased him most (largely because they were new to him). He added: 'I had always thought that Patricia Craig, from her reviews and from her promised book on Ulster fiction, might turn out to be a head-mistress who would chastise me. However, I met her in London recently and was quite enchanted by her . . .'[10] This was encoura-ging, even though I knew he'd liked me partly because I reminded him of one of his favourite MacNeill cousins. However, it wasn't for another eight years or so that I wrote to him to sound out his attitude to a potential biography. To my immense gratification, he was enthusiastic about the idea; and some time later, with his full co-operation, I began work on the project. The Moore trail took me to Clifton Street in Belfast – sadly depleted from its days as a doctors' enclave – and the Lower Antrim Road, where his hated school is situated; to darkest Antrim (Ballymena) and the furthest reaches of Donegal; to New York, Los Angeles, Montreal, south Nova Scotia (not to mention Calgary where the Moore Papers are located).

Along the way – as well as experiencing the legendary Moore hospitality – I received an enormous amount of help from a number of individuals. Brian Moore's nephew Brian O'Hara, for example, proved an invaluable source of information about the Moore family background. And I am immeasurably indebted to Brian Moore's Montreal friend Bill Weintraub, who supplied me with photocopies of the entire correspondence between the two of them, from the early 1950s to 1979 (alas, after that date they kept in touch mostly by telephone), as well as taking me on a guided tour of

Brian Moore's haunts in Montreal, complete with compelling commentary. Brian's sister, Mrs Una Maguire, provided sparkling reminiscence, letters and photographs. Brian Moore himself and his wife Jean could not have been more co-operative, or more concerned to keep me on the right track (if I've got off it at any point, it's in spite of their best efforts, and because of my own foibles).

I remember an evening in Nova Scotia, the three of us, myself, Brian and Jean, seated at the dinner table, the bay outside the windows behind us luminescent in the fading light, and Brian suddenly turning to me: 'You know, you're a bit like the skeleton at the feast.' Jean immediately began to remonstrate with him, fearing he'd spoken out of turn: but it was plain what he meant, he was expressing a measure of apprehension over the prospect of having his life dug into, raked over, even possibly misrepresented, by someone who barely knew him. He was trusting me not to make a hash of it, but obviously he had no guarantee that his trust was not misplaced. And, when he mentioned the skeleton at the feast, it's possible he was thinking more along the lines of skeletons in cupboards; well, everyone's life contains episodes they'd rather not dwell on, along with material just too personal to warrant exposure to the public view. (It's perhaps not without significance that a few of the novels begun and abandoned by Brian Moore, during the 1950s, for example, were more overtly autobiographical than those he completed – well, with the exception of the glorious *Emperor of Ice Cream*. It seems he needed a certain distance between his own experiences and the events he depicted to raise the narrative to a level of imaginative authenticity.)

On the same occasion, we got talking about Brian's relative by marriage, one-time President of University College Dublin, Dr Michael Tierney; and Brian made some comment to the effect that Dr Tierney's credentials included the possession of a gold *fainne* (ring), signalling fluency in the Irish language; I couldn't help chiming in that I had one of those too, having learned to speak Irish at the age of sixteen (and forgotten most of it since). Some months later, in London – again out of the blue – Brian said to me, 'You know the thing about you that impressed me most?' I hadn't the least idea what he was going to come out with, but it turned out it was that gold *fainne*; clearly, this was not an uncomplicated individual I was dealing with. The truth was that five of Brian Moore's six sisters were Irish-speakers, though he and his brothers weren't (the way the children were educated is one of the Moore family mysteries). He could, indeed, have learned the language if he'd chosen – and late in life he regretted not having done so; but, at the time, proficiency in Irish was tied up with the rest of the provincial Catholic package that caused him so much angst. The fact that it had become a cause of approval was indicative of the unending complexities in his attitude to Belfast, and Irishness, and his upbringing, and the whole Gaelic heritage.

On top of the shock occasioned by Brian Moore's death (since I'd got to know him slightly, as well as getting to know a fair amount about his lifetime's experiences), came the sense of a setback, on the professional level. I had of course intended to submit the completed manuscript to his scrutiny, in order to ensure, as far as possible, that puzzling matters might be addressed, and errors of fact got rid of. This I was not able to do. Fortunately, I had completed many hours of taped interviews with him (most quotations in the text which are not attributed come from these); and also the testimonies of friends, relations, professional associates and so on have – I hope – helped to produce a reasonably rounded-out portrayal. Then – as I've indicated – I was given exclusive access to a solid block of correspondence, and to the work diaries which he kept for many years, as well as other documents at his Malibu home. The Brian Moore Papers at the University of Calgary are, of course, a primary source of material for any student of his life or work; and my researches there were greatly helped by the kindness of Appolonia Steele and Marlys Chevrefils. My greatest debts, however, are to Brian Moore, and to Jean Moore, whose instinct for self-efface-ment[11] is only equalled by her wish to see her husband's achieve-ment properly acknowledged and upheld. If this biography goes any way towards furthering that objective, then it will have fulfilled an important part of its purpose.

Success did not come easily to Brian Moore: it required work, work, work, stubbornness and perseverance. At the same time, he led an intriguing life, first in the unruly city he turned his back on, then in locations as far removed as possible, geographically and spiritually, from the exactions and exacerbations of his birthplace.

The Second World War got him out of Belfast, and in on the edge of historic events, delivering some of the drama he'd craved as a thrill-deprived boy. Each phase of his life is marked by a distinctive outline and atmosphere, from the indefatigable days at the *Montreal Gazette*, all ebullience and journalistic banter, to the Hollywood of Hitchcock and beyond. A measure of social uncertainty, the lot of any Belfast boy let loose in a larger world, came out in incidents such as his nervous insistence to an interviewer scanning the bookshelves in one of his rented Hollywood houses that the books in question were absolutely nothing to do with him; however, as the years passed and his place in the world became unassailable, he acquired correspondingly exalted tastes in food, clothes, hotels and so forth, along with the confidence to take the smartest of literary and social *milieux* in his stride. He never steered clear of a risk; indeed, in retrospect, his life can be seen to arrange itself into a series of decisions which seemed fearfully dodgy at the time, but actually proved to be propitious. A talent for self-regeneration kept him always on the right path, even if the way forward sometimes seemed a bit indirect. What follows is basically a success story, the story of someone who achieved almost everything he set out to achieve: literary recognition, prosperity, sexual fulfilment, love, fatherhood, the exhilaration of a full engagement with his proper work. But obstacles aplenty, along with idiosyncrasies both circumstantial and temperamental, save this story from being in any sense bland; it has, on the contrary, a pungency and an edge of precariousness extending beyond Brian Moore's own lifetime into a hazy realm of Irish political history and social advancement.[12] It begins – or one strand of it begins – in Ballymena, Co. Antrim, Northern Ireland.

I

OLD BALLYMENA

They all knew him, or knew of him . . . yes, his mother was a Henry on her mother's side – his father passed away some years ago; every one of them had read the funeral report at the time. They were great readers of obituaries. They could, with their inexhaustible genealogical knowledge, have traced Mr Devine's family back for three generations; and most of them, seeing him enter, assembled the opening moves of this favourite game.

The Feast of Lupercal

A cobble thrown a hundred years ago
Keeps coming at me, the first stone
Aimed at a great-grandmother's turncoat brow.
The pony jerks and the riot's on.
She's crouched low in the trap
Running the gauntlet that first Sunday
Down the brae to Mass at a panicked gallop.
He whips on through the town to cries of 'Lundy!'

THERE'S A TYPICAL NORTHERN Irish story behind this poem[1] of Seamus Heaney's. The poet's Protestant great-grandmother, whose name was Robinson, married a man called McKeever and converted to Catholicism. The first Sunday she set out in pony-and-trap to attend Mass at Milltown Chapel on the road between Castledawson and Magherafelt in Co. Derry (opposite the present 'County Grounds' of the Gaelic Athletic Association), a minor riot was sparked off, complete with the usual taunts and stone-throwing. (This would have been in the 1860s or '70s.) The incident passed into family lore[2] without being magnified or excessively dwelt on. It was no big deal. You have only to consider the numbers of Protestants bearing Catholic surnames (Mahon, MacNeice) and vice versa (Carson, Adams) to twig the pervasiveness of ancestral exogamy. We're a more cross-bred lot than some of us care to acknowledge. And the initial transfer of allegiance, given the inflammable nature of conditions prevailing in the North, can't be hoped to take place painlessly.

Heaney's pungent set-piece, in other words, encompasses an outbreak of sectarian outrage which is doomed, it seems, to be enacted *ad infinitum*, and in every corner of the province. Some fifteen miles to the north-east of Castledawson is the Co. Antrim market town of Ballymena (population in the nineteenth century between 4,000 and 7,000), and here, in the 1850s, the homes of a law clerk named James B. Moore and his wife Eleanor, or Ellen, O'Rawe – first at Lawn View Place, and then at Bryan Street – were subjected to a ritual stoning by Orangemen each year on the Twelfth of July. James B. Moore (1832–80) was a Protestant, or Presbyterian, turned Catholic: and his family was made to suffer accordingly. Not that they made any more of this than the Heaney– McCann–McKeever contingent mentioned above; they simply sat it out, or rose above it. Everyone in Northern Ireland knew the Twelfth was a time of the year when passions ran high; and in the late 1850s these were possibly running higher than ever, due to the religious fervour which suddenly overwhelmed the district. 'From the North of Antrim, where the first manifestations were displayed, the fire spread rapidly south, until by midsummer, 1859, the whole of Presbyterian Ulster was ablaze.'[3] The social commen- tator James Winder Good is describing here not an actual con- flagration, but the outbreak of swooning and vision-seeing hysteria which briefly displaced the Calvinist element in Presbyterianism – whipped up, at least in part, by the anti-Papist outpourings of such intemperate clerics as the Rev. Henry Cooke (1788–1868), who waged incessant war 'against fierce democracy on the one hand, and more terrible Popery on the other'.[4]

It wasn't, on the face of it, an expedient move on James Moore's part to convert to Catholicism.[5] He was the son of a Ballyclare shoemaker, another James Moore, and his wife Catherine Bing- ham; for some reason, James junior became apprenticed to a

Ballymena solicitor named Alexander O'Rourke who happened to be a Catholic, though his own interest in that religion seems to have predated this career move. It also predated his marriage to Ellen O'Rawe, so we can't look to that to explain his conversion. A genuine theological conviction must have been at the root of it. Ellen O'Rawe (1836–1924) was the granddaughter of a Bryan O'Rawe (c.1750–1831), a Ballymena businessman, after whom a street in the town – Bryan Street – is said to be named.[6] This naming, or renaming, must have taken place after 1798, when the town consisted of Bridge Street, Mill Street, Castle Street, Church Street and Linen Hall Street, the last ending in an area known as the Shambles, the slaughtering ground of pigs and cattle. Bryan O'Rawe was one of only two Catholics among the crowd of loyalists who defended the Market House[7] against the raggedy troop of insurgents storming into Ballymena armed with pikes, muskets and whatever else they could lay their hands on, and making a fearful racket by blowing glass-trumpets, French horns and conch-shells. The date was 7 June 1798. Amid episodes of farce and confusion – at one point half the population seemed to be lying about the street, non-combatants having been knocked off their feet by charging Unitedmen, as they tried to remove themselves from the scene of action[8] – the victory went first one way, as a barrel of blazing tar was flung at the Market House, and then the other, as bit by bit the rebels were overmastered. These Antrim rebels, according to Moore family lore, included John O'Rawe, a son of Bryan, who was captured by yeomen and taken to his home to be executed. Fortunately his mother (née Nellie McManus) – so the story goes – was sufficiently in control of her wits to ply her son's captors with food and drink, while he escaped by hightailing it over a back wall, lying low for a time, and eventually making it to America.[9]

Ellen O'Rawe and her younger sister Mary were the children of Bryan O'Rawe's son Bernard,[10] who must have been pretty elderly (sixty at least) by the time they came along; it is possible that this was a second marriage for him. His wife, the mother of these late daughters, was Margaret Jane McAuley (d.1845) of Randalstown, whose father, Thomas McAuley, had been a Protestant; the further back you go in Moore family history, it seems, the more denominationally tangled it becomes. (You also get the same names recurring: McNally, McAuley, McManus, O'Loan.) Brian Moore's grandfather (on his father's side), then, was a Protestant-turned Catholic, while his O'Rawe grandmother was a Catholic with a Protestant grandfather, one of the – apparently – well-to-do McAuleys of Crumlin, Co. Antrim. Margaret Jane – Brian Moore's great-grandmother – was an O'Loan on her mother's side, grand-daughter of a Ballylesson farmer named Lawrence O'Loan, who is buried in Ballyclug[11] graveyard beside the ruins of a tiny school-house now almost entirely obliterated by ivy. (He'd have been the novelist's great-great-great-grandfather.) The resting place of Bryan O'Rawe, and at least one of his sons (William), is in Skerry graveyard on a hillside beyond Broughshane. Skerry, which faces Slemish Mountain, is the ancient burial ground of the Ulster O'Neills, and a place from which you get stupendous views of the mid-Antrim countryside rolling away in all directions. It's hard, indeed, to understand why this windswept height was chosen as the setting for a church (now a ruin) and graveyard (now overgrown, and with only a handful of weatherbeaten gravestones remaining upright); difficulties faced by funeral processions, especially in winter, heading upwards bearing a coffin through narrow, twist-ing, muddy, gorse-strewn pathways, over stiles and ditches, must have been nearly insurmountable.[12] Perhaps respect for the dead was incorporated into the feat of getting them buried. More likely, Skerry's inaccessibility is a legacy from the Penal days, when Catholic Ireland had to keep its rituals well away from public view. At any rate, in 1831 – two years after the Catholic Emanci-pation Act, and with violent clashes between Orangemen and Ribbonmen taking place all over the North – the body of Bryan O'Rawe, one-time defender of the Ballymena Market House, was escorted up here. The remains of a good many of Brian Moore's ancestors and relatives are dotted about this part of Antrim, down to his parents and (most recently) his sister Grainne, who died in 1997. (The last three are less picturesquely interred at Crebilly, Ballymena.)

A couple of Bryan O'Rawe's grandsons entered the church: Father William John McAuley, nicknamed 'the Big Priest', and his brother Father Bernard McAuley (sons of O'Rawe's daughter Catherine, or Kitty[13]). The latter pops up in 1827, representing his church in a three-day debating contest held at Ballymena, with a

Protestant clergyman, the Rev. Robert Stewart, as his opponent.[14] (These theological disputations, open to the public, were popular at the time.) The McAuley priests were Ellen O'Rawe's first cousins – though considerably older – and they survived long enough to make an impression on the next generation, as we shall see. The third – non-surviving – McAuley brother (Dan) was a doctor who practised in Ballymena, and – with only three associates – treated victims of the cholera epidemic which followed hard on the heels of the Famine. (This would have been in 1848 or '49.) Every town and village in Ireland has its Famine stories and this is one of Ballymena's: four brave men doing what had to be done for the sick and dying, while ostracised by their panic-stricken neighbours as fear of infection held the town in its grip. Among these Good Samaritans was Archie MacNeill, who went on to marry Rosetta McAuley (a cousin of the priests and Dr Dan) and, in due course, became the father of Eoin MacNeill – 'Uncle John' to Brian and the other young Moores. Archie survived, but Dr Dan paid the price for his foolhardy humanity. Like the poet John Hewitt's great-grand-mother, who, for a charitable action, 'accepted in return the Famine fever',[15] Dr Dan came home one day, threw up all over the dress of his cousin Rosetta, collapsed and died shortly afterwards.[16] (This incident was often recalled emotionally by Rosetta MacNeill in her old age.)

Ballymena in the mid-nineteenth century was a rather Calvinist, sobersided sort of place (except on Saturday evening, when drunkards flocking in from the surrounding countryside created a different impression),[17] not too clean – in wet weather, women could hardly walk the narrow streets without ruining their skirts and petticoats – and not much given to amusement or sociability, preferring instead to concentrate on trade and commerce in the interests of getting ahead. All Ballymena's energies went into money-making (well, leaving party politics aside). Unforthcoming, plain and inurbane, the town has never attracted many tourists or newcomers into its environs. It keeps itself to itself. A shopkeepers' and businessmen's centre, it goes about its affairs without fuss.

Ballymena was among the towns of the North whose development was hastened by the Industrial Revolution, as mills and factories became an inescapable ingredient of Ulster life – a circumstance that benefited some, and disadvantaged others. The local poet David Herbison, for example, who was born in 1800, takes a poor view of what he sees as progress gone haywire, applauding the simpler industrial arrangements of the past – 'We then had nae drapers the poor to oppress' – and crying out, at the same time, against newfangled enormities:

> Could our forefathers rise frae the grave whaur they lie
> And see the steam engine at speed passing by,
> They surely wad say that the foul fiend himsel'
> Was stealing awa' the big bellows o' hell;
> Or could they be here on a wild wintry night,
> When Luna is wrapped in her shroud frae our sight,
> And see the gas light in its glory burst out
> Dispelling the danger o' darkness and doubt
> Again they wad say owercome wi' surprise
> That we had brought down a' the stars frae the skies . . .[18]

Trains and gas lighting had reached Ballymena by 1853, the year in which Herbison composed his exercise in nostalgia. He looks about him and what does he see but streets being widened everywhere, buildings under construction, the 'auld clock', the castle and its garden swept away, cars and coaches, women in hooped frocks wearing silly plumes on their heads. The pretentiousness of it all provokes him to mockery (artless but ardent):

> They [i.e. Ballymena's *nouveaux riches*] winna sit down as our
>   forefathers sat
> On cauld flags o' whinstane to hae a while's chat
> Their seats maun be cushioned, or sit they'll not sit,
> At them I aft laugh till my sides like to split . . .

What he wants is to restore to Ballymena a rosy rural past, full of spinning-wheels and apple-sellers, thatched houses with straw- and heather-strewn floors, and kindness to the poor. It was never like that, indeed; it's just a poetic conceit to formalise the backward look. But Herbison is an astute social commentator nevertheless, and this poem in particular is abundant in local detail.

As Herbison noted, new stone-built houses, of one, two or three storeys, some thatched but mostly slated, were going up rapidly to accommodate the influx of mill employees, traders of all kinds, business and professional people, whose arrival was accelerating the pace of life in Ballymena. By 1849 – with the town still reeling from the effects of the Famine – the seventeen-year-old James Moore must already have come over from Ballyclare to take up his apprenticeship. It's likely that he lodged with his employer Alexander O'Rourke – who, noticing the young Presbyterian's sympathetic interest in Catholicism, loaned him books on the subject.[19] According to family lore, this is the year in which James Moore first caught sight of his future wife Ellen O'Rawe, who – at thirteen – was teaching a class of younger children in a Sunday School. Ellen and her sister Mary were only nine and six years old, respectively, when their mother died; at this distressing moment, their Aunt Mary McNally (born O'Rawe) treated them with great kindness.[20]

She might, indeed, have been their great-aunt; her own daughter Ellen was born in 1812, which makes her twenty-four years older than her cousin Ellen O'Rawe.[21] This Ellen (McNally) went to school at the Moravian Settlement at Gracehill,[22] just outside Ballymena, which seems to have operated a non-denominational policy; at any rate, some Catholic children, in the pre-Emancipation era, acquired some learning there. Ellen McNally grew up resolutely spinsterish, set up home with her brother Frank at a house called Wilderness Lodge, and scuppered Frank's one matrimonial bid – whereupon he took to drink. *She* lived on and on, surviving to attend the wedding of James and Ellen Moore's youngest daughter Agnes, who married Eoin MacNeill in 1898. 'Cousin Ellen': it's like something out of *Cranford*.[23] However, it should be remembered that this is Victorian Ballymena, distant and provincial and a bit uncouth, with cobbled streets and a smell of turf smoke pervading the atmosphere, and a Catholic *bourgeoisie* only just beginning to acquire a measure of self-confidence. All these O'Rawes and McAuleys and McNallys were solid citizens, well integrated into their community, wearers of buttoned-up waistcoats and frock-coats, employers of a good many domestic servants.

Some of them even got away from Ballymena. Francis O'Rawe (Ellen Moore's uncle) kept an apothecary's shop in Donegall Street, Belfast, where he practised as a doctor. Because of his good looks, the place was known as 'the handsome doctor's shop'. After Francis's death in 1860, the practice was taken over by a Dr Mulholland[24] who was equally handsome – so the tag still applied. Unfortunately the next incumbent, a Dr McWhirter, was a man of exceptional plainness. People went on referring to 'the handsome doctor's shop', but now the phrase, in a typically Belfast manner, was uttered with a derisive ring.

Francis never married. On his death his effects – 'under £450' – passed to his niece Ellen Moore, who also inherited her father's effects ('under £100') some years later. This would suggest her relatives had got over their disapproval of her marriage to James Moore, to which they'd put up a stiff opposition at the time, probably considering themselves a cut above a shoemaker's son and Presbyterian to boot. James, however, had been received into the Church by the time his marriage took place, on 3 September 1856, at All Saints, Ballymena, with the parish priest, the Rev. John Lynch, officiating. The young couple moved into a house at Lawn View Place and promptly set about the business of procreation. True to their time and place, they displayed a striking fecundity, engendering eleven offspring over a period of seventeen years. Indeed, this wasn't unusual. With a high infant mortality rate hanging over them, many Victorian parents must have felt they'd be back where they started if they didn't insure themselves against childlessness by being perpetually in a state of gestation. And – typical in this respect, as in many others – the Moores didn't succeed in keeping the family of eleven intact. Four never reached the age of three, and one died at fourteen. One became a nun, and one ran away from home.

The first four were girls. Elizabeth, born in December 1857, only lived until 1860. She was followed by Mary (Minnie) and Margaret (Maggie), both of whom lived to a ripe old age. Then came Elizabeth the second (Lizzie), a very plain girl who grew up religious and entered a convent in France. The first boy was John, born in 1865, who has all but disappeared from the family records – or at least, about whom conflicting stories are told. Johnny (as he was known) was the wayward one, the runaway, according to family tradition – though he's back home and among those present at the Moore/MacNeill wedding in 1898. He was possibly a gambler, or a drunkard: one story has him disappearing for years, only to be spotted eventually at a racetrack acting as a bookie's tout. It's a good story – however, what's more likely is that Johnny Moore held a respectable, if unexalted, position in a bank, and died fairly young. Did he really run away – and if so, was it family piety, overcrowding or small-town restriction that drove him to it? Did he give in to the lure of independence or adventure? Was he cleverer and more spirited than his younger brother, or less clever and not so well adjusted to the life around him? Was he greatly missed? What steps, if any, were taken to bring him home?

These questions are unanswerable. A whiff of the racetrack or stableyard is all that remains of Johnny Moore (well, in one version of the story), as he merges into the back lanes and outbuildings, the shabby lodgings and makeshift employments of late-nineteenth-century provincial Ulster. What's beyond conjecture is that it wasn't like this for his brother, the next in the family line. James Bernard, or James Brian,[25] the sixth Moore child, the great exam-passer and eventual father of the novelist, was pragmatic and self-reliant by nature. He was also a survivor. Born on 11 November 1867, James B. nearly got himself added to the family's casualty list before he was a year old. It wasn't long after the Fenian uprising, and although the movement[26] never really caught on in the North, where it had to contend with other forms of nationalist agitation such as Ribbonism,[27] it resulted in ' "Fenian" joining "Taig" at the top of the list of hostile epithets Protestants used for their Catholic neighbours'.[28] No doubt 'Fenian' was among the taunts hurled at the home of the turncoat James Moore the following Twelfth of July (1868), when the annual stoning of the house by Orangemen was taking place. It was a particularly vicious attack that year, probably in response to the recent – suppressed – uprising; and a huge stone smashing through a window narrowly missed the infant James B.[29]

The family home, this year at Hill Street, contained five children under nine, at least two adults and the usual contingent of servants: was it their proliferating progeny that caused the Moores' frequent moves? Five changes of address occurred over fourteen years – however, by 1870, when William Moore was born (he died in 1884), we find them established at High Street, Ballymena, and there they seem to have stayed. The family wasn't yet complete – Ellen Moore was born in 1871 (but died two years later); then came twins, Catherine and Agnes, of whom one lived for ten months, and the other for eighty-one years. The last child was the short-lived Alexander (Feb–Oct 1874). For a period of ten months, there were nine children in the house – but then two died in the same year, 1873. Those left behind must have gained a powerful sense of the precariousness of things. Contemporary photographs show an unsmiling, well-wrapped-up lot (apart from one of the three young brothers – $c.1875$ – in which James B. has a grin on his face). One of Minnie with a toddler on her lap – one of the twins, Taddie – shows a timorous, rather delicate face. Minnie, the oldest of the children after the death of the first Elizabeth, must have had to shoulder a fair share of the child-rearing burden. But it wasn't all infant burials, cowering under the table while drunken Orangemen rampaged outside, or learning by rote the Catechism of the Catholic Church. There were visits to Antrim Town to stay at Great-Aunt McNally's hotel, and other excursions. Agnes Moore – who was always called Taddie – recalled summers at a farm named Carnegies, in Glencloy,[30] the property of a relative, a Captain McAuley, whose ship had been used as a transport vessel during the Crimean War.[31] The little girl – this would have been during the 1870s or early '80s – was sent out with the maid each day to bring coffee[32] to the men working in the fields. On one occasion, Minnie went to Belfast to stay with her father's sister, a Mrs Ferguson, who lived in the Old Park district of the city. Once she got home, however, and reported that she'd been made to read the Bible every night before going to bed, her father put his foot down and refused to let her go there again. No doubt he feared that, given any encouragement, ancestral Presbyterianism might come out in her. He needn't have worried. Minnie eventually became a Dominican Tertiary, a kind of lay nun – indeed, a nun in all but the habit.

Though he did, in fact, breed a family of devout Catholics and nationalists, James Moore – the convert – was constantly on the look-out for proselytisers with designs on his children's allegiance, whether spiritual or political. There were dangers all around them. Taddie, his youngest daughter, was forbidden to join with her (Protestant) school choir in singing 'God Save the Queen' – and consequently forfeited the right to a solo performance at the school concert. Protestant schools still offered the best primary education in Ballymena; later, Taddie was packed off to school in Normandy, to continue her education with the Canonesses of St Augustine, where her sister Lizzie was a member of the Order.[33]

Interesting relatives came to visit the Moores, including the Big Priest ('Uncle Priest' within the family), Father William John McAuley, who frequently walked ten miles from his home at Glenravel to Ballymena for a chat with James and Ellen; and then thought nothing of walking back again. The Big Priest was something of a tease and joker. An old nurse of the Moores, Kitty Taffe by name, once went to Confession and was given the Seven Penitential Psalms as a penance for some transgression. Father McAuley got to hear of this and took great delight in interrupting her as she struggled through the fearsome imposition, only to announce that she must get the whole thing said in one go. The Penitential Psalms became a family joke. On another occasion, the Big Priest, turning up at High Street late in the evening, pretended to be very shocked to find young James B. still running about the place. Insisting that the child should go to bed immediately, he rang the bell for Kitty. However, when Kitty appeared, before Father McAuley had a chance to utter a word, the little boy piped up, 'Kitty, put Uncle Priest to bed.'[34]

Children's *bon mots* are always fun for adults in the family, and this one has survived to testify to the brightness and precocity of James B. Moore at the age of three or four. Nothing more is known of his early childhood; when he next comes into focus it's as a boy of thirteen, a pupil at St Malachy's College, Belfast and a recent semi-orphan. To go back a year or two, to 1877 – his father, after years of being a law clerk, had at last become a full-fledged solicitor and set up in practice on his own in Ballymena.[35] An announcement in the *Ballymena Observer* for Saturday, 10 February 1877 goes as follows: 'We are glad to understand that our townsman Mr James Moore of High Street has been admitted an attorney of the Courts of Common Law and Solicitor in Chancery'; and a month later, in the same paper, we find a reference to his first appearing for a defendant. But he didn't have long to enjoy his enhanced position. He caught pneumonia and died on 14 March 1880. He was forty-eight. His death marked the end of a chapter for the Moores – nothing was the same again. A week earlier, he'd made a will leaving everything he possessed to his wife Ellen. It's said he was building a house at the time of his death, and had sunk a good deal of money in this project – however, 'effects' in the region of £2,000 passed to Ellen and the rest of the family – quite a substantial sum in those days.[36]

In the autumn of the previous year – 1879 – James B. Moore, then aged twelve, had become a boarder at St Malachy's College in Belfast. St Malachy's – the diocesan college for Down and Connor – was established in 1833,[37] which puts it among the oldest Catholic secondary schools in Ireland.[38] It was essentially a training-ground for would-be clerics, but also catered for future professional men. In those early days, the school was virtually out in the country; the Crumlin and Antrim Roads, one to each side of it, had yet to be built. Pupils were marched down to Donegall Street, towards the city centre, for the bulk of their lessons, before the main school buildings went up in the late 1860s. After that date St Malachy's became a proper school, all-of-a-piece, with classrooms, refectory, chapel, library and study hall, and top-floor dormitory accommodation for a hundred boys. When James B. arrived in 1879, the college President – or Headmaster – was Dr Henry Henry; and a public examination system, with Exhibitions and prizes awarded to successful candidates, had just been set up.[39] James B. Moore, a natural scholar, an honours student and a boy unfazed by inter-schools competition, was an early beneficiary of this new system. It wasn't long before he gained an Exhibition in the Intermediate Examination, worth £15 a year and tenable for three years. This saw him through the rest of his schooling. Latin, Greek, English, Euclid, algebra, natural philosophy, chemistry: these were no trouble to him. In every respect he seems to have been an exemplary schoolboy, a champion of the examination halls.

In the autumn of 1881 James B. was joined at St Malachy's by his exact contemporary John, or Eoin, MacNeill (who went on to marry Taddie Moore). MacNeill, from the town of Glenarm on the Antrim coast, was already distantly connected to the Moore family through his mother Rosetta McAuley, and it's likely that the two boys already knew one another; at any rate, Taddie remembered visiting the MacNeills at Glenarm when she was very young, and being pointedly ignored by John and his brother James – both of them at an age when the society of girls was an embarrassment and annoyance. One, she said, 'nearly rubbed his clothes off against the wall, while the other walked off the sidewalk in the gutter in their anxiety to keep their distance'.[40] No doubt James B. was present on this occasion too. But it wasn't until they met at school – both boarders, and both Antrim men – that he and Eoin MacNeill became fast friends. ('They always told each other everything. They were . . . Cushendall boys together,' wrote James B.'s son in his second novel.) On Saturday afternoons, they'd have taken part together in the weekly boarders' walk, tailed by a teacher to ensure that order was kept: out the Antrim Road, down Gray's Lane, back again via York Street, turning up Donegall Street and into the newly built Clifton Street, thence reaching Carlisle Circus and the school. Dr Henry himself scrutinised the boys each week for signs of untidiness before they could set out and disgrace St Malachy's by looking less than spruce. Wearers of slovenly breeches were humiliated by being sent upstairs to change into something decent. Impeccable appearance, as well as behaviour, was required of these privileged, middle-class Victorian Catholic schoolboys.

The Belfast riots of 1886, following on from the defeat of Gladstone's first Home Rule Bill, brought a stop to these boarders' walks; the town was in uproar, as the worst violence of the nineteenth century got under way. Uprooted 'kidney pavers' (paving stones), a traditional Belfast form of rioting ammunition, were gathered in the aprons of 'vicious young women'[41] whose function was to egg stone-throwers on. Donegall Street, York Street, North Queen Street were all affected. In the dormitory at St Malachy's, according to Eoin MacNeill, 'night after night, we could listen to the sounds of war in the town outside'.[42] The excitement for pent-up boarders must have been tremendous. But it didn't keep St Malachy's seniors from getting on with their work. Both MacNeill and James B. were in the small university class (no more than six or seven pupils), along with Alexander Blayney, who went on to become a distinguished surgeon in Dublin, and Joe McNabb, later a Dominican writer and preacher (under the name of Father Vincent). By this stage, pupils had been whittled down to those likely to make their mark in one or other of the professions.

Ellen O'Rawe's sister Mary, three years her junior, had married a man named James McAllister, also to the consternation of her relatives; McAllister was a 'grocer's curate'[43] and considered vastly inferior to the important O'Rawes. When Mary finally agreed to marry him, the story goes, McAllister walked in triumph through the streets of Ballymena with his umbrella up, even though there wasn't a cloud in the sky.[44] It turned out, however, that James McAllister was a man of considerable commercial drive; he became a publican and importer of wines and spirits, and was soon considered exceedingly prosperous in the town. After James Moore's death in 1880, the McAllisters took Ellen and her children under their wing (they had a good many children themselves, and the cousins all seem to have knocked about happily together); it wasn't long before the Moores were installed in a semi-detached house, of recent construction, out on the Broughshane Road, the other half of which was occupied by the McAllisters. The families, indeed, became so intertwined that Taddie's and James B.'s children referred to Mary O'Rawe as 'Granny Callister' – though she was, of course, their great-aunt. The house, called Ardnagreina,[45] was a very substantial, suburban, three-storey, more or less inelegant, typical family villa of the period, complete with gables and glass-roofed porch. It's the kind of house outside which, in summer, you'd expect to see an assembly of well-dressed figures – the *paterfamilias* wearing a top hat even in his own front garden, a couple of matrons in black dresses with white lace collars, a nonchalant-looking youth or two, girls in leg-o'-mutton sleeves (one, clearly a hoyden, perched insecurely on a windowsill), the elderly relative with his blackthorn stick and huge St Bernard dog, the odd female visitor wearing an ornate hat: and, indeed, this describes Ardnagreina as it appears in a number of photographs.[46] It's a far cry from the sardonically rechristened Clabber Street,[47] for example, in the town centre – or for that matter from sectarian rumblings in the lower-class districts of Belfast.

Taddie, the youngest and prettiest of the Moore girls, was only eight years old when her father died. At the time, she would have had three brothers at school (Johnny, James B. and William); a sister (Lizzie) either already ensconced in the convent in Normandy, or about to renounce the world of Ballymena for ever; another sister (Maggie) also shaping up to go abroad as a governess; and a third sister (the oldest, Minnie), whom family pressures were impelling into the arms of a lunatic. Minnie's travesty of a marriage to a rich Glasgow 'flesher' named Thomas McNally took place in Ballymena on 11 July 1882, and was over a few weeks later. No one, neither her mother, nor her uncle James McAllister, nor anyone else with Minnie's interests at heart, seems to have twigged that the bridegroom was off his head. It probably looked like an opportunity to get the twenty-two-year-old girl settled for life. A wedding photograph shows McNally the flesher looking stolid and grim, and Minnie looking apprehensive, as well she might. The story, or a version of it, gets into a novel, *Fergus*, of 1971, written by Minnie's nephew Brian nearly ninety years after the event:

'The story I heard,' Fergus said, 'was that Daddy's mother, old Grandmother Fadden, married you off to this Christie, who was a Scottish shipbroker who came over to Killiney on a holiday and acted as though he were a millionaire. Anyway, he swept you off your feet.'

'Swept me off my feet?' Aunt Mary laughed, a false laugh, coquettish, to cover her embarrassment.

'Anyway, he married you, and Daddy went over to Scotland to give you away at the wedding in Glasgow. It was a very grand wedding, and apparently Christie *was* well-off. But the other thing about him was what his family didn't tell you. Which was that he was insane.'

Aunt Mary shrugged. 'Fergus Fadden!' said she, mock stern. 'Where did you get hold of a yarn like that?'

'It's true,' Fergus said. 'You went on your honeymoon to Europe, and in Paris, the first night of your visit, you and he were alone in a box at the Paris Opera when he got the idea that some man in another box was making eyes at you. So he took you home the very next day, straight back to Glasgow, and as soon as he got you there he locked you up in a room in his house, and you were a week locked up before you managed to smuggle a letter out with one of the maids, telling my father to come and get you.'

Far from giving his older sister away, and then doing an about-turn and hastening to retrieve her, Brian Moore's father, who was then a schoolboy of fifteen, would likely have been kept in the dark, as far as possible, about Minnie's misalliance. In essence, though, the passage above recounts what actually happened.[48] That was Minnie's great adventure, the single dramatic episode in her life.[49] The maid and the smuggled letter make it sound like something out of Mrs Braddon or Mrs Henry Wood. But the reality is dispiriting. It was an incident fit to be discussed only in whispers, a cause of chagrin for the family. It's hard to understand why some of Minnie's relatives didn't contrive to get the marriage annulled; Catholic or not, there were surely unimpeachable grounds for wiping the whole thing out. The bridegroom was soon taken into an asylum; husband and wife never saw one another again. But Minnie, home with her tail between her legs, continued to be known as Mrs McNally. She was married, and that was that. No doubt some people took her for a widow – but it can't have been pleasant for her to be an object of rumour and commiseration; or to remain financially dependent on her relatives. '. . . because you left him,' Fergus goes on, 'his family never gave you a penny.' As his wife, though, wouldn't she have been legally entitled to an income? Looked at from today's perspective, Minnie Moore's passivity in this matter seems inexplicable. There she is at twenty-two, legally tied to a lunatic, and refusing to do a thing about it. But this was a different century, with standards and orthodoxies unavailable to the present. It's easy enough to admire those, especially women, who step out of line and adumbrate attitudes we take for granted now. But bygone lives of quiet integrity, like Minnie Moore's, tend to go unrecorded and unappreciated. Sweet-tempered Minnie would eventually find a role to suit her disposition, the role of aunt. And Minnie she might have been, but never a moaning Minnie. ' "Waste, what's a waste about it?" ' her *alter ego* declares; ' "I had my life, I had my health, I helped with you children, oh, you were the funny wee articles, the four of you. God is good, Fergus. Yes, God is good." '

Old Moores and their extended family connections: these might be said to exemplify the rise of a respectable contingent among the Catholics of Antrim during the nineteenth century. Businessmen, solicitors, priests, nuns, farmers, sea captains, governesses, doctors – they were solid citizens, nearly the whole lot of them, worthy and industrious; church-goers, founders of families, fulfillers of obligations, and undisturbed, for the most part, by intellectual passions or radical views. They're not too far, in spirit or appearance, from the Antrim Presbyterians conjured up by R.N.D. Wilson, in his elegy for the poet John Lyle Donaghy:

> . . . the elders came out, to draw the shafts of the traps up,
> And load their wives and children into the well
> With their Bibles and their black dresses and farmyard
>   faces . . .[50]

Their Bibles and their black dresses and farmyard faces. For all his affection for any individuals among them who lived long enough to make an impact on him, the young Brian Moore felt himself to be powerfully dissociated from these paternal relatives and ancestors, whose experience – in so far as he was aware of it at all – smacked of stodginess, conformity and a provincial outlook: the very qualities he was keenest to repudiate. It's not unusual for a spirited adolescent to be addicted to the avant-garde, and unintrigued by the *passé*; and for Brian Moore, at thirteen or fourteen, the older generation, at least on his father's side, was so very much older that they all seemed mired in a hopeless fustiness.

2
THE GREAT EXAM PASSER

'. . . When I was your age, anything but honours marks would have been inconceivable to me. I was, as you know, a gold-medalist, a bursary-holder, and a scholarship winner.'

The Emperor of Ice Cream

PUPILS TAKING THE UNIVERSITY course at St Malachy's were all keen workers, and James B. Moore was as diligent as any. He was capable of immense application. A boy of steady temperament, he seems never to have got on the wrong side of his teachers. The Rev. Dr Henry was pleased to describe him, in 1892, as 'a young man of far more than average ability and acquirements, and . . . as amiable, gentlemanly, and correct in his conduct as he is able and accomplished': not a bad tribute to a past pupil. Other testimonials endorse Dr Henry's enthusiasm. 'Industrious and attentive';[1] 'an ornament to his profession';[2] 'sound knowledge and ability'.[3] It reads like a Victorian success story in the making. After the Exhibitions, Gold Medals and whatnot obtained during his schooldays, James B. went on to Queen's College, Cork, where a further succession of honours awaited him. He started by taking an Arts course in conjunction with his Medical Degree course, but found the double grind insupportable and dropped the former – though not before he'd gained a fourth place and certificate in English (1886–7). Logic, zoology and botany, practical anatomy, anatomy and physiology, surgery, midwifery and medical jurisprudence: in all of these he distinguished himself, coming top of the class more often than not. Throughout the late 1880s he was engaged in postgraduate work at various hospitals in Cork and in Glasgow, where the Professor of Surgery at St Mungo's College and Senior

Surgeon to the Royal Infirmary[4] commended his 'earnest work and intelligent appreciation of the details of Anatomical Science'; and a St Mungo's Lecturer on Pathology[5] said much the same. It's a record of unobstructed achievement.[6] In 1890, Degrees of Bachelor of Medicine, Bachelor of Obstetrics and Bachelor of Surgery were conferred on him at a public meeting of the Royal University held in Dublin on 29 October. By 1896, James B. – loaded down with qualifications – had been appointed Assistant Surgeon to the Mater Infermorum Hospital in Belfast; and in 1909 he became a Fellow of the Royal College of Surgeons.

At the same time the career of his friend Eoin MacNeill was also forging ahead. In the past, when the pair of them were brainy schoolboys at St Malachy's, it was possible to learn Irish, or 'Celtic' as it appeared on the syllabus; but in fact, in the entire school, only one pupil opted to do so, and it wasn't either James B. or Eoin MacNeill. MacNeill's interest in the language seems to have burgeoned only after he'd been awarded a B.A. Degree by the Royal University of Ireland (with Honours in economics, jurisprudence and constitutional history), and considered himself entitled, for the moment, 'to follow any line of study, or none, as it might please me'.[7] He was twenty-one years old, and it was possibly during that summer – a cold wet July if the year is right – that he and his brother James, in company with the future naturalist Robert Lloyd Praeger, repeatedly tested their courage by diving off a rock at Glenarm into a freezing sea, after which came the headlong 'scramble to get out of the icy water as quickly as arms and legs could accomplish it'.[8]

There were remote parts of Antrim in which Irish had remained the predominant language up until the last quarter of the nineteenth century (Eoin MacNeill's mother, not herself an Irish-speaker, remembered Glenspeople from her childhood who hadn't a word of English). But towns like Ballymena and even the much smaller Glenarm were thoroughly Anglicised, and MacNeill had to start from scratch in his newest enterprise. First he advertised for a tutor (he was living in Dublin, to which he'd come in 1887 to take up a post as clerk at the Four Courts); and then he discovered the native-speaking districts of the West, preceding Synge to Aran, and immersing himself to the full in the *dinnseanchas* and the *dearscnaidheacht* of the place. It wasn't long before his interest in 'the living Irish language' merged with that of another scholar and linguist, Douglas Hyde; and between the two of them – and in the wake of the latter's seminal paper on 'The Necessity for De-Anglicising Ireland' – the Gaelic League came into being. And everyone is familiar with the outcome of that crucial turn of events. 'I have said again and again,' stated P.H. Pearse, 'that when the Gaelic League was founded the Irish revolution began.'[9]

Those were heady days. The movement to uphold all forms of Irishness was under way, as the country rebelled against the incessant ridicule inflicted on it in the pages of *Punch* and else-where. The pig-and-shillelagh image purveyed from abroad was no longer an insult to be swallowed passively. You had Yeats and Lady Gregory bending over backwards to add dignity and gran-deur to Ireland, the beginnings of an Irish theatre, the glamour of a sorrowful past contributing to a growing nationalist consciousness. Pride in the Irish language, in the rediscovered treasure trove of Irish literature, from the Fenian and Red Branch sagas on, pride in a kind of Catholic integrity and Celtic distinctiveness: all these were coming together to bolster up the separatist ideology, and in the thick of the new catalytic goings-on was Eoin MacNeill – and along with him, and influenced by him, his friend and brother-in-law James B. Moore. (' "I was fortunate in my schoolfriends," ' says the resurrected father-figure in Brian Moore's novel *Fergus*, going on to single out ' "my friend John MacEoin, a man of European reputa-tion in Celtic scholarship." ') It is likely that the two[10] were among the frequent visitors at a house called Ardrigh (literally, high king) on the Antrim Road in Belfast: the home of a Protestant solicitor and cultural nationalist, Francis Joseph Bigger, and a non-sectarian gathering place for advocates of the Irish Revival in all its forms – literary, political, social, journalistic, antiquarian, revolutionary.

In 1896, MacNeill had become engaged to James B.'s sister Taddie, and the two were married in Ballymena in April 1898, after a rise in salary had enabled the chancery law clerk to take this step.[11] The couple set up house at Monkstown, Co. Dublin. James B., in the meantime, had been appointed Assistant Surgeon to the Mater Infermorum Hospital in Belfast, after a stint as a general practi-tioner in the Mountpottinger district of the city, where his duties included a spot of dentistry whenever required. A doctor was expected to cure all ills, from the mundane to the horrific – and

James B.'s impressive qualifications didn't exempt him from routine work. No doubt he was pleased to join the Mater's staff, when the Assistant Surgeonship came up in 1896.

The Mater, described in 1902 as 'a new, priest-owned hospital for Catholics, managed by nuns',[12] had actually existed in a small way since 1883; but it wasn't until 1900 that the new hospital building (in 'institutional Tudor'), with adequate accommodation for patients, was formally opened by the Lord Mayor of Belfast. It was sited on the Crumlin Road, near the original building (once a 'gentleman's residence'), and run by a religious order, the Sisters of Mercy. Belfast Catholics disinclined to trust themselves to the non-sectarian Royal Victoria Hospital were treated at the Mater whose central block reassuringly contained a chapel. If all other shifts failed, supernatural aid could be invoked.

There's a moment in *Fergus* when the central character cross-questions the ghost of his father, demanding to be told whether or not Fadden Senior has had a happy life; after some thought, the wraith[13] comes up with a memory of a cycling tour in France, on which he was accompanied by his friend John MacEoin, another character named Davy McAusley and Fadden's sister Kate, 'before she entered the convent'. Leaving aside the fact that no young nineteenth-century Catholic Ballymena woman, let alone an intending nun, would travel abroad unchaperoned with three men (even if one of them was her brother) – the recollection does have a basis in reality. Brian Moore must have listened to his father reminiscing about a trip to Normandy, in the summer of 1899 (which may well have included a visit to his sister Lizzie's convent), with Eoin MacNeill and another – male – friend making up the party. MacNeill jotted down his impressions of France. Expecting people there to be mean and feckless, for some reason, he found them, on the contrary, hard-working, vigorous, generous and mannerly. On his return, he published these impressions in Irish in the Gaelic League journal *An Claidheamh Soluis*.[14]

The trip reinforced MacNeill's devotion to Ireland, by making him aware of the extent to which the character and appearance of *Englishmen* were imposed by the French on himself and his companions. ('*Voici les Anglais*, oh yes,' chortled a little boy in the street, making fun of them.) Ireland had made so little impact on the world at large that people of other nations simply declined to distinguish between it and England. This is a cause of chagrin to MacNeill – however, 'With the help of God we won't be thus for ever.'

The *Claidheamh Soluis* may have dictated the slant MacNeill gave to his notes on the Normandy trip; but it's unlikely that the consciousness of being an Englishman's clone dampened down his spirits altogether. 'We laughed a great deal that summer,' muses the shade of Dr Fadden, before his son's probing knocks his concentration askew. (All this is taking place in Fergus's mind.)

> 'So, that summer you were happy,' Fergus said. 'Is that the only time you can think of?'
>
> His father grew agitated, his fingers knotting and unknotting. He looked at Fergus, cleared his throat, and said deferentially, 'Yes, the . . . the question is a multipart question, is it not, sir?'
>
> He thinks I am an examiner, Fergus decided. He nodded to his father. 'That is correct.'

Dr Fadden's allusion to a bygone cycling holiday is an answer of sorts, if a meagre one – gaining his son's grudging approval. ' "I mean, if that's as much as you can say?" ' The father's response – in this self-reflexive piece of fiction – as well as reversing the characters' roles for a moment, provides a warning for novelists, and by extension for biographers, against the dangers of putting words into another person's mouth, or thoughts into their head:

> His father coughed, then rose, adjusting the skirts of his plaid dressing gown. 'No, no,' he said quietly. 'Not I. *You.* It is, perhaps, as much as *you* can say.'
>
> 'What do you mean?'
>
> 'It's not very difficult,' his father said. 'I'm sure that with reasonable application the meaning will become clear to you . . .'

With this impersonation, we catch the authentic tones of the didactic father mildly exasperated by his son's obtuseness – and this, indeed, no doubt was an element in the personal relations between James B. Moore and his son Brian (as we shall see).

However, while the latter is a novelist who deals only sparingly in wholly invented characters, preferring instead to home in on the core of authenticity suggested by the real-life prototype, he is all the time sufficiently in control of his material to cause the emphasis to fall most tellingly in relation to the needs of a particular plot, adjusting a trait here, scrubbing out potential *longueurs* there. Subtle distortion is, in a sense, the fiction writer's business.

By the late 1890s, Dr James B. Moore had been joined in Belfast by his mother and his sister Minnie, who kept house for him at 4, Mountpottinger Road. The address wasn't especially convenient for his work at the Mater Hospital, but it wasn't until 1908 or '09 that he was able to move into No. 11, Clifton Street, virtually a stone's throw away. Clifton Street, an extension of Donegall Street,[15] had been developed in the 1870s, and the first occupant of No. 11 was a Dr David Johnston (whose executors still owned the building as late as 1930). The editor of the *Belfast News Letter*, Richard Lilburn, lived in the house in the 1880s, and he was followed by a couple of medical practitioners in succession (Drs Speer and O'Brien), before James B. Moore acquired the lease. A rather imposing, three-storey, red-brick building, No. 11 contained at least six bedrooms, along with waiting-room, surgery, dispensary and so forth on the ground floor, and drawing-room, breakfast-room, etc above. However, only a tiny dirt garden at the front separated the house from a busy city-centre street, and behind it was nothing but a yard. It was directly opposite an Orange Hall (built in 1889), complete with bronze equestrian statue of King Billy, sword in hand – ready to fight, as Louis MacNeice has it in a poem, 'till the blue sea turns to orange'.[16] Just round the corner, fronting on to North Queen Street, was the graceful old Poorhouse (1774; now Clifton House); while west of the junction between Clifton Street and Donegall Street – just a few minutes' walk away from the middle-class doctors' enclave – were the slums of Carrick Hill. The area was full of churches of all denominations, including St Patrick's Roman Catholic Church (in Donegall Street), while North Queen Street had a slightly dicey reputation harking back to the Rev. W.M. O'Hanlon, one-time minister of the local congregationalist church, who, in the 1850s, proceeded gingerly along it, counting public houses as he went, and succumbing to outrage on reaching the figure of twenty-two.[17] This small locality, you might say, contained in a highly concentrated form some of Belfast's most striking features – sectarian and social distinctions; middle-class affluence and the ultimate in privation; religion and conviviality; elegance; a sense of history; disaffection and squalor. Decidedly untypical as a family home, No. 11, Clifton Street was nevertheless an interesting place for the young Moores – still some way in the future – to grow up in.

It was at the Mater Hospital, some time around 1909 or '10, that James B. met a young Donegal woman, a staff nurse there named Eileen McFadden, who became his operating-theatre nurse. In 1910, she would have been twenty, while he was forty-three. It was pretty late in the day for James B. to start paying attentions to any woman, if indeed he did start then; we have no information about any earlier entanglements he may have entered into. Looking for something to explain James B.'s prolonged celibacy, his children have cited an early obligation to support his mother and sister; but even if this were the case, his income, especially after 1900 when he was promoted to the Senior Surgical Staff of the Mater, should have been sufficient to meet all demands on it. Whatever the reason, he remained a bachelor until he was forty-eight, apparently content with the role of uncle to his sister Taddie's and Eoin MacNeill's children.

Eileen McFadden was born on 1 February 1890, at Cashel, near Creeslough, in the district of Dunfanaghy in Co. Donegal. Socially, her background seems a bit of a hotch-potch. According to her birth certificate, her father Pat McFadden was illiterate (in place of a signature we get 'Pat McFadden – his mark') – yet the same McFadden had a couple of brothers, or cousins, who were parish priests, one of whom, indeed, attained some local celebrity after he'd accompanied evicted tenants from Glenveagh as far as Liverpool on their way to a new life in Australia.[18] This melancholy exodus took place in 1861, nearly thirty years before Eileen McFadden came on the scene: here we have another instance of the kind of generational overlap we've already seen with the young O'Rawes, Ellen and Mary, and their very elderly aunts.[19] It's true that she came at the tail-end of a large family, which included a brother nineteen or twenty years her senior, whom she never met, since he'd emigrated to America before she was born.[20] Her mother was Grace McGee (1852–1936), also a Donegal woman, who lived long enough to form an acquaintance with her grandson Brian Moore – who, in the late 1920s and 1930s, would spend summer holidays with his Donegal relatives – 'real country people' – at a place called Duntally, near Doe Castle, not far from Creeslough. These were small farmers and had been for generations – not the poorest of the poor, indeed, but a world away from the comforts of urban professional life.

Patrick McFadden, farmer – illiterate or not – seems to have been of sufficient standing in the neighbourhood to become a JP before he died in 1905,[21] when his daughter Eileen was fifteen and a pupil at St Louis's Convent in Letterkenny. After this she went to live with her uncle Father McFadden (not the Glenveagh priest but his brother – or possibly his cousin?), to act as his housekeeper. When he died three or four years later, she came into a small inheritance which paid for her nurse's training. It shows a certain amount of gumption, on Eileen McFadden's part, to leave the security of rural Donegal and set out to earn her living in a large, unknown, industrial city; but this is precisely what she did. Early photographs show a rather pretty, slightly plump, dark-haired girl gazing steadily at the camera, looking unlikely to be daunted by anything life might throw at her. You would judge serenity and confidence to be among her traits. It didn't take her long to qualify as a nurse – and then came an abundance of hard work, mostly at St John's (a private nursing home attached to the Mater). A nurse's tasks, in those days, included scrubbing floors and doing an awful lot of fetching and carrying. Eileen McFadden was shocked by some of the things she saw – including patients in the throes of delirium tremens. One of these once cornered her in a lift, and gibbered at her to such an extent that she was left with a horror of alcoholism for ever after.

Said to have at least one broken engagement behind her, Nurse McFadden was, at any rate, free to accept the courtship of Dr James B. Moore, when the latter found himself bowled over by some fundamental quality he discerned in his young theatre sister. The two of them were about to act out the stereotype of every hospital romance, in which the comely nurse without social pretensions carries off the most distinguished doctor about the place. The

Moore–McFadden wedding took place in Dublin, on 26 October 1915. The bride wore a white, two-tier, ankle-length dress and veil, and carried a bouquet of calla lilies. The church, St Joseph's, was in north Dublin, in Berkeley Street, the celebrant a Father Joseph Sheridan. The best man was David McCloskey, a whisky importer from the Antrim Road in Belfast and an old school chum of James B. Moore's from his St Malachy's days, and the bridesmaid Theresa Fitzpatrick,[22] a nursing friend of the bride's. Guests on the groom's side included Aunt Minnie (McNally), Aunt Taddie (MacNeill), and Canon John O'Neill, founder of the (Irish) Knights of St Columbanus.[23] Eileen McFadden's sister and brother-in-law, Agnes and Michael Duffy, were present. Eoin MacNeill was there, taking time off from Ireland's business. So was his brother James, lately returned from India where he'd held a post as Deputy Governor of Bengal. All in all, it was an impressive gathering. Two senior figures were absent, however: the mothers of the bride and groom. Possibly, at their age (sixty-three and seventy-nine respectively), the journey to Dublin would have been considered too much for them.

In the autumn of 1909, Eoin MacNeill, who was by then the father of seven children, had been appointed to the Chair of Early and Medieval Irish History at the new University College, Dublin. It was a felicitous choice. MacNeill was, as many commentators have pointed out, by temperament a scholar rather than anything else. However, events in the early part of the century, from the introduction of the Third Home Rule Bill on, were impelling him into the armed resistance camp along with Padraig Pearse and others. Towards the end of 1913, he played a leading role in the setting up of the Irish Volunteer Force, which came into being directly as a counterblast to Carson's Ulster Volunteers and their impassioned anti-Home Rule activities.[24] After having consulted his wife, and with her support, MacNeill accepted the presidency of the Irish Volunteer Force, and, according to the historian F.X. Martin, 'continued as its head up to Easter 1916, and not merely as its figure-head'.[25]

The situation changed, indeed, with the outbreak of war in 1914, which some Irish patriots saw as an opportunity to gain their ends, by force if necessary, while others, under the leadership of John

Redmond, believed the Home Rule question should be shelved for the moment, while support was lent to England's – for once – undeniably just cause. Constitutional nationalism or revolutionary nationalism: you could take your pick. The Volunteers were split in two, with MacNeill on the side disinclined to come to England's aid. But then a further split occurred, as MacNeill repudiated the 'blood-sacrifice' rhetoric promulgated by Pearse. As a pragmatic Northerner, he held that any proposed rising should take place only in circumstances that gave it a fair chance of victory; however, by February 1916 the Military Council, which included Pearse, Clarke, McDonagh and Connolly, had made its plans, and Mac-Neill – despite frequent assurances from Pearse and the others – had the feeling that he was being kept in the dark (as, indeed, he was). He was still Chief of Staff of the Irish Volunteers, and in possession of an agreement to the effect that no order would be issued to members in the absence of his countersignature. Believing, as he did, that a premature and foolhardy uprising could only result in the decimation of the whole Volunteer Force and the end of Ireland's hopes, he took what steps he could to stop the insurrection, once he got wind of what was actually going on. On the eve of the uprising, a countermanding order from Eoin MacNeill went out to Volunteers in Cork, Limerick, Galway, Waterford, Wexford, Tralee, Tyrone and Tipperary, causing terrible confusion and ensuring, basically, that only those insurgents stationed in Dublin itself would actually take military action as planned. As a consequence, and with considerable simplification even of the facts that were known at the time, MacNeill went down in history (well, in some circles at any rate) as the man who wrecked the Rising,[26] and it's only comparatively recently that his motives, and his tactics, have been cleared of unsoundness.

The Rising went ahead, in spite of MacNeill's efforts, and after its suppression MacNeill himself was arrested 'for being a rebel'.[27] He was taken first to Arbour Hill where, from his cell, he could hear executions taking place in the prison grounds. On 24 May 1916, he was sentenced to life imprisonment for his part in organising the Volunteers and fomenting rebellion.[28] It was probably at this point that his friend James B. Moore, who must have been following these events with deep apprehension from his home in Belfast, resigned from his wartime post as Surgical Specialist to the Victoria Barracks. This was a gesture of protest against the British treatment of the Easter rebels, and of solidarity with MacNeill (who, in prison in Lewes, near Brighton, was put to weaving hearth-rugs on a loom).[29]

The Ballymena solicitor James Moore was dead at forty-eight; at the same age his son's married life was only just beginning. James B. went on to equal his father's reproductive feats (and to beat the total of his friend MacNeill, who stopped at eight children, the last born four years before James B.'s first). Eileen McFadden gave birth to nine children over a period of twelve years (as well as suffering a couple of miscarriages). By the early 1930s the Clifton Street house was bursting at the seams, what with offspring, aunts, nursemaids, domestic servants, and, we may suppose, at set times, patients trooping in and out.

The first child, Eibhlin,[30] was born in 1917. She was just old enough[31] to remember the baptism of her second brother Brian, whose birth date was 25 August 1921 (between him and Eibhlin came Grainne and Seamus), at St Patrick's Roman Catholic Church in Donegall Street. The fourth Moore child arrived at an exciting time, with 'murders, burnings and other outrages'[32] taking place all over the country. Pogroms, curfews, night raids, assassinations . . . these were the order of the day. It was less than a year since the first 'Bloody Sunday', when the shooting of fourteen British agents had been followed by a massacre at Croke Park, Dublin. In that same month, November 1920, 'Uncle John', who had resumed his post as history professor at UCD, was arrested for the second time, released and then re-arrested. While in Mountjoy Prison, he immersed himself in five volumes of the *Ancient Laws of Ireland*, which no doubt helped to take his mind off its present unsatisfactory government and state of lawlessness. But things were coming to a head. In June 1921, under the Government of Ireland Act, the Northern Parliament was opened in Belfast by King George V; and a few days later, political prisoners, including MacNeill and the acting president of the Irish Republic, Arthur Griffith, were released. The terms of the Truce, enforcing a complete cessation of military activity, came into effect on 11 July. Bonfires, tricolours and the chanting of republican slogans made it feel like a victory – but it wasn't. 'In Belfast,' wrote Dorothy Macardle grimly, 'there was no rejoicing over the Truce.'[33] Partition was impending, and by the end of the year, with the Treaty signed in London, republicans were split, once again, into two factions, and a bloody civil war was about to replace the war with the British.

Brian Moore's first year in Belfast was marked by unrest and upheaval – so much so that the nickname 'Bomber' was bestowed on him by his mother, who gave birth to him thinking a bomb had actually exploded outside the window, as a volley of rifle shots rang out in Clifton Street. Many Catholic families were driven from their homes in those days of disruption. From the roof of the Orange hall, snipers would train their guns on known Catholics in the street below. The inhabitants of nearby Carrick Hill took their lives in their hands if they stepped outside – in fact, to get in and out, it was necessary to crawl on hands and knees through yards and entries. The poet John Hewitt, born in 1907, recalled this violent era:

> Once, from front bedroom window, I could mark
> black shapes, flat-capped, across the shadowed street,
> two policemen on patrol. With crack and spark
> fierce bullets struck the kerb beneath their feet;
> below the shattered street lamps in the dark
> blurred shadows crouched, then pattered quick retreat.[34]

During the first week of June, 1922, according to Dorothy Macardle, the Mater Hospital resembled a war hospital, filled with bullet-wound and shrapnel-wound cases.[35] On the night of 4 June, many hospital windows were shattered by gunfire, while doctors and nurses rushed through the wards dragging patients from their beds to the comparative safety of the floor. Dr Moore, who had been promoted to Senior Surgeon in 1919, was no doubt among them. To get to the hospital, he'd have had to walk up dangerous Clifton Street – but he was a well-known figure in the district, and exempt from assault. One particular sniper, who'd positioned himself by the statue of the Rev. ('Roaring') Hugh Hanna in the centre of Carlisle Circus, in order to be able to take a pot shot at anyone approaching from Catholic North Queen Street, used to lower his rifle to greet Dr Moore – 'Good evening, Doctor. How nice to see you. How are you?' If the doctor had to make a night call at this period, he was often ferried to his patient under police guard in a Crossley Tender. You will always find dramatic ironies and complications in Irish sectarianism.

The Civil War divided families, including the MacNeills, who allied themselves with the pro-Treaty faction, apart from the second son Brian, who'd persuaded himself that the terms of the Treaty fell short of the republican ideal to which he had sworn an oath of allegiance. He was, at the time, a medical student of twenty-two, and would really have liked nothing better than to get back to his studies.[36] After a talk with his father in Dublin, he had almost resolved to remove himself from the armed struggle – but then decided that to do so would be to let down his fellow republicans. He returned to his IRA column in Sligo, where, on 20 September 1922, along with five other volunteers, he was shot dead by Free State forces. His Belfast cousin and namesake was just over a year old.[37]

All these things – impassioned politics, patriotic funerals, stones, rifle-shots, angry voices, family scandals and secrets like Aunt Minnie's marriage, triumphs and social advances, Donegal versus Antrim, the Irish Victorian inheritance, siblings older and younger – all these were strongly in the background as the infant Brian Moore began to sit up and take note of his surroundings. By the time he was eighteen months or so, he'd acquired a quantity of lightish-brown hair, cut pudding-basin style, and some little knitted suits, tied with woollen bobbles at the neck. He was already learning how to charm those around him, including his mother, who referred to him as 'the wee son'. Even his brother Seamus, not by and large Brian's greatest admirer, admits that he was an attractive child.

3

A HOUSE OF CHILDREN

He looked into the looking-glass. In that world, encircled by the looking-glass frame, he had acted and reacted, had left his mark, and had, in turn, been marked. His bare knees had helped wear down the old Turkey carpet, battleground of a thousand childhood games of Snap. A Hornby locomotive, thrown by him twelve years ago, had made a big dent in the brass fender in the fireplace . . . Night after night, during the family rosary, he had knelt at those chairs and sofas, until now, eyes shut, he could see the shape and colour of each faded rose on their slipcovers.

The Emperor of Ice Cream

THE MOORES WERE WELL enough off to employ a nursemaid, and, like many another middle-class child, Brian Moore in his earliest years had trouble distinguishing between his nanny and his mother. Eileen Moore claimed, jokingly, that it was the nanny who brought him up. One family story has him sitting in the drawing-room at Clifton Street buttoned up to the neck in his outdoor clothes ready to be taken visiting. When his mother came to collect him – 'Come along now, Brian' – she got the firm response, 'No, no, Mama, I can't come now.' 'Why not?' 'Nellie – Nellie said I had to stay here.' Nellie Ritchie was the nanny whose word was law, even though she must have been a very young woman at the time. She came from the Falls Road and would often talk to Brian about her family there, with the result that he developed a pretence about having an alternative family on the Falls Road, and would threaten to go and live with them if he was scolded or punished at home.[1] Another of Brian's *bon mots*, which his brother Seamus remembered, occurred when the Moores were visiting the MacNeills in Dublin. 'Go and call the others in for their tea,' Aunt Taddie said to Brian – who was about four or five at the time – whereupon he went out into the garden and shouted, 'Others! Come in for your tea.'

The Moore family was continuing to expand. After Brian came Marie-Therese, and then Una. By the time of Sean's arrival in 1926 Brian would have been enrolled in a little kindergarten run by Mercy nuns. Their achievement was to train a naturally left-handed child to use his right hand, which they did by binding the left hand behind his back with a piece of raffia. 'I write with my right hand because I was taught to,' he said – but every other activity, drawing, catching a ball, and so on, was performed instinctively with the other. These nuns were obsessed with the strait and narrow; no leeway was allowed for doing things differently. By the time he got to Newington,[2] the next stage in his education, Brian Moore was apparently right-handed like everyone else. But something in him had been knocked out of kilter.

The Holy Family School at Newington Avenue in the Antrim Road district of Belfast was opened in 1914 with Mr Fitzsimmons as headmaster of the boys' section, a post he held until 1940, by which time the nickname 'Baldy' had become appropriate. It was a Public Elementary school, but considered a good one, and catered for boys of all social classes, sons of bank managers and those of flax roughers alike. Pupils were made to stand on benches to recite their tables or answer questions from the *Penny Catechism*. Knowledge was dinned into their heads, a method of teaching to which Master Brian didn't take kindly. However, it was here that he first fell under the spell of fiction. One of the Grimm Brothers' stories is 'The Valiant Little Tailor', in which a puny young man gets the better of a giant by exercising his wits to create a wondrously false impression. The first thing he does is drape a banner around himself inscribed with the words, 'Seven at One Blow'. A mighty fighter indeed – however, what the tailor doesn't specify is that the slaughtered seven are *flies*. This story, read by a teacher called Paddy Woods to a class of senior infants, *c.* 1927, instantly captivated at least one of them, and stayed with him for the rest of his life. Brian Moore claimed not to be able to remember much about his early childhood reading, or indeed about his early childhood,[3] but he did remember the impression made on him by this intriguing tale.

It was also at Newington that his gift for English composition was first appreciated. Instructed to open their exercise books, take up their pens and write on the topic 'What I Did on My Summer Holidays', or 'The Adventures of a Threepenny Bit', most of the class of seven- or eight-year-olds would groan inwardly, wriggle about on their seats, chew their pens, drop ink blots, and finally plod through the task with reluctance and without finesse – but not Brian. Brian really came into his own with this routine piece of schoolwork – and basked in the kudos it earned him. Mr Fitzsimmons, the discerning headmaster, spotted his natural talent and, at one point, let him off the rest of his classwork for a whole week. During this time he simply sat at his desk and wrote non-stop, until seven or eight of the little school essays had mounted up. As each was completed it was passed to a boy whose special skill was handwriting, and the resulting pristine copy was then held up to the rest of the class as exemplary work. It's unlikely that this endeared Brian to his schoolfellows, but it did give him a certain amount of confidence in his abilities – 'I got the idea, early on, that I was pretty good!' – before this was undermined by his lack of success in other subjects, particularly maths.

The boy with the good handwriting was Niall Dempsey, who lived opposite the Moores at No. 36, Clifton Street, and was a friend of the whole family, but particularly of Brian, his exact contemporary. Niall and his sister Clodagh were the only children who lived near by (well, the only middle-class children). The young people of both families were constantly in and out of one another's houses. The Dempseys' father was also a doctor employed by the Mater Hospital – in fact he took over a lot of Dr Moore's duties when the latter became Senior Surgeon in 1919. Niall's grandfather was Sir Alexander Dempsey (knighted for his work on the Irish Universities question[4]), the original owner of *their* Clifton Street house which passed to his son when he died and hence became the home of the Moores' young friends. Another grandfather came to live in the Dempsey household in the mid-1930s: 'old' J.B. Hearne, a grain exporter from Southern Ireland and victim of de Valera's economic war with Britain. His business went bankrupt and he and his wife came North to Belfast. He was a very religious man, and Brian would often see him leaving the house opposite, wearing an old green overcoat that looked as if it was covered in verdigris, and making his way down to early-morning Mass at St Patrick's. Like Dr Moore, old J.B. Hearne was a figure in the neighbourhood. His contribution to literary history was to bequeath his surname to Brian Moore's first significant character.[5]

Life was pretty formal then. The Dempseys had a maid, Mary, who wore one uniform during the daytime, and another in the evening, and referred to the children as 'Master Niall' and 'Master Brian'. Master Brian was very agile and reckless at this time and got up to all kinds of acrobatic escapades, sliding down banisters, shinning up ropes and so forth, which sometimes caused Dr Dempsey to succumb to jocular exasperation and pack the delinquent off home: 'Go and break your neck in your own house!' Once, on holiday in Portstewart,[6] Brian nearly gave his parents a heart attack by hoisting his young brother on to his shoulders and inching the pair of them up a steep rock face – Sean holding on for dear life, and the parents open-mouthed below. He did this to get himself and Sean a better view of people diving into the sea from high rocks as part of a swimming exhibition. Scoldings and chastisements didn't curb his high spirits.

By the time the two youngest Moores, Clodagh (always called Peggy) and Eilis, were toddling about, their middle brother was known in the family as 'big boy Brian', and he was looked up to by them on account of his story-telling abilities. He used to spend hours devising little dramas involving toy soldiers and doll's houses to entertain his younger siblings – at the same time exercising his narrative bent. He always had some character represented by a toy soldier 'falling out of a window or being hanged or something like that'.[7] (One of the soldiers was called Darkie.) None of the adults about the place was particularly adept at making things up, so his was a vital role in the household. He would also set up toy racing tracks on the nursery floor and re-run famous races on them, with his own commentary. On one occasion, a doll's pram got rammed into the gas fire in the nursery, which caused a panic among the children, but fortunately no damage was done.

The children took their meals in the nursery until they reached the age of seven or so, by which time it was supposed they could be trusted to behave properly at the dining-room table. Their behaviour was overseen by an imposing aunt – Aunt Maggie, who joined the household some time in the 1920s. Aunt Minnie was already installed at Clifton Street, having moved in after the death of her mother in 1924. Maggie Moore had been educated in France, at the convent where her sister Lizzie later became a nun; and for a good part of her life she was employed as a governess to the children of various aristocratic French families, including those of the Duc de Levis-Mirpoix (a cousin of the Duc de Guise) and the Marquis de Chaponnay. Brian, in later life, regretted not having derived more benefit from the presence of his Aunt Maggie with her impeccable French – or from having an incomparable tutor on the spot – but he did, through her, learn to appreciate the language and the culture in which she'd been immersed for thirty-five years, even though he had all the normal spirited child's resistance to being subjected to anything smacking of schoolwork in his own home. Aunt Maggie tried to teach him French, 'But I didn't want to know!' She did, however, instruct him and his sister Marie-Therese in verse-speaking, 'And we won prizes at contests in Ballymena and Belfast. I have medals for verse-speaking . . .'

Aunt Maggie, like her sister the nun, was extremely plain in appearance and made up for it by cultivating a formidable manner. When her usefulness as a governess was at an end, after years of service, she was packed off home with what Brian Moore called 'a little purse' – in other words, a totally inadequate recompense. 'And where did she end up? In our house in Clifton Street – so we had *two* old aunts living with us.' This circumstance may well have created some tension in the household. Eileen Moore, by all accounts, wasn't especially maternal and must have welcomed whatever help she could get in raising her expanding family; however, the continuous presence of a couple of elderly sisters-in-law can't have been always easy to tolerate. These were, after all, middle-class women and she was a farmer's daughter from Donegal; and she had it in her head, rightly or wrongly, that they were for that reason inclined to look down on her. Social distinctions mattered, at the time. There were occasional failures of tact on both sides – for instance, Minnie and Maggie, both living on reduced incomes, or possibly no incomes at all, once clubbed together to buy Brian an overcoat – 'And my mother was furious! Because she thought that, you know, it was an insult to her.' She may also have felt that the aunts were, in a way, sabotaging the slight distance she tried to maintain between the older and younger members of the household: the children were in a subordinate position and had to mind their manners, no doubt about it. And there were Minnie and Maggie – Minimus and Maximus, a humorous relative dubbed them – one with her caches of Fox's Glacier Mints kept under her pillow to encourage young visitors, and the other considering herself exceptionally well versed in the management of children.

Through Aunt Maggie, the young Brian Moore found himself connected to a hitherto unimagined world: the world of Marcel Proust, Parisian *noblesse* and luxury, aristocratic attitudes, the great and the rich, family *châteaux*, travels abroad and so forth. Miss Moore the governess had accompanied one family to Brazil, and another to Russia, where, on one occasion, she had actually come face to face with Rasputin. All this was heady stuff for a small boy already dissatisfied with the prosaic quality of his surroundings, even if it only came to him in whiffs and glimmers. Aunt Maggie took over the spare room, and whenever Brian was unwell he was put to sleep with her, in case he might need attention in the night; he remembered her head of white hair, unpinned for bed, full of great yellow streaks which he attributed to strong tropical sunlight – a far cry from Belfast's tentative rays. 'She was very French,' he said: smoked herbal cigarettes and wore frightfully formal clothes, a black neckband and so forth. She kept silver-topped jars and bottles on her dressing table. 'Of course she thought we were absolute savages – Brian's[8] children were absolute savages.' In the *bien élévés* stakes, they compared very unfavourably with the young de Chaponnays, whose photograph Aunt Maggie guarded carefully: a group of dark-complexioned nineteenth-century French children wearing immaculate cream sailor suits. (Her brother annoyed her greatly by once remarking that one of them 'looked as if he had a touch of the tar-brush'.) She did her best to amend the Moore children's manners. 'Don't look at me over your plate like a cow looking over a whitewashed wall,' she would scold. Mealtimes must have been something of a strain.

One of Miss Moore's aristocratic ex-pupils had actually had a couple of novels published – at his own expense – and these she displayed proudly in their exquisite leather bindings, not having the least inkling that an infinitely more talented future novelist was developing under her nose. The self-published author – Antoine de

Chaponnay – actually arrived at Clifton Street one day to take tea with Miss Moore, having sailed to Bangor in the family yacht and then driven up to Belfast to look up the old governess. It cannot have been a happy social occasion, with Miss Moore's Donegal sister-in-law thrown into a state of consternation by the unexpected visitor, and her brother disapproving of the way her services had been dispensed with – to say nothing of the language difficulties. However, it was an incident that Brian remembered, his fancy being tickled by intimations of a world beyond Newington, the Mater Hospital and the Cave Hill.

In the meantime, he developed an aversion to going to school, succumbing for a time to what the family dubbed 'Monday morning sickness'. It wasn't long before he was rumbled. There was nothing for it but to get dressed and leave the house with his satchel. 'If you don't go to school and learn your lessons,' his mother told him, 'you'll be good for nothing but opening car doors and holding umbrellas over old ladies.'[9] (He remembered this admonition when he came to create the character James Madden in *Judith Hearne*.) So, he remained a Newington pupil until the age of eleven, spending half his tram money on sweets and having to foot it there or back. Money was important. 'Brian was quite a character even at school,' his sister Eibhlin remembered. 'He was known as "Ikey" because he would not contribute to the Black Baby Fund . . .'[10] There was clearly a core of stubbornness in him. Outside of school hours, there were walks along the Lagan tow-path, excursions to the Zoo and Bellevue Pleasure Grounds on the slopes of the Cave Hill, or, more often, trips to the nearer Water-works or Alexandra Park, with Nellie Ritchie wheeling Sean, Peggy or Eilis in a big black pram, while holding Marie-Therese or Brian by the hand.

Years later, in the story 'A Vocation', Brian Moore uncharacter-istically evoked the atmosphere of these early childhood activities, all of them overshadowed by elementary Catholic teaching:

Q. *Who made the world?* A. *God.* The world was sweetie shops, Alexandra Park, the Antrim Road, Newington School, Miss Carey's garden, and the big pond in the Waterworks . . .

So it goes on. Anxiety of influence led him to discard the Joycean manner pretty quickly, but it serves very well to illuminate some particulars of juvenile Belfast life:

> There was sin. It was an awful thing in the sight of God. Lies were sins, losing your temper was a sin, calling Mary a dirty pig was a sin. It was a sin to tell a lie . . . It was a sin to steal Rory O'Hare's bike . . .[11]

It was, in many respects, an enviable upbringing, even if it wasn't geared to satisfy the requirements of a gifted child. Not that Brian would have been encouraged to see himself as such, even if anyone (aside from Mr Fitzsimmons) had spotted his talents. A facet of the Belfast Catholic education was its insistence on the unimportance of the individual; anyone who looked in danger of acquiring a swelled head was promptly sat upon. 'Who do you think you are?' was the usual taunt, with its implication that the person in question was very small beer indeed. And it wasn't only a playground gibe, but filtered down from higher authorities. It produced an atmosphere of suppressed self-assertion.

Brian Moore has described the way in which his past might suddenly flood into his mind in 'a jumbled kaleidoscope of images, fond, frightening, surprising and sad'.[12] One of these images was of his father sitting in the breakfast room at Clifton Street reading the *Irish News* while Brian's canary sang its heart out in a cage above Dr Moore's head. The *Irish News* was, of course, Belfast's morning newspaper for Catholic readers; you wouldn't have caught Dr Moore perusing the *Belfast News Letter*, the paper for the other lot. This attitude infected everything. On one occasion, according to his son, Dr Moore was affronted by a *Protestant* loaf of bread. 'Where did we get this?' the maid was asked. She couldn't provide a satisfactory answer.

> My father is puzzled. My mother is summoned. 'Hughes and Kennedy are the Catholic bakers,' my father says, holding up the offending loaf. 'But Ormeau is cheaper, and they say their bread is very good,' my mother tells him. 'Hughes' bread is very good,' my father says. 'I don't care if it's a few pennies

more. We shouldn't buy from Ormeau. They're Protestant bakers.'[13]

That the spirit of intolerance and sectarian back-scratching pervaded even so comparatively enlightened a middle-class home as the Moores' tells us something about the strength of the schism afflicting the North of Ireland in the pre-war era (and later). The Moore children were forbidden to have Protestant friends – given strict instructions not to speak to any Protestants they might meet on the way to school. Bigotry of this kind was so ingrained that it actually became equated with moral superiority: sticking up for one's faith and one's culture. The 'other side' was consequently demonised; only a renegade would take the ecumenical view. Catholics on the receiving end of Protestant animosity – and vice versa – would dub the offender an 'oul' bigot', while remaining blissfully ignorant of any equivalent prejudice in themselves. Of course, as with any highly charged situation, this one was fraught with ironies and ambiguities, and allowed for the day-to-day suspension of bigotry (as we've seen in the case of Dr Moore and the mannerly Orange sniper, p.39 above). It was pretty ironic that the ultra-Catholic Moores should be domiciled directly opposite the Clifton Street headquarters of the Orange Order – however, the location probably helped to keep their sectarian instincts up to the mark.

'When I looked out of my bedroom window on the top floor of our house,' Brian Moore wrote,[14] 'across the street I could see, graven into a stone plinth on top of a building, the figures 1690. On the plinth, a cavalier stood in stirrups, brandishing his sword over his head . . . in triumph at the chimneys of the York Street Flax Spinning Mills. He was William III of the Dutch House of Orange . . .' He goes on:

The Glorious Twelfth. It came during school holidays, but we weren't allowed out. Unlike other Catholic children, we didn't mind being kept in on that day. For we had the rare distinction of being the only Papishes in the world with a grandstand viewing position, right across from the balcony where Sir Joseph Davison, grand panjandrum of the Orange Order, watched the men set out on their march to Finaghy Field. A thrilling day for me, and I mean it, for what better excitement for a schoolboy than to have all those wild men, thousands strong, parading under your window and to know that you and yours were the very enemy they seek to destroy?

Enmity, bitterness, triumphalism, injustice, disaffection: these ingredients of a desperately riven community were constantly at the forefront of people's minds, whether through direct experience or observation. You had to be on one side or the other. The young Moores' allegiance was never in any doubt – at the same time, though, gathered at the top-floor window for the march-past during more than one 'Glorious Twelfth' of the 1930s, they must have been susceptible in some measure to the pageantry of the occasion, even if an atavistic reflex didn't cause their hair to stand on end. 'Every now and then the melodious procession is punctuated by the tyrannical thunder of the Lambeg drums . . . their reverberations drown every other sound, set windows chattering in their frames and print a stunned smile on the face of the onlooker.'[15] It would have been a thrilling enough occasion for a child, even without the overtones of intimidation savoured by the young Brian Moore.

Photographs of Dr Moore show him looking a bit like an authoritarian *paterfamilias*, and a bit like an Edwardian cad – both misleading images, as it happened. 'My father was the kindest man alive,' Brian Moore has stated – so kind he could never bring himself to mete out corporal punishment to his naughty offspring. 'If one of us had misbehaved, and my mother instructed him to give the culprit a good spanking, he would go into another room, take the strap and whack his own hand, so that it sounded as if we were getting it in the neck . . .' His daughters remember him as a jolly, happy sort of person. There were great holidays for the whole family at Portstewart, in the course of which Dr Moore would sport his summer garb of white suit and panama hat, and go about with binoculars and a camera slung around his neck. (He was an enthusiastic amateur photographer, who developed and printed his own films and spread them out to dry on a back windowsill at Clifton Street.) A box of chocolates, offered by Cadbury's as first prize in a sandcastle competition, had Brian out on the sands for a whole day constructing an elaborate sculpture – though whether it did the trick or not he couldn't recall. Sandcastles, picnics, donkeys, bathing pool, Punch-and-Judy, jellyfish . . . these were sufficient to keep the children engrossed, under the watchful eye of Nellie Ritchie or some other Moore employee. It was a world of seasonal treats and rituals, 'Strung chestnuts every autumn; kites in spring', as John Hewitt has it.[16] At Christmas the children, under the direction of Aunt Maggie, would put on a play to entertain the adults. 'Daddy sat in an armchair with his cigars and a box of chocolates,'[17] and various unattached family friends were invited for Christmas dinner. Among the latter were a widow named Mrs Shaw and an old acquaintance of Dr Moore's, Miss Keogh of Ballymena (who was later to gain a revised incarnation in the fictional character Miss Judith Hearne). Miss Keogh, who would have been around seventy at the time,[18] was partial to the colour red and never tired of talking about the 'dear aunt' who had brought her up. This lady was musical, and for her party piece would sit at the piano and belt out a hearty version of 'One More River'. There was a bit of a niggle between Miss Keogh and Mrs Shaw, each vying with the other to be the favoured guest. The children would have been under strict instructions to behave themselves, being mostly (in the early 1930s) of an age to find adults' foibles either tedious or hilarious. Certainly a few of Miss Keogh's peculiarities remained with Brian, to be turned to good account when the right moment arrived.

Between 1930 and 1936, Brian was sent each year to spend part of the summer with his Donegal relatives, his mother's brother James McFadden and his wife Annie.[19] (It seems likely that his grandmother Grace McGee – Granny McFadden – lived in the house as well, but he didn't have much recollection of her – or, indeed, of the plethora of cousins who were mostly a generation older than him and his sister Marie-Therese, who often accompanied him on these visits.) The farmhouse was called Duntally and stood above a glen; it contained a stone-floored kitchen with huge iron cooking-pot; it was pervaded by the pungent smell of turf-smoke, and not far away was the fifteenth-century Doe Castle, an enticing ruin in those days, though now tidied up by the Department of the Environment. Brian would go out to the fields in the mornings with his uncle to watch the men work, the turf-cutters and sheep-shearers and ploughmen and so forth; coming back riding a donkey or horse, bare-legged and happily unkempt, he'd consider himself privileged to be connected to this vivid Irish world with its bogs and heather and changeless customs and tangy air. It was all tremendously exhilarating for a city boy susceptible to changes of atmosphere – and everyone was kind to him and made a fuss of him, except for one occasion when he fell over in a cow-byre and ruined his sandals, obliging his aunt to take him into Creeslough to get him a new pair which she could ill afford. 'She was really cross!' he remembered. However, Aunt Annie was reimbursed by Eileen Moore when the latter travelled from Belfast to retrieve her offspring at the end of the summer and take them home on the Letterkenny bus. Aunt Annie was a big, rangy, skinny-looking woman, always wrapped in a patterned overall to protect her clothes and permanently tanned from working out of doors. She catered for everyone. Dinner, which generally consisted of potatoes and buttermilk, was eaten at midday and shared with any vagrant or passer-by from Creeslough who happened to show up at the right time. 'I seemed to be in an older Ireland,' Brian Moore has written:

> a place where life was elemental and harsh, yet close to a reality which was timeless and true. I would see a pig slaughtered, its blood running in rivulets in the yard outside the kitchen door. I would see a stallion mount a mare, its hooves scraping at the barrel of her rib-cage . . . I would be butted by yellow-eyed goats, kicked by donkeys when I tried to climb on their backs. I would see people drink tea, not from teacups as in Belfast, but from large china bowls in the eighteenth-century manner. I would sit by the hob of the kitchen turf fire watching as floury potatoes were doled out to the men coming in from the fields for their noonday dinner . . . I would see long white clay pipes and plugs of tobacco laid out near jugs of poteen at my aunt's wake.[20]

Actually, it is likely that the wake he refers to was his grandmother's; she died in 1936 and he has said he was there at the time. She doesn't seem to have made much impression on him as a personality; in fact, the whole mass of Donegal relatives are somehow lumped together under the heading 'real country people' and merged in his mind with the intoxicating landscape. Together these add up to a kind of psychic inheritance from his mother's side of the family; he has paid tribute to his mother's poetic sensibility,[21] along with her 'wicked' turns of phrase and countrywoman's shrewdness – in contrast to his father's practical, if unoriginal, intelligence and his rather surprising financial inexpertise. The McFaddens were greatly in awe of the debonair Dr Moore and extremely ill at ease in his presence. Probably without in the least intending it, he seems to have caused them to feel they stank of pig shit and had clay on their boots. But Brian – straddling two worlds – relished the chance to try out the role of a country boy, standing in the main street of Creeslough holding a rope attached to the neck of a calf, 'waiting for my uncle to come out of the pub where he was celebrating the calf's purchase'.[22]

If the Donegal McFaddens were not well off, the Moores could claim at least one rich relation: Uncle Jim McAllister. Uncle Jim, who lived in a house called Tullyglass, outside Ballymena, was actually a cousin of Dr Moore's[23] and had inherited his father's wine-and-spirit business, as well as owning a mineral-water company and seventeen pubs.[24] He was married to a woman considerably younger than himself, 'Aunt Sheena' to the Moore children, an archetypal 1930s fashion-plate in the eyes of Brian, thin as a rake (the story was that she refused to have children for fear it would spoil her figure). Aunt Sheena's frocks came from Paris, she wore a thin silver chain around her ankle and smoked Abdullah cigarettes. She kept a couple of Pekinese dogs as pets, and had picked at least one of the McAllister chauffeurs for his good looks. (Brian's description makes her sound like something out of Vicki Baum or Richmal Crompton.) Arriving on the Belfast-to-Ballymena train, the Moores would be met at the station by the current chauffeur and driven to the house with its great sweep of a drive, its paddock stocked with horses (just for show, Brian Moore recalled), its conservatory and private electricity generator. Luncheon guests at Tullyglass might include a local librarian named Pagan Cameron and a cultured priest or two: Aunt Sheena kowtowed to priests. She was *not* fond of children. It was always, 'Oh – give them some more strawberries and cream – keep 'em quiet!' When they couldn't feed their faces any more they were packed off to the housekeeper, Bea, with a couple of shillings to give her as a tip (there was no getting out of this embarrassing duty) – whereupon she would present them with a bag of sweets. These were small ritual courtesies which had to be observed. The practice of tipping servants, inculcated in Brian Moore at an early age, stayed with him all his life. It was also common practice for adults to dole out monetary handouts to children in return for some small service or just to mark an occasion: for this reason, if no other, the Moores were always pleased when they were visited by generous Uncle Jim.

Their own family's financial position, during the 1920s and '30s, is hard to gauge. Dr Moore's work at the Mater Hospital, as a GP with private patients, as St Malachy's medical officer, as a Queen's examiner, should have ensured a fairly high standard of living – and indeed, for a time at least, they enjoyed all the trappings of middle-class life, the nannies, servants, outings, seaside holidays, family celebrations and all the rest of it. They even employed a chauffeur of their own from time to time – Dr Moore being an appalling driver. The Clifton Street house itself seemed positively magnificent to awestruck visitors such as Marie-Therese Moore's Newington friend Aimie Clarke, from proletarian Annadale Street.[25] However, all the brothers and sisters remember their childhood as being not particularly affluent: 'There was not a great surplus of money' (Eibhlin); 'We didn't have a terrible lot of money' (Seamus). Of course, after primary level, there were school fees, including boarders' fees, to be paid for all nine of them; and Dr Moore it seems was in the habit of making regular donations to various Catholic charities (though surely even the most careless of fathers would not have imposed this pious obligation on himself to the detriment of his own family?). According to Brian, the first five children came in at the tail-end of a kind of quasi-Edwardian abundance, while things were different for the younger ones, especially after Dr Moore's death in 1942 when the extent of his improvidence was revealed. At that stage, with all but three of her children still at school or university, Eileen Moore must have faced a very uncertain future. They were living in Camden Street at the time, having been evacuated from Clifton Street after a bomb had fallen and damaged the house (which, some time after 1930, had passed into the ownership of the Mercy Sisters). As it happened, things didn't fall out too badly; but this was a very low moment in the family's fortunes.

* * *

Ardnagreina, *c.*1890. The semidetached house in Ballymena which became the home of Brian Moore's paternal grandmother after her husband's death. Her sister Mrs McAllister lived next door. *Courtesy Mrs Eilis McDowell.*

above left Aunt Maggie Moore.
Courtesy Brian O'Hara.

above right Dr James B. Moore
(top left) and a couple of
medical friends.
Courtesy Brian O'Hara.

Mary Judith Keogh, the
'friend of the family' and the
inspiration for Judith Hearne.
Courtesy Brian O'Hara.

Dr James B. Moore and Nurse Eileen McFadden in 1914, the year before their marriage. *Courtesy Brian O'Hara.*

Brian with Grainne, *c.*1923. *Courtesy Mrs Eilis McDowell.*

Brian catching a ball with his left hand. *Courtesy Mrs Eilis McDowell.*

Five young Moores by the railings in Henry Place, off Clifton Street, *c.*1926. (Brian second from right.) *Courtesy Mrs Eibhlin Darbyshire.*

Nellie Ritchie (holding Sean) and assorted Moores outside No.11, Clifton Street. (Brian on extreme right.) *Courtesy Eilis Moore.*

Clifton Street in the early part of the twentieth century, showing Brian Moore's birthplace on the extreme right. *Lawrence Collection. Courtesy National Library of Ireland.*

At the seaside. Aunt Minnie, Mrs Eileen Moore, Brian, Seamus, Eibhlin and Grainne. *Courtesy Brian O'Hara.*

Brian as a shepherd in the school Nativity Play, *c.*1929.
Courtesy Mrs Eibhlin Darbyshire.

Antrim Road, Belfast, *c*.1930. A children's party in full swing. Brian is among the young guests playing with balloons. *Courtesy Mrs Clodagh Hopkirk.*

Brian (third from right) with some young friends. *Courtesy Mrs Clodagh Hopkirk.*

St Malachy's seniors enjoying the snow, 1938. Brian at bottom on left, smoking a cigarette. 'The only photographic record of myself and the boys I palled around with for many years,' Brian wrote. *Courtesy Bernard McCloskey.*

Dr J.B. and Mrs Eileen Moore with family, summer 1941. (Brian on extreme right.) *Courtesy Brian O'Hara.*

There was Belfast, and Ballymena, and Portstewart, and Cree-slough; and there was also Dublin. Dublin had a much more cosmopolitan feel to it than any of these other places. It was a capital city; it should have been the capital of the whole of Ireland. It was freer and brighter and infinitely more full of possibilities than the North. Even its Catholicism had an edge of picturesqueness, and seemed less sour and dour than that of Belfast. Though it was 300-odd miles to the south, you always went 'up' to Dublin.

The Moores kept in close contact with the MacNeills, and Brian enjoyed a couple of summer holidays with his cousin Niall Mac-Neill and his family at the Ordnance Survey house in Phoenix Park,[26] which was – delightfully – surrounded by a moat. (Niall's children would have been his near contemporaries.) When he wasn't bicycling into town to see his Uncle John and other members of the family, or going to one of the cinemas near O'Connell Street, Brian would be out with brushes and paintpots helping to paint the black-and-white barriers which went up in the park during the annual international motor race. Niall MacNeill was president of the Irish Motor-Racing Club, as well as owning a Bugatti; on one occasion he allowed his young cousin to accompany him in this vintage car on its official journey through the park to signal the start of the race – 'a great moment!'. Racing became a temporary enthusiasm; it was his Dublin experiences that prompted Brian, back in Clifton Street, to entertain the younger children by setting up toy tracks on the nursery floor.

In his review[27] of Michael Tierney's biography of Eoin MacNeill, Brian Moore recalled earlier childhood visits to Dublin:

I remember that he [Eoin MacNeill] liked to break the long hours in his study by coming out to work in his garden and it was during these breaks that I discovered him to be infinitely more interesting than other grown-ups, for he treated children as his conversational equals, an unheard-of thing in Ireland in those days. He also, in some ineluctable way, communicated an impression of complete integrity and truthfulness.

He goes on to describe his Uncle John as 'the physical opposite of the trench-coated revolutionary of popular fancy', as he pottered about in his sobersided suit and old-fashioned wing-collared shirt, incessantly puffing away on an enormous pipe. There was, however, the evidence of a British Army bayonet, discovered in a garden shed, to remind young Brian of his uncle's far-from pussyfooting past. He liked and admired his Uncle John, no less than his father, and would have been – at the very least – intrigued by the upright old professor's one-time involvement in historic events. This was before Brian grew into an exasperated adolescence and washed his hands of the whole irksome business of Ireland's squabbles and fixation on its past. Even then, however, he didn't disclose this attitude to older relatives to whom he had no wish to cause distress.

The South, still known in those days as 'the Free State',[28] was the political entity to which Dr Moore and his family, in common with the majority of Northern Catholics, felt they owed their allegiance, even though an Act of Parliament had cut them off from it to leave them marooned in a morass of Orangeism. The Free State embodied self-determination, national confidence and the freedom to foster indigenous cultural resources – in the eyes of Northern nationalists at any rate. Once outside the six Northern counties, you weren't affronted at every turn by the sight of the Union Jack waving triumphantly above your head; the air wasn't tainted by sectarian rancour. Heading South, you moved into an altogether more glamorous and accommodating zone. And yet: Brian Moore has testified to feeling 'very much an Ulster person', and even a bit repelled by Southern loquacity and *plámás*.[29] His roots were in the North – even though Donegal was technically part of the Free State – and a Northern outlook, with its pragmatism, enterprise, aversion to cant, its self-mockery and general drollness, was an inescapable inheritance.

4

ST MALACHY'S ALUMNUS[1]

An electric bell, deafeningly loud, screamed out into corridors, crying unheard in empty dormitories, echoing across wet playing fields to die in the faraway mists over Belfast Lough.

Boys of all ages crowded corridors and stairs as though the buildings were on fire. Priests, wearing black soutanes, appeared at doors and turnings, swishing canes to restore order, harrying stragglers in transit from classroom to classroom. It was ten minutes to three. All were eager to finish the day.

The Feast of Lupercal

IN *LIES OF SILENCE*, published in 1990, Brian Moore singles out 'a school where teaching was carried on by bullying and corporal punishment and learning by rote, a school run by priests whose narrow sectarian views perfectly propagated the divisive bitterness which had led to the events of last night' (i.e. the capture by IRA gunmen of a youngish couple and the forcing of the central character to drive a bomb to a designated spot). It's not the first time he's had a go at his own and his father's Alma Mater. His second novel, *The Feast of Lupercal*, published in 1958, features a school, Ardath College, whose effect on its pupils is to muck up their lives: 'Ardath cared little for appearances or social graces. No wonder those boys weren't fit to go out with girls when they left school. It was a matter of ignorance, pure and simple.' (When the novel came out and some St Malachy's authorities actually considered initiating some kind of lawsuit, the then headmaster quashed the idea with the phrase, 'Boy's merely biting the hand that birched him.'[2]) Everything about the place is uncouth: the boys, the masters, the teaching methods, above all the ideas disseminated.

St Malachy's College in the 1930s was awash with Catholicism and coercion, qualities guaranteed to breed a critical attitude in a fairly recalcitrant pupil who found himself in an awkward relation to the school system almost from the word go. In the school records you find a note to the effect that Brian Moore left St Malachy's in June 1940, without formal qualifications, having failed his Senior Certificate Examination for the second time. This was not the ending to his school career that would have been predicted for him when he arrived at St Malachy's as a bright day boy in September 1933, shortly after his twelfth birthday; at that time, all the signs would have suggested a meritorious progression through the school, with exam-passing at intervals a trouble-free prospect. The son of the school doctor and President of the Old Boys' Association, the younger brother of a diligent worker, himself possessed of an uncommonly good mind: such a boy ought to have been able to take every academic requirement in his stride. What went wrong? With hindsight it's easy enough to regret the liberal education that would obviously have suited him better, the kind of education that wasn't available in Belfast at the time, and would never, in any case, have been available to his father's son.

What emphatically didn't suit him were the rote-learning and regimentation, the practice of knocking knowledge into boys' heads by whacking them on the palms of their hands, the endless intoning of prayers and precepts. Brian Moore believed himself to stand in something of an anomalous relation to his family and most of his contemporaries, and religion was one of the major issues on which his mind diverged from theirs. He claimed to have been a sceptic from the start. Unlike other members of his family, indeed, he didn't inherit a religious temperament; however, there's a slightly defensive element to his early agnosticism. He had to cultivate an attitude of disbelief in order to preserve a certain peace of mind. If you declined to take the whole caboodle seriously, then you didn't have to worry about unavoidable transgressions, such as constant self-abuse.

Brian Moore has always described himself as a highly sexed child, who discovered masturbation at an early age – 'almost from the time of my First Communion' (i.e. six or seven). This was something he could never speak to anyone about, least of all the priest in Confession – though some instinct alerted him to the fact that it counted as a 'sin'. Doing it was bad enough, and failing to confess it compounded the business: according to Catholic dogma, failure to disclose every item of wrongdoing meant you'd made a bad Confession, and hence were in a state of mortal sin. Your soul, as a consequence (Catholic children were assured), instead of being all bright and shiny as it should have been, was as black as soot.

Lumbered with an indelibly black soul, then, the young Brian Moore – 'as most children would do in that situation' – began to distance himself from the Church, and from religion. It was easier to jettison the dogma than to take it all at face value, including the prospect of damnation. For a time, it's true, he was terrified of Hell, but it wasn't long before he was able to discard this figment of Catholic faith as his natural rationality began to assert itself. There was never, he insisted, any great drama or moment of crisis about his loss of faith – just a gradual withdrawal into a state of more-or-less happy secularism.

The thing that troubled him most, he said, was having to lie to his parents all the time, the sense he had of 'letting them down' by virtue of his unspoken apostasy. It was necessary to pretend. He couldn't possibly have got out of the Family Rosary, for instance, the nightly ritual which took place with the entire household on its knees in the drawing-room clutching rosary-beads and intoning Hail Marys with more or less fervour. This communal praying was a source of terrible embarrassment to Brian as he knelt there doing his best to efface himself in the back of an armchair. (Later on, he might have had a couple of allies within the family – Sean and Una – but they'd have been too young at the time to take any kind of independent attitude.) Sunday Mass, fortnightly Confession, Holidays of Obligation, Evening Devotions: these were other ingredients of a Catholic upbringing there was no getting out of.

I stand with my brothers and sisters [he recalled] singing a ludicrous Marian hymn in St Patrick's Church at evening devotions:

> O virgin pure, O spotless maid,
> We sinners send our prayers to thee.
> Remind thy son that he has paid
> The price of our iniquity.[3]

Seamus Moore was enrolled in St Malachy's Preparatory Department at the age of five, progressed to being a First Year Junior, and never attended any other school. All the rest of the family got their primary education at Newington,[4] after which Brian and Sean went on to St Malachy's, while the girls, starting with Eibhlin, were sent as boarders to the Cross and Passion Convent at Kilcullen, Co. Kildare. The exception was Una. By the late 1930s, Eileen Moore had made up her mind that the younger girls should be educated in the North, nearer home, at a school in Ballycastle, Co. Antrim, where Una went. However, the war intervened, and because of food shortages and dangers, it was decided that the two youngest, Peggy and Eilis, would be better off in the neutral South. Una stayed where she was, however. The Moore girls who were educated in the South learned all their lessons through the medium of Irish, and consequently became fluent pretty quickly, while the boys in the family all failed to acquire any Irish at all. It's hard to see any consistent educational principle operating here. According to Eibhlin,[5] the decision to educate the girls in the South was strongly influenced by Eoin MacNeill,[6] but why only the girls? And if the Irish language was so important, why wasn't pressure put on the boys to acquire it? Why divide the family by ensuring that half its members could list among their resources a language which remained a closed book to the others? Brian claimed that Irish was 'compulsory' at St Malachy's and that he was therefore 'against' it; but, as in his father's day, you had a choice about whether to study it or not.[7] Seamus didn't take it as a school subject either, though he remembers briefly attending Irish classes at the Ard Scoil in Divis Street, and deriving very little benefit from them.[8] So – we have the three Moore brothers enrolled as day boys at a school that was virtually on their doorstep, while their sisters, during term time, were away in different parts of the country. Things reached such a pitch that the youngest child, Eilis, hardly knew who her sisters were – who were these big girls, she'd demand to be told, coming in as if they owned the place: 'Why can't they go to their own homes?'[9] Eilis herself, in due course, went off with her school trunk to the Cross and Passion Convent, where she acquired such a taste for the religious life that she fixed her sights on it. Endowed with a full measure of Moore obstinacy, Eilis overrode every objection raised to her taking the veil. She became a Cross and

Passion nun herself (taking the name of Sister Anne), and eventually a headmistress – based in Manchester – until her retirement in 1990. She and Brian, at opposite ends of the religious spectrum, retained some affection for one another, as well as some mutual respect. A kind of wary politeness, though, came into their rare encounters in later years. Family affections didn't stop each being totally bemused by the other's way of life.

Brian Moore's arrival at St Malachy's coincided with preparations to celebrate the school centenary. Local bishops and cardinals,[10] got up in full religious regalia, took part in the Solemn High Mass to mark the occasion, which was held in the College chapel on Friday, 3 November 1933, with the school choir performing at the top of its bent. The previous Sunday, 29 October, designated 'Staff and Students' Day', had started with another High Mass celebrated by the College President and attended by the whole school. At six in the evening, the day boys were back in the chapel, along with the boarders, for Solemn Benediction; and afterwards, as a great treat, the whole school assembled for high tea in an 'improvised banquet-hall' (the Lower English classrooms), 'a feast well calculated to make the teeth of any schoolboy water, and we were no exceptions to the rule'.[11] The buns, we're told, were well up to standard. It sounds like a very jolly occasion, especially for those with a relish for pulling crackers and wearing funny hats. Even at twelve, though, it's unlikely that Brian Moore would have entered whole-heartedly into these proceedings. Throughout his life, he resisted the temptation to be part of a clique, setting himself first of all slightly at odds with his family,[12] holding himself a bit aloof from the Catholic cosiness and partisan school spirit that prevailed at St Malachy's, and eventually – in later life – making his home as far as possible from centres of literary freemasonry.

His brother Seamus was a year ahead of him at the school, but more important, at the time, was the continuing friendship and support of his neighbour Niall Dempsey, a fellow new boy and constant companion. It was, perhaps, proximity rather than natural affinity that drew the two of them together, but for all that they got on well enough and remained friends throughout the whole of their schooldays, even if their interests diverged in certain respects. Niall Dempsey, for example, was a keen tennis player and champion runner, whereas Brian took very little interest in school sports[13] (well, aside from swimming). Whenever he was questioned about his schooldays, Brian Moore tended to lump the whole period together into a kind of blur of dreariness and disgruntlement: it's only in his fiction that he singles out remembered incidents and details. However, it can't have been completely as dismal and unmemorable as he registered it. He remembered having made very few friends at St Malachy's,[14] mentioning in this connection only the Casement brothers, Rory and Enda, along with Niall Dempsey. When pressed, though, he came up with a kind of mildly disruptive group within the school, a group which took a certain pride in its rather blasé orientation, in being firmly opposed to everything authoritarian, hearty and conscientious about St Malachy's. 'It doesn't seem terribly significant now,' he said, looking back on it; and it probably only existed during his first or second year, after which it would most likely have looked a bit childish. But while this rebel faction was going strong it was led by him, and frequently he'd be driven to fisticuffs to defend its principles, while his second-in-command Niall Dempsey backed him up to the extent of volunteering to hold his jacket.

This subversive element may not have amounted to very much, as he implied, but it shows how his mind was shaping: when faced with any kind of establishment stuffiness, his instinct was to go in the opposite direction. ('If the left wing had been in power, he'd have been right wing,' observed Niall Dempsey drily.)[15] He was never, of course, completely an outsider, even during his schooldays; restless, dissatisfied and critical he may have been, but he was also amiable, humorous and quizzical, and it was the latter qualities that came to predominate. The nickname Ikey, or Isaac, followed him from Newington; but it was, one of his contemporaries insists,[16] always affectionately applied. And, as at Newington, he took the star place in at least one lesson. His was usually the essay that was read out and praised before the class – though now he had competition from a boy named Brendan McGarry[17] whose English was considered equally good. Each week, one or other of them would have written the top composition, and it turned into a kind of horse race between them. The English master then was a Father Crossin – 'a terribly Uriah Heepish sort of person', according to Brian Moore, and probably, he added, a repressed homosexual to boot; however, it's unlikely that he is the model for the odious schoolmaster in that untypical Moore story, 'Preliminary Pages for a Work of Revenge',[18] the one who reads out the narrator's essay to a class of thick-witted boys, in a spirit of sneering sarcasm ('Oh, what a fine foil I must have seemed for the exercise of his lumpish pedagogic wit . . .'). Even if this story was sparked off by remembered wrongs and slights, which is debatable, these would have been inflated in the interests of a dramatic impact. (Brian Moore did come in for some teasing at home on account of his literary interests, but this was a very minor vexation.) The villains of this short piece, the betrayers, taunters, traducers etc, are clearly no more than pretexts for an exercise in recrimination. The effect of the whole thing is rather odd, as though a naturally good-humoured person were assuming a posture of rancour and bitterness; and it's framed in a style which is a far cry from Brian Moore's usual lithe and relaxed narrative practice.

Niall Dempsey remembered Brian and the French master – unoriginally dubbed 'Froggy' – exchanging jokes in French, while no one else had a clue what they were talking about. This is borne out by a letter of 1957, signed 'Your old friend Charlie Lenaghan',[19] written to Brian Moore after the publication of *Lupercal*,[20] which looks back nostalgically to 'Froggy's French class in 1935–6', recalling ruefully: 'You were somewhere near the top of the class . . . while I only had one poor chap as a cushion at the bottom.' (The writer was ordained a priest in 1958.) French and English – though not the dull parts, like grammar – were the two school subjects that captured Brian Moore's interest, and at which he was happy to excel. His deficiency in other subjects, though, is a complicated matter. He conveyed to his friends an impression of being indifferent to success or failure, as far as schoolwork was concerned; but his apparent insouciance was covering up a very real dread of failure, of being the only one in the family to make a poor showing at exams, of disappointing his parents and condemning himself to a twopenny-halfpenny future. And the more he did badly at certain subjects, the more his self-mortification drove him to do even worse. The practicalities of the situation didn't help. Because of his family connections, and his own evident intelligence, he was always placed in the 'A' division – alongside boys whose adroit mathematical brains only reinforced his sense of inadequacy.

He couldn't compete, so he didn't try. And he was always badly taught. Long after he'd left St Malachy's, he came to the conclusion that he'd been what he called 'dyslexic in numbers' (this may have had something to do with the left-hand right-hand switch), and the very rough-and-ready teaching methods to which he was subjected could never have coped with any such anomaly. Mathematical propositions weren't explained or discussed; you learnt the rules by heart, and if, after that, you failed to work out the correct answer to a sum, you held out your hand to be lashed with a cane. That was how it was.

The school president, or headmaster, in Brian Moore's day was Dr Hendley, 'a small little grey man', very strict and authoritarian, who taught maths and Latin and used to suffer shaking fits in the classroom as a consequence of having contracted malaria; this would no doubt have reinforced his unsettling effect on the boys. ('Peculiar sort of man', Niall Dempsey summed him up.) Dr Hendley wasn't popular – he's remembered as a useless and arrogant headmaster, and held to blame for the intimidating atmosphere which prevailed at the school. (Things changed greatly for the better when his successor, a Father McMullan, took over in 1939.) That was St Malachy's then in the early 1930s: utterly lacking in social polish, often freezing cold (efficient central heating wasn't installed until 1936), a place of constant beatings and endless apprehensions, filled with withering religiosity and overbearing pedagogy.

A BBC discussion of *Lupercal*, broadcast in 1958, included as one of its contributors a Mr J.J. Campbell, one-time mathematics master at St Malachy's who'd been responsible in his day for administering a great deal of corporal punishment. Campbell's extraordinarily crass verdict on the novel[21] was as follows: 'This is an unpleasant book or rather unpleasing book with an adolescent touch. The author is a young man who did not like school. He has not outgrown adolescence.'[22] Nothing about the book's remarkable liveliness, its breathtaking set-pieces and technical expertise, its moments of comedy, its absolute trueness-to-life, the way it puts its finger on every essential shortcoming of the mid-century Belfast Catholic education. Instead, Mr Campbell is very much on the defensive about the amount of caning sanctioned by the school (Moore has exaggerated it, he says), driving even Seamus Moore –

the 'good' brother Seamus, the one who sailed through St Malachy's without coming a cropper in any exams or setting himself at loggerheads with his teachers – to counterattack by recalling 'the sadistic regime that I encountered during twelve years' penal servitude at school'.[23]

The first hurdle in the race to achieve a place at university was the Junior Certificate Examination, undergone at fourteen or fifteen and requiring a pass in every subject to get you through to the next level, the preparation course for the crucial Senior Certificate. A maths coach was hired by Dr Moore to provide extra tuition for Brian, and he just scraped through the Junior Maths paper (he did well in every other subject). In the meantime, he'd devised a scheme for earning extra pocket-money. There were boys among his classmates who were unable, or at any rate unwilling, to grind out the weekly composition prescribed by Father Crossin; and he undertook to do it for them – for a fee of something like a shilling a time. 'I was,' he reminisced gleefully, 'a professional hack from the word go!' He was terribly chuffed to find he could get away with it; it was easy enough for him to imitate other boys' styles, even that of a dunce named Hugh Burns who could hardly read, let alone write. His exercises on behalf of Burns were not only convincing but actually gave Father Crossin the impression that this incorrigible dimwit was improving throughout the year.

It was an eccentric form of literary apprenticeship, indeed, but it had its uses, introducing young Brian to the art of impersonation, of writing as though you were someone else. It was also a thrill to discover this way of undermining school discipline. Contempt for his teachers was a sentiment he probably wouldn't have articulated at the time, but it was seething away. Uninspired teaching at St Malachy's extended even to the English lessons, which took no account of any book or author not on the school curriculum ('Mark that, boys, that's a likely passage for the Examination!'), bludgeoned pupils into learning set texts by heart, and nearly destroyed any feeling for poetry that might have existed. 'I remember our English master,' Brian Moore wrote,[24] 'droning these lines from "The Lake Isle of Innisfree": "Nine bean rows will I have there, a hive for the honey bee/And live alone in the bee-loud glade." "That is onomatopoeia, boys. You can hear the sound of the buzzing bees." I did, and for years associated Yeats's poetry with the memory of falling asleep.' It took him a long time to reinstate Yeats.

St Malachy's was, of course, a fee-paying establishment in those days, with only a handful of scholarship boys to temper the middle-class tone. On the social scale, pupils ranged from the sons of rich Catholic bookies, who arrived at the college gates each morning in chauffeur-driven cars, to the socially disadvantaged day-boys from the Lower Falls, whose twice-daily trek lay along Dover Street, across the Shankill Road, through a couple of other streets to Carlisle Circus, and hence to the school. Almost the only good word Brian Moore had to say about the place concerned the absence of snobbery: an equality of treatment prevailed, whether your clothes came from Brands & Norman's or the local St Vincent de Paul depot. 'We were all badly dressed, dirty and unkempt,' he recalled; however, it was plain that the Falls Road boys were worse dressed than the others. (He also remembered a brilliant classics scholar, Johnny Something-or-other, whose blinkered working-class family forced him to relinquish a Queen's scholarship in order to go out to work as a labourer: a common enough story at the time.)

Some of the scholarship pupils were country boys and had to board at the school. One of these, of a slightly earlier vintage than Brian Moore, and an altogether more tractable student, was the future novelist and headmaster Michael McLaverty, whose por-trayal of St Malachy's is framed in an uninquisitorial manner.

Outside in the grey evening lay two playing-fields, black with mud, the goal-posts white and dirtied by smacks from the ball. On one side was the dark jail wall, and on the opposite side the top windows of terrace houses overlooked the grounds. The fields were desolate and already the gulls were swarming and calling as they lit on the ground.

Inside, the Study Hall glowed with dry warmth from the hot pipes. All the boys stood at their yellow desks waiting for the priest to enter. Some were combing their wet-streaked hair and others exchanging twopenny detective stories. Father McGorey came in. The fellows were glad: he was an easy man that read his breviary all the time, or maybe perused a book that he'd find on a boy's desk. He ascended the rostrum. They blessed themselves. The priest began:

> *Direct, we beseech Thee, O Lord, all our actions and carry them on by Thy gracious assistance, that every prayer, word and work of ours may begin through Thee, and by Thee be happily ended through Christ our Lord . . . Amen!*

There was a loud shuffling of feet, a creaking of desks, and a turning of pages. Then silence.[25]

It's an evocative account. McLaverty's Belfast is a good deal simpler and more decorative than the city recreated in the novels of Brian Moore. His first and best novel, *Call My Brother Back*, records Belfast's idiosyncrasies with all the keenness of a child's vision, without ironic or critical counterpoint: the holy-water fonts and plaster statues, brickfields and dumps and factory chimneys, hens poking about in the dirt, ill-lit churches and deprived children hawking bundles of sticks in battered prams from door to door. The hero of the novel, young Colm MacNeill, spends a term as a boarder at St Malachy's before his family's move to the city enables him to enrol as a day-boy.

> Colm stood behind Chit, both of them watching with patient regret the day-boys running down the straight avenue, and out through the open gates. They could see an odd tram passing, and they envied the day-boys their freedom.
> 'It's as bad as the jail in here,' Chit squeaked, his hands in his pockets, his face ink-spotted.[26]

With this novel, and to a lesser extent with its successor, *Lost Fields* (1942), McLaverty achieved an extraordinary delicacy and lucidity of tone – qualities which evaded him for ever after.[27] McLaverty as a novelist is in nearly every respect the opposite of Brian Moore – parochial, devout and decorous, while the other, a product of the same scholastic regime, is an expatriate, a sceptic and an outspoken social commentator. As a sidelight on Irish literary history, however, it's worth noting that the two came briefly in contact in the mid-1930s, when one was a young schoolmaster, as yet unpublished, and the other a restive and dissatisfied schoolboy. Neither had much effect on the other, it's true, though Brian read *Call My Brother Back* some years later and judged its school section authentic enough, with the country boys coming in as boarders, the airing of trivial grievances and all the rest of it – but totally anodyne in relation to the school's defects.

Dr Moore was President of the local branch of the St Vincent de Paul Society, a Catholic charity which dispensed help of various kinds to the needy, and constantly required volunteers to assess degrees of neediness. Michael McLaverty played a part in the work of this organisation, and through it he became acquainted with Dr Moore and his wife, and also with Brian, who was roped in – though he was only fifteen or sixteen at the time – to accompany SVDP officers visiting working-class homes to gauge the genuineness or otherwise of pleas for help. If satisfied, they would hand out half-crown vouchers for food which could then be exchanged at the grocer's. A lot of this evaluation work was carried out with the utmost insensitivity, and put people's backs up by exposing them to humiliation.[28] It can't have helped anyone's morale to have a young schoolboy come round with the charity workers and stand there scrutinising the details of pauperdom. (This was during the Depression, when unemployment was rife and poverty escalating.) However, Brian quite enjoyed the experience, he found it interesting enough and he came to believe it was good for his character to get a glimpse of the troubles and privations some people were forced to endure. (He wouldn't otherwise have had much of an *entrée* into lower-class homes.) The experience may even have contributed to his later socialist leanings – though these were no doubt more strongly connected to a sense of enlightenment, a forward-looking way of ducking out of Ireland's impasse.

He never actually joined a left-wing organisation, 'Belfast and my childhood [having] made me suspicious of faiths, allegiances, certainties . . .'[29] but he was sufficiently committed to the socialist ideology to stand in the streets of Belfast flogging copies of a Trotskyite news-sheet. This was quite an audacious undertaking, in the face of general Catholic teaching and the particular Catholicism of his own family. Of course his revolutionary leanings, political and religious, were cultivated clandestinely. Among the limited social activities available in Belfast at the time were marathon walks along the Lagan Towpath, up the Buttermilk Loney or the Cave Hill; Brian's friend Rory Casement remembered the endless discussions and arguments about religion, socialism and life in general which enlivened these outings. Brian would always take the atheist position, and, when it was pointed out to him that he still went regularly to Mass, and asked how he thought this tied in with his claims to be a free-thinker, he'd explain that he kept up religious observances solely for his mother's sake. It was better to conform outwardly than precipitate a domestic furore.

Sometimes the Casement girls, Maire and Eily, would come along on these walks; and other boys' sisters or cousins might occasionally join in, but attempts at dalliance never amounted to very much. ('Ardath cared little for appearances or social graces. No wonder these boys weren't fit to go out with girls when they left school. It was a matter of ignorance, pure and simple.')[30] Girls, though, were the chief thing on Brian Moore's mind at the time; he was possessed by carnal desires and desperately unhappy about his looks. 'He was . . . an inch or two smaller than most other fellows of seventeen,' thinks his *alter ego* Gavin Burke. 'Had masturbation made him pale, or was that just a stupid yarn? God, not self-abuse, had given him his face, all beaked nose thrusting out blindly like a day-old bird's, his thin lips which seemed to bite each other, his hated girlish hands. If he were a girl, would he go with him? He had to answer: no.'[31] It was just another of the crosses he had to bear, along with the bad schooling, the need to share a bedroom with his brother Seamus, the oppressive religion and the evidence proving him insufficiently endowed in the brains department (though he knew this wasn't true). Summoned to Dr Hendley's office, after yet another flunking of a maths exam, he was rather surprised to be let off with the words: 'I suppose it's not really your fault, Moore – it's not laziness, I think, just a want of intelligence.'

What was going to become of him? It was all very well to cultivate an unconcerned appearance for his friends, but the day of reckoning wasn't too far away, the time when he'd have to accept that a university course and a degree in medicine were not for him. The 1930s were wearing on, with Belfast engendering the usual eruptions: if its riots weren't sectarian, they were Communist-inspired[32]

– though the latter never came to anything, since the Communist Party of Ireland didn't stand a chance against a powerful, if unusual, united opposition from *both* religious factions. Angry voices, shots ringing out, police baton charges, sore heads, cracked ribs, blood running in the gutters, looting, barricades . . . all these features of endemic unrest were constantly enacted not a stone's throw away from Clifton Street, whose professional families were brought up smack against commotions they'd rather not have known about. Belfast was embedding itself in Brian Moore's consciousness as a place of tedium and stress. Its excitements were of a despicable kind, and its boredoms were bottomless.

Changes were taking place in the home – 1936, for instance, saw the deaths of both the resident aunts. Aunt Minnie was the first to go, and Brian was in the room with her when she died. She'd been put in a bed in the day-nursery, and he thought this very odd: to see an adult in these unsuitable surroundings, and in bed. (All the family took their turn at sitting with her.) As her breathing became more laboured, worried about upsetting the child (he was fourteen at the time), Aunt Minnie took up a book in both hands and pretended to be reading it. However, it wasn't long before he spotted that she was holding it upside-down. It was a book about Ireland, and there was a tricolour on the dust-jacket: green, white and gold. These details stayed with him, along with an image of his aunt's chalk-white face, pouring with sweat, and her terrible efforts to get her breath, which stopped before long. Much later, the episode took on a kind of symbolic resonance for him:[33] the dying woman, thoughtful to the end, the upside-down Irish flag, the noise of the death rattle, which terrified him. And more was to come. Being a Dominican Tertiary, Aunt Minnie had the right to be buried in a brown nun's habit; seeing her laid out in it, in her coffin, he was more than ever conscious of the gulf between himself and his father's generation, and it gave him a strange feeling, a *frisson* of incomprehension – 'It was almost as if these people had been members of some kind of secret society, with weird esoteric rituals and beliefs.' He consigned the lot of them, in his mind, to a dark, claustrophobic and backward past, something he preferred to have no truck with.

The ritual of the funeral, however, was a different matter: 'Funerals were a big event in our lives.' The words of the burial service impressed him with their sonorousness and implacability: 'Remember man that thou art dust, and unto dust thou shalt return.' Little boys were involved in these ceremonies (unlike women and girls), accompanying funeral processions right to the graveside where they stood ready to hold the men's top hats whenever they took them off as a gesture of respect. Brian and Seamus performed this task quite often, usually in Ballymena at the family plot. They were there for Aunt Minnie, and again for her sister, only a few months later. Aunt Maggie had died while on a visit to relatives in Dublin; the body was sent home on the train, and the Moores, including Brian, were at Great Victoria Street Station to receive it. 'I remember seeing the train come in and waiting and seeing her coffin brought off.' It was a dull dry day, overcast and gloomy. Then came the burial in Ballymena followed by funeral meats – fruit cake and whisky – at the home of a distant relative. A drunken doctor among the mourners ('Dempo' Redden was his name) came over to have a word with young Brian. 'Well now,' he said. 'There's two of them in your house – Minimus and Maximus. Minimus has gone, and now Maximus has gone too.' From that point on, Brian said, 'They've always been Minimus and Maximus – Minnie and Maggie.'

'One thing he [Brian] and my father had in common,' observed Seamus Moore,[34] 'they were both voracious readers.' Not that they went in for the same kind of reading material. Brian remembered virtually nothing that came into his hands between the *Magnet* and the *Gem*[35] and *Ulysses* – but he was sure of one thing, that his taste in literature was always superior to his father's. Dr Moore enjoyed certain unofficial privileges through being a person of note on his home ground, and one of these was the right to have first choice of new books coming into the Falls Road Library, where his friend Joe Fitzsimmons was head librarian. The Moore children would frequently be taken there, or sent over with a suitcase to borrow recent acquisitions on their father's behalf. (The arrangement worked for them too; they had the run of the juvenile section before the local hordes of grubby fiction-addicts were allowed in.) Agatha Christie, A.J. Cronin, P.G. Wodehouse, Maurice Walsh . . . all these made their way to Clifton Street, to be fallen upon by Dr Moore. Anything Irish was especially welcome: he relished Forrest Reid and George A.

Birmingham, and considered Kate O'Brien to be a great novelist. Ferocious arguments with his middle son ensued. Brian detested all this bland, middlebrow, middle-of-the-road stuff. 'He was a young teenager,' his brother Seamus recalled,[36] 'and my father was getting on, and they didn't consort together all that well . . .' Fiction, indeed, was only a minor cause of friction. The great exam-passer couldn't, and wouldn't, understand his son's apparent lack of academic drive. Why on earth didn't he pull himself together and put in a spot of work, at those subjects at which he was weakest? Work, hard work, was the only way to get on in the world.

Brian Moore would often become tremendously irritated by those, particularly critics, who read into his fictional fathers – Dr Fadden in *Fergus*, and Burke Senior in *The Emperor of Ice Cream* – a direct portrayal and indictment of Dr Moore; and it was even worse when they went on to superimpose a heavy-handed Freudian gloss over the novels' postulations: 'Having tasted his own death, Fergus can at last demythologise his father, accept him as a man, release him from the role of tyrant and god he has held for so long in the depths of his son's being.'[37] Not only is such phraseology at odds with the high comedy of *Fergus*, and the rueful exuberance of *Emperor*, but it inflates unacceptably the pretty down-to-earth, at times discordant, but basically affectionate relationship that existed between Dr Moore and his second son. ('My father was the kindest man alive.') Of course the novelist ransacked his past, his exclusive store of raw material, for his books; of course he worked up all kinds of remembered, or half-remembered, incidents, conflicts, *idées fixes* or idiosyncrasies into a fine-tuned piece of fabrication. The end result rings true, that's the main thing. If it's necessary to go through the novels searching out pieces of unadulterated autobiography, and drawing inferences from them, then one would probably have to say that the clashing viewpoints of father and son (to take that example, which looms pretty large among critical strategies) were ultimately of less significance than certain commentators have suggested, but produced more tension and acrimony than the novelist cared to recall.

Dr Moore is remembered by his son's contemporaries as a pleasant enough individual, but undeniably 'stern and strict . . . Victorian [in outlook], no question about it!'[38] During the Christmas break of 1938–9, a crowd of St Malachy's boys took advantage of unusually snowy conditions to indulge in a bit of sliding and tobogganing down the Buttermilk Loney in North Belfast. About ten or twelve hefty seniors took part in this piece of seasonal skylarking, which ended, hilariously, with everyone thrown together at the bottom of the toboggan-run in a tangled heap. A passing photographer from the *Belfast Telegraph* recorded the blithesome moment for posterity. One boy had managed to keep his head above the mêlée, and a lighted cigarette stuck to his lip – Brian Moore, whose father was said to have given him a good hammering the next day when the photograph appeared in the evening paper: he'd been caught out smoking. This doesn't, indeed, accord with his own version of his father's attitude to corporal punishment, but it seems a very likely action, at that time, on the part of an angry parent faced with indisputable evidence of his son's delinquency.

Smoking was forbidden, but the practice was widely indulged in, even in Michael McLaverty's day – 'Fellows rushed out to the daffs for a quick smoke and then hurried back to the refectory for a cup of cocoa and hunks of bread.'[39] Everyone did it – pupils, teachers, parents, priests. Rory Casement remembered a camping holiday in the summer of 1939, with the same group of St Malachy's seniors ensconced for six weeks or so in a bell tent in a field near Newcastle, Co. Down, in an increasingly smoky atmosphere. All of them puffed away incessantly – but only Brian, it seems, possessed sufficient nerve to essay a further approximation to the grownup state. With only a couple of Guinness to bolster his resolve, he'd take himself off every now and then to a dance hall in Newcastle, returning home 'at God knows what hour of the night'.[40] The scope for misbehaviour wouldn't have been unrestricted, though, and he didn't add sexual braggadocio to his parade of audacity and devilmay-careishness. He was seventeen, had just failed his Senior Certificate Exam for the first time and was about to put in another futile year at school before the same thing happened all over again. (He was just two months short of his nineteenth birthday when he finally left St Malachy's, marked as 'Failed'.) In the meantime, the Second World War had broken out, and Dr Moore the Irish patriot was no doubt giving vent to a few of the aberrant opinions attributed to Mr Burke in *The Emperor of Ice Cream*.

5

BOMBS OVER BELFAST

Two more explosions boomed on the far side of the city. The guns were silent. Then, beautiful, exploding with a faint pop in the sky above them, a magnesium flare floated up in the stillness, lighting the rooftops in a ghostly silver . . . And in that moment, within Gavin, there started an extraordinary elation, a tumult of joy. He felt like dancing a Cherokee war dance on the edge of the parapet. The world and the war had come to him at last . . . Tonight, history had conferred the drama of war on this dull, dead town in which he had been born.

The Emperor of Ice Cream

BRIAN MOORE HAS ALWAYS agreed that *The Emperor of Ice Cream*, his fifth novel, is the most directly autobiographical, in its depiction of the events which took place between his leaving St Malachy's, and, a few years later, washing his hands of Belfast. At the start of the novel his *alter ego* Gavin Burke is about to join the ARP in the face of some opposition from his family – ' "Gracious God, [his Aunt Liz exclaims]. Did I ever think I'd live to see the day when my own nephew would stand in this room dressed up like a Black and Tan" '; and the book discloses straightaway its hero's secret, almost shameful glorying in the new, anarchic state of affairs: 'War was freedom, freedom from futures. There was nothing in the world so imposing that a big bomb couldn't blow it up.'

With 'the grown-ups' world [reduced to] ruins', he thinks, it hardly matters a jot if Gavin Burke has failed his School Leaving Certificate, and if, as a consequence, a sober professional future is unavailable to him. It's true that the Second World War was, in a sense, Brian Moore's salvation; it was certainly the most crucial event of his early life. A week after war was declared, however, he was back at school and accepting a challenge from the history master – a Dr Rogers – that he'd not be able to take up history at that late stage and pass an exam in it, which he proceeded to do, winning the five-shilling bet that the other had initiated. Dr Rogers, a one-time pupil of Eoin MacNeill's, had expressed the view that a nephew of MacNeill's ought to be ashamed of himself for being ignorant of history; Brian was in a mood to agree, and to offer to make good the deficiency. He worked hard throughout the year and got a good pass mark in history – but the terrible maths paper was his downfall again. That summer (1940) he went to Dublin with the idea of urging his MacNeill connections to exert a bit of pull to get him into the Irish Army; in fact, he was accepted on to the equivalent of the OTC,[1] but while he was waiting for the papers to come through it became very clear that De Valera's policy of neutrality was never going to be jettisoned. 'So I simply never reported for duty.' Disgusted by the Free State's – as he saw it – pig-headed refusal to ally itself with the forces for democracy and right-thinking, he caught the first train back to Belfast and offered his services to an ARP unit. It was one thing to have contemplated joining the *Irish* Army; to become a British soldier[2] was simply unthinkable, given the Moore family's cultural and political in-heritances. The ARP – civil defence – was a kind of compromise.[3]

It was hard for Irish nationalists to concede that Britain could ever be wholly in the right; in many cases, opposition to the war effort was prompted by nothing more cogent than atavistic hosti-lity. The First World War slogan, 'England's difficulty is Ireland's opportunity', was deeply engrained. 'Your Man Gallagher', the nationalist ARP recruit in *The Emperor*, stands for a whole com-munity whose feelings about the war 'could be summed up in the fact that they considered it a point of honour to leave a light shining in their upstairs windows at night in case any German bombers might come over the city'. Such people do, in the event, get more than they bargained for; but in 1940, even in more sagacious circles, the received wisdom was that Hitler would never bother to attack an outpost such as Northern Ireland; and that defence organisations like the ARP, with their drilling and scurrying and pretend emergencies, were both ridiculous and redundant. The battledress uniform didn't help to create a serious impression ('His older sister Kathy came into the room, stopped, and shrieked: "God help us! Charlie Chaplin!"'), nor the fact that the ARP was largely made up of misfits, the chronically unemployed, boozers and bletherers and bullies like the Crummick Street Warden in *The Emperor*, Mr 'There's a war on' Craig. At theatrically low moments the nineteen-year-old exam-failer would have felt he was in the right place, among the feeble, the futile and the no-hopers.

Brian Moore's ARP unit was based at the Mater Hospital, not Crummick Street (his youngest sister Eilis, who was still at home, remembered carrying his lunch up there to him every day); and in the novel he has, naturally, tampered with reality in other ways consistent with obtaining a piquant effect. Many of the characters, though, he admitted, 'had sort of semi-models in real life', and one at least is almost a direct portrayal – Freddy Hargreaves, the nearest thing to a kindred spirit encountered by Gavin Burke at his make-shift place of employment. A 'tall man in a tweed jacket, well-cut flannels, and highly polished brogues', aged about thirty and wearing thick-lensed glasses which 'did not seem to belong on his handsome face': this is Teddy Millington, 'a failure in life and a drop-out', but, for Brian, a person wonderfully *au fait* with current literary departures. It was Millington who introduced the avid teenager to the *Faber Book of Modern Verse*, edited by Michael Roberts, and first published in 1936 – a book which showed him a whole new side to W.B. Yeats, and, even more importantly, brought him face to face with Eliot and Auden, and thereby gave him a taste for poetry which stayed with him for the rest of his life. 'They were all there!' he recalled exuberantly in later years: Hart Crane, Wallace Stevens, even the Ulsterman MacNeice, all the new (new to him) and exhilarating writers whose modernist procedures were a world away from the suffocating axioms of Catholic nationalism. He couldn't get enough of urgent, up-to-date, non-provincial literature and allied cultural pursuits, even in the watered-down version in which the latter were available in Belfast; and Teddy Millington, though never exactly a mentor, was instrumental in gaining him an *entrée* into Belfast's more progressive milieux.

He'd already had a clandestine encounter with *Ulysses*, an experience he's recounted in several different versions. As far as one can judge, the authentic version seems to be the one in which his cousin Tom Graham,[4] who lived with his parents in a house on the Antrim Road in Belfast, brought a copy of the book back from Paris and recommended it to his young relative as a salacious read. Going through it avidly in search of the supposed 'dirty bits', Brian, before long, found himself reading in an entirely different spirit, as the power of Joyce's vision was transmitted to him. It's a moment akin to the one in which Virginia Woolf and Katherine Mansfield were fooling around with the manuscript of the same work by Joyce, skimming through it in order to pick holes in it, when Mansfield suddenly stopped and said, 'But there's something in this.'[5] Brian had no qualms about appropriating Tom Graham's copy of *Ulysses* (the Odyssey Press edition), because he understood that his cousin, having read the book once without appreciating it, would have no further use for it. It was, he said, 'the only book I've ever stolen!'; and it sat on his bookshelves for the rest of his life. Another seminal experience, around this time, was reading Hemingway's *The Sun Also Rises* on top of the Cave Hill overlooking Belfast, 'lost in [the] perfect evocation of a Spanish bullfight fiesta and the Left Bank café life of expatriates in the 1920s'.[6] Joyce, Yeats, Hemingway, Scott Fitzgerald's *Gatsby*, Dostoevsky's *Notes From the Underground* . . . These were thrilling discoveries for a literary-minded Belfast boy without straightforward prospects, and with an instinct for the durable as opposed to the merely meretricious in his reading matter.

Between September 1940, when he joined his ARP unit, and the following April, when the first bombs fell on Belfast, Brian Moore would have had to take his share of the scoffing and annoyance directed at these – as it seemed to many – meddling and officious enforcers of wartime impositions.[7] What with being virtually branded a traitor to Ireland by his more nationalist relatives, and being subjected to rude remarks by fed-up civilians in the streets, he can't have had an easy time of it. The companionship of Teddy Millington was important during these months, even though Teddy was quite a dissolute character, with louche habits that slightly shocked the well-brought-up nineteen-year-old – going with whores, for example, whom he'd pick up in Belfast's rudimentary 'red-light' district centred on Amelia Street opposite the Great Northern Railway Station. Brian wasn't tempted to follow suit; he'd acquired a girlfriend – despite his continuing dissatisfaction with his looks – and hence an improved outlet for his sexual aspirations. It was his first encounter with someone who – as he put it – 'wasn't too inhibited in a sexual sense', even if Catholic morality was still primed to clamp down on the pair of them at a certain point. This girl was the daughter of an old nursing acquaintance of Eileen Moore's, and was herself a nurse – though not in any sense a model for Nurse Sally Shannon in *The Emperor of Ice Cream. That* particular character was totally invented, Brian Moore said: an embodiment of the frustrating force every reasonably lusty Catholic boy would find himself up against, sooner or later. The real-life girlfriend was 'just the opposite'. The two of them would go to dances at Bellevue's Floral Hall, up the Cave Hill, or Saturday-night student hops at Queen's University. 'We did a lot of dancing in those days.' The combined effect of this girl and Teddy Millington was to buck up his social life. At the same time, to mollify his family, he was studying for the London Matric. (said to be an easier prospect than the Northern Ireland Senior Certificate Examination); and – he recalled – he succeeded in getting through the first part of this correspondence course, before more crucial concerns supervened.

There was more to Belfast, Brian Moore was finding out, than he had realised. A couple of socialist bookshops,[8] for example, in Howard Street and Union Street, provided a haven for those averse to atavistic allegiances; and Campbell's Café, opposite the City Hall, was another refuge for the level-headed. There were flats in leafy areas of the city in which joss-sticks were burned – amazingly – and Chinese screens formed a part of the decor. The Belfast Theatre Guild, run by actor-manager Harold Goldblatt, specialised in staging plays with a left-wing orientation, such as those by the Jewish-American Clifford Odets, in one of which Brian Moore had a part. He was introduced to all these places and activities by Teddy Millington; and though he later referred rather dismissively to the people he met during the second autumn of the war as 'drinking companions' ('That's all they were to me'), there's no doubt that they, and their comparative sophistication, enthralled him at the time. (He seemed to have grown estranged from earlier friends such as Niall Dempsey,[9] then a medical student at Queen's.) Gavin, in

The Emperor, articulates Brian Moore's feelings about this period, while standing for the whole mass of undirected but liberal-minded young, for whom a strong attachment to Ireland's cause – or Ulster's cause, for that matter – is associated with the previous, boring generation and their current idiocies: in Gavin's case, his father claiming to prefer Hitler to Churchill, his vehement Aunt Liz and all the others. As far as he is concerned, over-consciousness of nationality is just a part of the terrible provincialism he has to contend with; and when he gets a glimpse of a richer kind of life, surprisingly going on in his own dull city, it's the 'Protestant' aspect of the set-up that strikes him: 'Why was it that no Catholic could grow up in an interesting atmosphere?' You didn't catch Catholics, in other words, savouring the aroma of joss-sticks, discoursing wittily on the novels of Ronald Firbank or constructing puppet-theatres – though Gavin, as it happens, is a bit taken aback when it dawns on him that homosexuality goes with the rest of the bohemian package.[10]

At this point in the novel, Brian Moore imports a minor character directly from life: the puppet-maker Maurice Markham was in reality the manager of the Union Street bookshop, Terence Pim – also one of Belfast's few and flamboyant homosexuals, complete with peroxide hair and enormous polished leather boots.[11] It's easy to understand why such a figure should have fascinated – if only for a moment – a youth of the 1930s deprived of style. The novel also contains a homosexual padre, dubbed 'the Red Reverend', who owes something – though not his homosexuality – to the Rev. Arthur Agnew, unofficial pastor to the intellectual set and out-spoken opponent of sectarianism, vulgar prurience and narrow-mindedness of any sort. (It's encouraging to remember that Belfast threw up the occasional liberal cleric to balance all the noisy demagogues of one persuasion or another.) All these people, along with others like the essayist Denis Ireland, BBC men such as John Boyd and Sam Hanna Bell, the actors Joseph Tomelty and J.G. Devlin, poets John Hewitt and Robert Greacen: all these, and more, would have congregated at Campbell's Café, enabling the young ARP recruit to be in on the edge of an ebullient atmosphere (though his chief memory of Campbell's concerned a red-haired girl – some sort of ballet-dancer, he thought – with whom everyone was besotted). This was a time when a lot of people were trying to write the great Northern Irish proletarian novel and onslaughts on Ulster philistinism were coming from all sides. Belfast, though Brian Moore didn't exactly realise it, had been sympathetic to democratic ideas, since the days of the 1790s, when the radical paper *The Northern Star* circulated merrily among its more enlightened inhabitants, and religious liberty, not religious zealotry, was a cherished objective. His own experience of growing up in the city had, on the other hand, reinforced the sense of 'a small, narrow world', in which Protestants and Catholics didn't intermingle, in which values were askew and harshness and oppression prevailed. It was also a place that had denied him, personally, any scope for fulfilment. He may have gained a new angle on the city, for the moment, under Teddy Millington's guidance; but his aversion struck deeper. At his lowest, he felt a failure, unattractive to girls, in a false position at home due to his discarded Catholicism, unable to fit properly into any social niche. And 'poor old Belfast got clobbered with all that', he reflected ruefully, many years later – with even its supposedly miserable weather contributing to the overwhelming argument in favour of getting out of it at the earliest opportunity.

In 1940, the two oldest Moore girls, Eibhlin and Grainne, were employed by the Northern Ireland Civil Service[12] and Seamus was studying medicine at Queen's University, while Marie-Therese, Sean, Una, Peggy and Eilis were all at school. The question of evacuation had come up in relation to the younger children, and, according to Eilis,[13] they used to get down on their knees every night and pray to God that they wouldn't be sent to Tullyglass, where Aunt Sheena's foibles would have proved insufferable. In the event, Eilis went to live for a time with the Tierney[14] relations near Bray (outside Dublin), and attended a convent run by Loretto nuns before going on to Kilcullen.

By early 1941, a hundred thousand troops were stationed in Northern Ireland, where defence preparations had been stepped up following the Fall of France in 1940, and the increased likelihood of attack and invasion.[15] In fact the North's first Blitz occurred on 7–8 April 1941, and it was followed a week later by what became known as the Easter Tuesday Raid. Suddenly, people began to take the war seriously. The days of poking fun at the ARP were over.

Belfast was ablaze, whole areas were devastated, with many thousands dead, injured, or suddenly rendered homeless. It was chaos. 'Bodies were found in the streets, spread-eagled over pavements, even collapsed over roofs and buildings and trees, blown there by explosives.'[16] 'All was changed,' we read in *The Emperor* (which conflates the two raids).[17] 'The church was without its steeple. Bricks and rubble were strewn on the lawn of the adjoining manse. The steeple lay, like a great tree, amid the headstones of the old church graveyard.' Just for a moment, on the roof of the Nurses' Home with his chum Freddy Hargreaves, Gavin allows himself to glory in the liberating orgy of destructiveness being enacted all around him, raising his own voice above the noise of exploding bombs, the whine and crash and bang and the magnified shattering of thousands of panes of glass.

'Blow up a few capitalists,' Freddy shouted, suddenly.
　'And the Bishop of Down and Connor,' Gavin yelled.
　'And Stormont Castle and Lord Carson's statue and the House of bloody Parliament.'
　'Not with a whimper, but a bang.'
　'Right you are, Gavin boy. A big bang.'

But it isn't long before reality kicks in. The 'nasty job' for which Freddy and Gavin volunteer – placing the dead in coffins – was a fearsome *rite de passage* which the bloody circumstances foisted on the young Brian Moore (like Gavin, he spoke up bravely when volunteers were called for). Dr Moore, who, unlike Burke Senior in the novel, didn't scarper to Dublin but worked tirelessly throughout the Blitz attending to the wounded, took immense pride in his son's behaviour at this appalling moment.[18] It seemed that Brian – scholastic failure or not – was as well endowed with moral fibre as anyone else in the family.

The second Luftwaffe raid left the Clifton Street house badly damaged and uninhabitable, after a landmine had obliterated a police barracks near by. Fortunately the family had taken shelter and so escaped injury, but the experience was traumatic. Eileen Moore and Grainne worked hard to clear the house the following day, salvaging what they could; a dealer was called in and paid a ludicrously low price for some antique furniture that couldn't easily be transported to their new temporary home. They found a place to rent in Camden Street, near Queen's University (later to be the scene of Miss Hearne's tribulations), a rather depressing, three-storey house halfway along a red-brick terrace: aesthetically nondescript, socially a come-down and emotionally distressing, as any enforced rehabitation must be. This was the place in which Dr Moore, finding himself one day in the kitchen with his middle son while everyone else had gone out, made the innocent enquiry, 'Brian, do you know how to make a cup of tea?' Brian never ceased to feel a kind of indulgent amazement over the areas of incompetence peculiar to those of the previous generation who'd been acclimatised to a different way of life.

The following March (1942) Dr Moore died. He was seventy-four, and had continued working right up until the end; overwork, indeed, was held to have contributed to his sudden heart-failure – so he was, in a sense, a casualty of the war. The family was still at 13, Camden Street, and his body was taken to the nearest Catholic Church, St Brigid's in Derryvolgie Avenue, to await a Requiem Mass before the funeral and interment in Crebilly, Ballymena. Described in one of his obituaries as 'one of the best-known surgeons in the city, and for over half a century a leading figure in Catholic professional life',[19] Dr Moore's assets fell far short of what might reasonably have been expected of someone in this position: he left no property, no valuables, and only the trifling sum of £908 16s 7d to safeguard the future well-being of his wife and family of nine. On top of the natural grief occasioned by a death – and in this instance, the death of a much-loved husband and father, and a person, moreover, of such distinctive presence that the shock of his departure was all the more benumbing – the Moores had considerable financial worries to contend with, the burden of which would have fallen on the widow. Not that Eileen Moore ever thought of blaming her husband for having neglected to call in fees from private patients, or donated excessive amounts to charities, or whatever it was that had eaten up his income. She was simply inconsolable. When one of the children tried to comfort her by reminding her that she still had *them*, the response came back that none of them had ever meant a thing to her in comparison with him (or words to that effect).

The death of his father affected Brian Moore in ways that he'd hardly have been aware of at the time, in which guilt, chagrin, natural sorrow, resentment, anger and the sense of something uncompleted were all mixed up. Even in later life he was still articulating the thing that nagged away at him: the fact of his father's having breathed his last before he, Brian, had a chance to prove himself, in an intellectual sense. 'My father died thinking . . . I was a person who wasn't going to achieve anything in life . . .'[20] In the opening pages of *Fergus*, the beset protagonist glances across his Californian living-room and sees, with a jolt, his long-dead father sitting there on a yellow sofa. The vision promptly vanishes.

> How like his father to appear [Fergus thinks], and then dis-appear again without giving him a chance to say a word. That had been his father's style right up to his final vanishing trick, the night of his sudden death in the downstairs bedroom in Hampden Street in Belfast . . .

The apparition is Dr Moore to the life:

> He wore a suit of heavy tweed . . . His silk tie, in the green and red stripes of St Michan's Old Boys' Association, was knotted large and lax in the gate of his white, starched collar. His rimless pince-nez spectacles were fitted firmly on the bridge of his nose, the right eyepiece attached to a black silk ribbon which looped over his ear and was draped round his neck. His shoes were brown.

This is the image of his father that remained with Brian Moore for the rest of his life,[21] bound up with deference, remonstrance and affectionate exasperation. According to some members of his family, Brian ended up nurturing something of a father-fixation. Certainly his father's absence carried a greater emotional charge than that of his mother, when she too died in due course. In spite of his having been 'the wee son' in early childhood, and remaining 'the white-haired boy' even after he'd long left home, Brian's relationship with his mother, though amiable and dutiful, probably never struck as deep. With this family, too, ties of affection were tempered by a distinctively Northern Irish acerbity which included the unmalicious put-down. Brian's instinct for hyperbole was always noted. 'Whenever Brian tells a story,' his family would maintain, 'you can rest assured that it won't lose in the telling.'

After a stint with the National Fire Service, later that year, Brian Moore suddenly saw a chance to get away from Belfast and grasped it with both hands. Among his left-wing acquaintances was a young man called Norman Shrage, whose abilities he didn't rate all that highly. When Norman announced one day that he'd secured a position with the British Ministry of War Transport, and was just off to North Africa, Brian immediately grilled him over the details of this enviable appointment – 'I was sort of jealous, you know, because this would have been a way to get into the war, without actually joining up.' Running through his head was the conviction that if Norman Shrage was suitable for such a post, then so was he. He wrote out his application and, not long after, found himself summoned to London for an interview. He'd never before set foot on English soil. He had to make his way to the War Transport Headquarters in Berkeley Square, where he arrived at eight in the morning – his appointment was for ten – and sat in a state of nerves until the interview took place.

He recalled the episode later as being like something out of Evelyn Waugh. He was cross-questioned by a Mr Somerville who – he decided – 'could not figure me out at all'. Details of his education, the name of his old headmaster (the Rev. J.B. McMullan), and his father's position, seemed to suggest that he'd attended some sort of minor Irish public school, and this (he thought), combined with his proficiency in French (which wasn't actually put to the test), was sufficient to get him into this wartime department of the Civil Service. And 'the next thing I knew, I was on my way to North Africa with the troops'.

Before this, though, occurred the memorable departure from Belfast on the Liverpool boat.

I remember as the ship sailed up Belfast Lough . . . the fog-horn, the fog closing in – in third class, among the real emigrants, the

Irish poor who worked on English roads and in English kitchens, who lived in slums and sent their money home in postal orders – old hands had bagged the benches. The rest of us sat on our suitcases. Bottles of Guinness went round and a pale girl in black began to sing in a church contralto, 'Come Back to Erin, Mavourneen, Mavourneen'.[22]

It was a significant moment. However – as he did with the first two air raids on Belfast – Brian Moore has conflated two journeys by boat, the first one for the interview in London, and the second when, his appointment confirmed, he was actually leaving home, on the way out of Belfast for good, voluntarily relinquishing the security, along with the vexations, of his teenage years. He has also imposed an impossibly clear definition over the confusions of the time. Even his serious literary ambitions – which he kept to himself – must have taken a back seat in the face of impending travel abroad under the most hazardous of wartime conditions. But all his accounts of this moment of transition include the story – possibly apocryphal – of the man in the black overcoat sitting on a suitcase next to his, who offered him a drink from his whisky bottle and elicited a kind of crystallisation of his future plans.

'Your first time across the water, lad?' he said.
'Yes,' I said.
'What line of work are you in?'
Then I began to live out my private lie. 'I'm a writer,' I said.
'A ship's writer?' he said.
'No, just a writer.'
'Would that be good wages?'
'I don't know,' I said. Perhaps that's the way a lot of people become writers. They don't like the role they're playing, and writing seems a better one.[23]

In fact, he had just taken on a totally unfamiliar and exciting role; he was about to experience enemy action and witness prodigious dramas in locations far removed from fusty Belfast; and writing had to be put on hold for the time being. However, Brian Moore, in later life, would often quote Mauriac's observation to the effect that, for the writer, the door closes at twenty – meaning that a particular way of seeing and responding to events has already been determined by the forces and circumstances of one's childhood. It was something he held to be true in his own case, and it under-scored the ambivalence in his attitude to his upbringing – which he, possibly because of his temperament, had made more fraught than any of his brothers or sisters would have understood. (Even his view of Belfast was never static, but underwent various transfor-mations and modifications according to mood.) But at that mo-ment, aged twenty-one, sailing up the Lough bound for Liverpool and, ultimately, Algiers, when the door, in a more practical sense, had closed on a whole section of his life, he was conscious above all else of relief at having put behind him the shackles and inertia of provincial Northern Ireland.

6

GOODBYE TO ALL THAT

I didn't know that in a few weeks I would be in Algiers, that in six months I would see the Germans fleeing Naples, that I would see the dead brought off the hospital ships at Anzio, that I would land with the Americans in the South of France, that I would see collaborators shot dead in the streets of Marseilles – and the great death camps of Auschwitz – and watch the Russian armies roll back victorious through Poland on their way home.

'The Writer as Exile'

THE CONVOY IN WHICH Brian Moore was travelling was attacked by German bombers off the coast of Spain – an alarming experience, even though his particular ship wasn't hit. This episode of naval action made him understand, he said, that the Germans 'must have had some sort of base in Spain – so all those left-wing ideas you had were always being confirmed in the worst possible way'. (His left-wing orientation endured throughout the war.) A priest came round offering Confession to anyone who required it, with sudden death, as it seemed, in the offing; but Brian declined to take advantage of the offer, thereby consolidating his irreligion. The ship sailed on and reached Algiers, where his new assistant was standing at the dock to meet him: and what made him almost jump out of his skin was that the assistant was none other than Norman Shrage, who'd preceded him all the way from Belfast. Shrage, however, was moved on after a few days and disappears from the Brian Moore story. Brian, who described himself as a shipping clerk, was rather surprised to find himself treated like a British officer, with all the perks attached to that position. He was kitted out with a uniform which resembled a naval officer's uniform, and accommodated in superior quarters. There were servants aplenty to ease him into the new, paradoxically elegant social life of wartime Algiers. But things were not entirely trouble-free. He and his fellow civilian officials, he quickly realised, were not popular with the Army or the Navy – naturally enough, considering their non-combatant status.

The first night in Algiers, he slept in the officers' compartment of a train parked in a siding alongside the port, and was awakened in the small hours by terrible screams. It turned out that an Arab thief had attempted to board the train in search of rich pickings, but had electrocuted himself instead, with his body left on the line as a warning to others. Brian went back to bed wondering what kind of a brutal environment he had landed in. However, it wasn't long before he came to relish the exotic city, with its filth and daggers and all, and 'the disjointed, strange life I led just behind the front lines in a time when you felt you were a living part of history'.[1]

Algiers was a divided city – a bit like Belfast in this respect – with a white and a native population; at this time (1943) a question remained over the intentions of the French authorities, who might or might not be guided by the terms of the Franco-German armistice. In the event, Algiers became a centre for British and American forces engaged in extending the frontiers of Allied territory. Brian Moore, as it happened, was only in North Africa for a short time. He proved more than equal to the demands of his new job, which entailed, among other things, provisioning whole fleets of ships; and his boss, a man called Bill Loker – who wasn't much older than himself[2] – picked Brian out to accompany him to Naples,[3] as an Assistant Port Officer, in the wake of the Salerno landings in September 1943.[4] It was part of the Ministry's function to establish ports at places which came into the Allies' hands, and therefore, as he later recalled, Brian Moore was vouchsafed a spectator's view of historic events, as he moved from one place to another just behind the advancing front lines. He witnessed the German exodus from Naples, and watched the casualties of Anzio[5] – twenty-five miles south of Rome – being unloaded from hospital ships. All these things, inevitably, had a profound effect on him; however, his literary impulse was activated differently. Even at the time, he said, he made a clear distinction between journalism, even high-class journalism – 'that sort of *Black Lamb and Grey Falcon*[6] stuff' – and imaginative literature grounded in everyday life. It wasn't, as yet, external drama, major wartime actions, that suggested themselves to him as the stuff of fiction.

He was nevertheless extremely susceptible to the allure of foreign places, that 'amazing city of Naples', for example, where strings were pulled, once again, to get him and his colleagues into luxurious lodgings. The 'big boss', a one-time colonel in the Scots Guards, saw to it that his employees were well housed. Brian stayed, to begin with, at the home of the Duchessa di Bagnioli complete with white-gloved menservants waiting at table, and all the other trappings of the high life. This interlude made him feel a bit uneasy, as if he'd strayed into 'some kind of weird movie'. It didn't last long: the billet proved a bit too far away from the port itself, and soon he was transferred to an area called the Barberoni, and installed in 'a very nice little apartment', which suited him better.

It was a strange life: the heightened atmosphere, the exacting duties, the requisitioned resources, including a car and driver, and a couple of handsome motor boats belonging to the Crown Prince of Italy. Brian – the youngest in an office consisting of only three or four Ministry of War Transport employees – often worked a twelve-hour day, fit for nothing in the evening but to stagger home to bed. However, he wasn't always alone. Along with the other perks of the job and the change of scene had come the freedom to indulge his normal erotic instincts, and his first serious sexual entanglement had ensued – with a young colleague named Isobel Hammond, a Scot, and a Communist. He gained a reputation in the office for being a bit of a lothario, which probably didn't displease him too much, after the years of abstinence. He'd have been chuffed by it rather than not. The whole wartime experience he found fascinating – 'a kid who'd never done anything like it before' – and he soon took in his stride the routine of boarding huge ocean liners to interview the ships' captains about their requirements in the way of provisions, and arrange on-shore accommodation for sick or wounded sailors. For recreation there were night-clubs for Allied personnel only, with ten-piece bands, full of American, British, French and Polish officers, and hundreds of Italian girls. 'There was a cabaret which was all undressed girls dancing American, British, French and Polish national dances, and each time a girl waggled her bottom the Allies stamped their feet, yelled in hard animal voices, hammered their glasses and bottles on the tables and laughed like boys who have just been let out of school.'[7]

From Naples he was posted to Toulon, where he and Bill Loker were taken ashore from a British destroyer to investigate the possibility of setting up a port; however, they found that the Americans were already engaged in constructing docks by laying platforms on top of the French fleet – an entire fleet – which had been sunk at Toulon. On the morning they landed, Brian was impressed by the sight of a huge French battleship, one that had escaped the Vichy regime, towering over them like a skyscraper, while its decks were crammed with emotional French sailors cheering on the British and American invasion force.

Marseilles, along the coast, offered the best port facilities in France, and it was here that Brian Moore was stationed next, helping to obtain and direct supplies for the Allies throughout the autumn of 1944. He was quite an experienced administrator by this time, understanding a good deal about the logistics of wartime shipments. His confidence was growing. He was also, as well as having a pretty good time, closely observing the events being enacted around him, and making moral judgements. It was typical of the confusions of the time that collaborators, or those denounced as collaborators, were being executed by the thousand, while known Fascists were, in many cases, able to evade retribution and even find employment with such bodies as his own Transport division. 'At that point when I was in Marseilles,' Brian Moore recalled, 'we were hiring Fascists – a Fascist ship's chandler and suchlike – because they'd had connections with the British before the war.' It made him wonder what all the fighting had been in aid of. People in the know, even those who'd been on the wrong side, were able to prosper: it was a blow to his idealism, or naivety, as far as the idea of a totally just war, with which he'd belaboured his relatives back in Belfast, was concerned.

There are in existence a couple of rudimentary stories, or sketches, written by Brian Moore around this time, interesting items of juvenilia (something in very short supply), which indicate how his literary instincts were shaping up. No over-writing, no self-consciousness, no faked-up effects: all the usual demerits of the untried writer are, indeed, absent from these short pieces which exude professionalism, despite a certain, perhaps inevitable, skimpiness. The author's first address on the typescript, Ministry of War Transport, 102, Rue de la République, c/o Fleet Mail Office, Marseilles, crossed out and superseded by 17, Cliftonville Avenue, Belfast, N. Ireland,[8] suggests that he went on submitting them for publication for quite a long time, even though it seems nothing came of his efforts in this direction. Well – as with every other would-be writer – it was necessary for him to learn the importance of perseverance.

The first and more conventional of these stories (untitled) concerns an encounter on a train between a Catholic priest and a Jewish commercial traveller, both amiably presented, in which the former, through no fault of his own, is precipitated into an apparently discreditable and embarrassing position. Low-key though it is, this sketch has a degree of poignancy, as well as being admirably constructed. The twenty-three- or twenty-four-year-old author already has sufficient nous to shun prolixity and risk the abbreviated denouement. The other story, 'Roman Holiday', is more of a mood-piece, in which an unidentified young man, described in his papers as a British civilian, gets euphorically drunk in an imposing, domed city, very different from his home town with its forests of factory chimneys. He trails through the streets in the company of a lovely young English girl, a good sport, in a state of exhilaration sufficient to withstand confused encounters with an opinionated captain in the American Air Force, an English lieutenant colonel, some irate hotel guests, and even the *Carabinieri*.

The young lady suddenly said that she wanted to leave, and what the hell anyway. So they both said, what the hell, in loud voices and went downstairs again. Outside the moon was full and they decided to go for a walk in the Pincio Park. They walked slowly up to the park and he felt very sober as he looked down on Rome with its domes and spires in the cathedral silver of the full moon. The park was beautiful and he thanked the stupid people in the hotel for giving him this unexpected joy.

The young lady then said that she had never spent a night in a park before.

What the hell. Brian Moore knew he was cut out to be a writer of some kind, even if magazine editors didn't at present share his confidence in himself, and even if (which was true) the way ahead should prove exceptionally rigorous and roundabout. Some of the euphoria contained in 'Roman Holiday' has to do with the pleasure of getting his impressions of a drunken evening down on paper, in a more or less satisfactory way, as well as the state of light-headedness evoked.

In Marseilles his assistant was an English boy named Arthur, who'd had the misfortune to be working for a German firm in Holland at the start of the war, and consequently suffered internment in a concentration camp,[9] during which time he studied Buddhism and developed serious Buddhist leanings. Arthur eventually made his way back to England, only to be promptly dispatched to the South of France where it was thought he could be of some use to the Ministry of War Transport. Brian and he became quite friendly.

One Sunday – Brian having access to a fleet of motor cars but being a non-driver – the two of them commandeered a car without permission (Arthur driving) and went on a pleasure trip along the Riviera coast. Free-wheeling down a hill into Toulon, the engine switched off to save petrol, they hit a boy who had suddenly darted out from behind a parked bus. Horrified, they stopped the car and Brian ran back to see what damage had been done to the child. Having been through the Blitz and witnessed all kinds of injuries, he could tell that the little boy's legs were broken. He was also concussed. Brian, who – as a doctor's son, and a person trained in First Aid – should certainly have known better, picked the child up and bundled him into the back seat of the illicit car, then got in himself and held him while Arthur, exhibiting a true Buddhist detachment from the incident, cruised serenely around in search of a hospital. The first one, run by nuns, refused to admit the injured child; but they finally got him into professional hands. By this time he'd come round, and was able to give them his name and address. After a lot of telephoning, Brian succeeded in making contact with the boy's father, a farmer, whose entire interest proved to be focused on the amount of compensation he'd be able to claim as a consequence of the accident. Since they were under Army control, the British Army was liable for damages, though in the event only a small sum – about £150 – was paid to the grasping farmer. Brian and Arthur got into a certain amount of trouble for having taken the car out without an official driver. Their copybooks were well and truly blotted. But the thing blew over, and the boy recovered. While he stayed in hospital, Brian went to visit him bringing sweets and toys. The incident had shaken him, if not his companion.[10]

Arthur the Buddhist then developed an obsession with Brian's girlfriend Isobel Hammond, and used to follow her home after work and hang around outside her front door, hopelessly infatuated. However, after an evening's skinny-dipping in the Mediterranean in which the whole office took part, Arthur's attentions were shifted to another girl (whom he later married). Meanwhile, in the background to all these diversions, the war was grinding to a halt. Early in May 1945, the German Armed Forces surrendered to Field Marshal Montgomery at Luneberg Heath. Back in England, two months later, a Labour landslide victory in the general election enraged those who saw this unexpected result as a slap in the face for Churchill, after all his overmastering strategies and stalwart defence of the British Empire. 'That's it. You won't catch me working for Major Attlee – the war's over, and I'm going home.' This was the attitude of Brian's War Transport bosses, one of whom was Robert Campbell, a Scottish millionaire who'd been a colonel in the Scots Guards during World War I, and a big shipping magnate. Campbell had become fond of Brian, and, after the office had closed down, he decided: 'We'll take Moore with us.' ('As if I was a pet dog or something,' Brian later joked.) So they got in a car and set off across France, staying in plush hotels and eating meals in three-star restaurants – and Brian's first sight of Paris, even in its shaken and dilapidated state, initiated a lifelong enthusiasm for that city.[11] Continuing northwards towards the English Channel, driving through a blighted war zone, he saw on all sides 'the wreckage of abandoned German tanks, ruined farmhouses, bombed-out bunkers and military cemeteries that littered the roads of Normandy'.[12]

When they reached London, Brian was booked into what is now the Athenian Court Hotel, opposite Hyde Park (at the time it functioned as a kind of gentlemen's club, he thought), while his employers considered what to do with him next. Once they understood the strength of his reluctance to go home to Belfast, it was suggested that, as an experienced shipping clerk, he might get himself posted to the Far East. The idea quite appealed to him. It also made him very apprehensive – the prospect of going to the other end of the earth and being obliged to embrace a hoity-toity colonial life, at odds with his socialism. But he made up his mind to it. The alternative, as he saw it, was an unenterprising return to Northern Ireland, and some kind of footling job (if he was lucky) behind a bank counter. However, though he'd have been able to go out to China under the auspices of the Ministry of War Transport, once the war had ended he'd need to have a secure appointment with one of the great shipping firms located in the area – and when he went for an interview with a representative of one of these firms (Jardine Mathesons) he found, to his disbelief, that his nationality told against him.

His boss Robert Campbell had to break it to him that his application had been unsuccessful, despite his unimpeachable credentials and the testimonials in his favour. The only employable Irishman, as far as Jardine Mathesons was concerned, would have been an Ulster Protestant; they'd had so many bad experiences in the past with Irish troublemakers who allied themselves with the underdog (i.e. the local workforce), and otherwise failed to abide by colonial regulations, that the whole nation was now blacklisted. This was the explanation passed on to Brian, and he believed it. His first reaction was relief, that he hadn't travelled all the way to China only to find himself confronted with this kind of bigotry and blimpishness. But the fact remained that his future, which had been assuming a definite if not entirely desirable shape, was now amorphous once again.

So there he was at a loose end in London – twenty-four years old, no job, no degree, ineligible for a university grant since he couldn't claim to be an ex-serviceman, and disinclined to initiate a course of study that would lead, belatedly, to a medical qualification. It was 1945, a time of upset and dislocation. As happened with others in a similar position, he soon became conscious that his experiences abroad, on the fringes of the war, had temporarily unfitted him for a sobersided civilian existence. He went to Belfast to visit his family, and enjoyed being treated as his mother's white-haired boy – but only for a day or two. Belfast looked worse than ever: blitzed and battered and still irredeemably uncouth. While he was there, his uncle Eoin MacNeill died in Dublin (on 15 October) and Brian travelled South for the funeral, a large-scale affair. He felt completely at odds with the atmosphere in the Free State as well: 'Here in neutral Ireland, it seemed that De Valera and his political foes, kneeling in prayer at my uncle's funeral, were figures from a dead past.'[13] Once he got back to Cliftonville Avenue, he made some excuse and returned to London, where his ex-War Transport colleague and girlfriend Isobel Hammond came to the rescue. Back in London herself by this time and reinstalled in her pre-war job with the Civil Service, she first of all found accommodation for Brian in a flat in Swiss Cottage which was rented by her mother, and then put him in touch with the man who would arrange his next employment.

Brian's introduction to the Swiss Cottage flat was somewhat disconcerting. The first evening he was taken there by Isobel, they lit a fire, ate some sort of scratch meal, and went to bed. The following morning, Brian opened his eyes to an unexpected sight: a strange female figure was bearing down on him with a breakfast tray expertly balanced on an arm from which, he saw at once, the hand was missing. Isobel had failed to explain that her mother actually occupied the flat – though it turned out that Mrs Hammond's job as a cleaner at one of the ministries kept her out of it except at odd hours, such as early in the morning. It was quite a shock and embarrassment for a well-brought-up Irish boy: to be cornered in bed with her daughter by a one-handed charwoman bringing toast and tea. He ate his breakfast very nervously. Isobel kept telling him not to worry; her mother wasn't at all put out; but he couldn't throw off a feeling of desperate unease. True, Mrs Hammond hadn't thrown up her hands – hand – in horror on being confronted with her daughter's indisputably immoral behaviour; but that in itself was weird. Such maternal sang-froid, in these circumstances, was a reaction unattuned to suburban Belfast, whose mores Brian had not quite eradicated yet. A number of things about Isobel and her mother puzzled him. For a start, Mrs Hammond was not an uneducated woman, yet she earned her living cleaning the offices of civil servants (and this despite her handicap – how on earth did she manage? – which he judged to be an injury sustained in the Blitz). No father was ever mentioned: 'dead or disappeared', Brian surmised. Isobel was rather economical when it came to disclosing items of personal information. She was a small girl, with small neat features: very Scottish and precise, and adamant in her Communist beliefs. A number of Party members had established contact with her during her time abroad with the Ministry of War Transport. A sergeant in the Marines, or some such, would make himself known to Isobel, whereupon the two would fall into an intense discussion. It suggested to Brian a kind of freemasonry, a whole underworld from which he was excluded – by choice, indeed, since his socialist orientation fell far short of a commitment to Communism.

Isobel had other, non-Communist acquaintances, including an American who'd befriended her at an early stage in the war, and who now appeared in London as an attaché of UNRRA (United Nations Relief and Rehabilitation Administration). It seemed not unreasonable that Brian should apply for a post with this organisation, and – armed with references from Bob Campbell and others – he met up with Isobel's American friend at Grosvenor Square to discuss the possibility. That he was immediately judged suitable for the job was something of a boost to his morale, and also a relief, since his savings from the War Transport Ministry were running low; though it meant he'd be stationed in Poland, and not – as he'd hoped – in Italy. UNRRA's twofold purpose involved the repatriation of refugees and the transportation of vital supplies to the devastated territories of Europe – and it was in the latter area that Brian's recently acquired expertise lay. The new job would also entail a separation from Isobel Hammond, with whom he'd been co-habiting quite happily, if not ecstatically (mother and all). She, however, was eager for him to go, and not to miss such an opportunity, assuring him that they'd be able to keep in touch by letter, and eventually take up where they'd left off. So, as it happened, Isobel Hammond passed out of his life. Once he'd left London, in January 1946, he never met her again.[14] From Warsaw, he had to steel himself to break it to her, on the telephone, that their affair was at an end.[15] He had met someone else, whose effect on him there was no gainsaying. Margaret Swanson. Eleven years his senior, a Canadian economist from a secure middle-class background,[16] also attached to UNRRA, something of a beauty, a drunkard and a bit of a handful, Margaret Swanson was irresistibly alluring to a still comparatively inurbane, sexually and socially unpractised Belfast boy (though he was learning all the time). Isobel Hammond, attractive, good-natured and in every way unexceptionable, simply couldn't compete.

'Warsaw in January 1946 was no longer a city,' Brian Moore wrote in his Introduction to his friend John Vachon's *Photographs and Letters*. 'It was a grave marker at the boundary of the two very different worlds which had destroyed the armies of the Third Reich.'[17] The whole country was a shambles – its economy ruined, its population depleted, many of its towns reduced to rubble and ashes.[18] When Brian first set foot in Poland, an appalled spectator at the aftermath of the cataclysm, UNRRA work was being organised by an overall chief, Brigadier-General Charles Drury, and three Heads of Mission: a Russian, an American and an Englishman. Brian was first of all assigned to the British division under a Mr Mills, and posted to the Baltic seaport of Gdynia. However, his stay at Gdynia only lasted a week or so, after which he was summoned back to Warsaw to work as a statistics officer. (How he, the failure at maths, got into this position requiring considerable accounting skills was something that entertained him greatly in later years.) He took up his duties under a Russian named Colonel Poulnikov, Head of the Transport Section, happy to be back in the capital despite its wartorn state:

Warsaw – it was wonderful, like being in a Dostoevsky novel . . . Here were *droshka*, the horse-drawn street cabs we had read about in Russian novels. Here were filthy peasants in fur-trimmed coats, driving long carts through the muddy streets; here were Russian soldiers singing gypsy chants, bearded beggars (or were they priests?) begging for alms outside ruined churches. Here was the heart-stopping sound of a piano playing Chopin on a quiet Sunday morning in a deserted square.[19]

And here too was an incongruously stylish social life (as he'd found in Algiers, in 1943), carried on in the ruins of once-grand hotels like the Hotel Bristol, or the Europa with its intact dining-room complete with orchestra, still offering a menu of pressed duck, caviar, champagne and chocolate souffle; or the miraculously undamaged Polonia full of foreign correspondents, embassy officials and Russian officers all bent on having a whale of a time. These places provided a perfect setting for a sophisticate like Margaret Swanson – whose work involved preparing for Brigadier-General Drury a detailed report on the expenditure, resources and achievements of UNRRA in Poland. Like almost everyone else in those days, Margaret didn't have an extensive wardrobe – but nevertheless managed to look stunning when she made the effort, with her lovely face, elegantly greying hair (though she was only thirty-six or -seven) and confident North American manner. Brian was completely bowled over by her, and the feeling was in some measure reciprocated – God knows why, Brian said: Margaret was a person who'd had many lovers 'who must have been much more satisfactory'. ('She went for football players, that sort of thing,' he joked. 'And I didn't fit the bill at all!') It was an intense relationship, and never an easy one. Brian – sensitive and scornful, diffident and opinionated – respected Margaret's brains, all right, but deplored her taste in literature, as well as being far too sanguine about her drinking habits. (He tried to keep up with her, but found that his head wouldn't stand it.) It was true that she was never a falling-down drunk: just someone, he recalled, who managed to put away 'an awful lot of vodka'.

In the intervals between conducting an affair with Margaret Swanson, and compiling statistics relating to the numbers of locomotives, tractors, industrial machinery, farm supplies and so on coming into Poland to put the country back on its feet, Brian was taking private Russian lessons with a Jewish woman whose tales of the Warsaw ghetto,[20] recounted in English, proved so fascinating to him that he lost track of the original project and never did become a Russian-speaker.[21] He listened, engrossed, thinking: if only he were a writer; here indeed was an overwhelming subject. He didn't consider himself equipped to tackle anything on that scale; however, it seems that he wrote, or lent his name to, a couple of articles for the *Sunday Independent* in Dublin, detailing a few enormities of the Communist regime. The first, which appeared on the paper's front page on 9 November 1947, under the heading, 'Red Sabotage in Poland', and names Brian Moore as the '*Sunday Independent* Correspondent in Warsaw', concerns the disappearance from the country of the leader of the Polish Peasant Party (PSL), M. Stanislaw Mikolajczyk (misspelled Mickolajczyk), previously premier of the wartime Polish government-in-exile in London. The article shows an astonishing familiarity (for a mere relief worker) with the ins and outs of current policies and politics, not to mention the various opposition parties – the PPR, SP, PSL, SL, SD. The second article, two weeks later, is on an inside page and attributed merely to 'a special correspondent' who claims to have conducted an interview, recently, with 'a leading spokesman of the Catholic clergy' (what language did he do it in?). The principal grouch of this spokesman is the failure of the government to acknowledge a letter, signed by Cardinal Hlond, which condemns the current 'godless' policy of allowing work to be carried out on a Sunday to restore Poland's ruined towns and cities. The person quoted is very hot under the collar about the Church being treated with such disrespect, particularly by a government made up of foreigners including 'Moscow-trained Communists, many of whom are Jews of Russian origin'. The heading of this article, in which the Church spokesman's comments are presented sympathetically, is 'Poland – 96% Catholic – Is Run By Reds'.

There are a number of mysteries here. These articles, if genuine, represent a considerable *volte face* on the part of Brian Moore, whose early left-wing orientation bypassed Communism, it's true, to evolve into a kind of principled liberalism – but never, at any stage, got itself revoked in favour of the kind of proselytising Catholicism beloved of the clerically minded *Independent*. It is, indeed, also true that whatever remained of his idealistic socialism was shaken by his day-to-day experience of the way things in Poland were being run. However – as he says in his John Vachon Introduction – neither he nor the equally left-wing Vachon wanted 'to think that our allies, the Russians, were not the Soviet heroes we imagined them to be'. He imagines the Russians to be heroes, then, and he is dismayed to find that Polish Communists – this is the gravest charge he can level against them – 'were almost always as anti-Semitic in their views as the rest of their countrymen'. These comments, which he offers as a reflection of his state of mind at the time, do not tally with the tone of the *Independent* articles, which are themselves guilty of an Irish Catholic anti-Semitism (among the enemy are 'Jews of Russian origin'), and do not cast the Russians in any sense as 'heroes'.

The Vachon Introduction also claims that 'we foreigners lived insulated from the truths of recent history', which can hardly have been the case if Brian was dashing around battered Warsaw interviewing Cardinals' representatives, opposition party members and so on, and evolving political opinions. And *if* he was doing this, it would have endangered his position at UNRRA, since Brigadier Drury had decreed that his staff should keep its nose out of local affairs. He'd have had to have a powerful ideological incentive to disregard this embargo – and putting the case for Catholic Poland, in its opposition to the terrible 'Reds', hardly seems to constitute such a motive for a young left-winger. (It's also completely at odds with the stance Brian Moore took during the Spanish Civil War, when he and his father had ferocious arguments over the Catholic *Irish News*'s partisan coverage of events.)

If – *if* – he wrote the *Sunday Independent* articles, he must have done so in a moment of atavistic solidarity with beleaguered Catholics; and the action clearly came to embarrass him so much that he never referred to it in any of the numerous interviews he gave in later years, or used the status thereby conferred on him (our 'correspondent in Warsaw') to effect an entry into investigative journalism. And even if it was just a matter of allowing his name to be associated with this particular viewpoint – which would explain away certain difficulties of language, special knowledge, reporters' know-how, etc – it still seems an unlikely position for someone of Brian Moore's professed beliefs. It would have pleased his family and his MacNeill relations in Dublin – but nowhere does he indicate that this was something he was eager to do.

The affair with Margaret Swanson culminated in a trip to Scandinavia (her ancestral homeland) in 1947, a trip to which Brian Moore later, humorously, applied the adjective 'disastrous'. It was something of a disaster, at any rate, as long as they stayed in

Sweden, a country whose inhabitants they disliked ('terribly rude, the Swedes'), and in which they started not to get on too well with one another. There was something of a fracas in one hotel in Stockholm – probably caused by one of Margaret's alcoholic episodes – which ended with the pair of them having to pack their bags and find alternative accommodation. On another occasion, they were doing the tourist thing of traipsing through a pleasure garden (Luna Park), when they somehow got separated. A couple of hours later, Brian – by now seriously worried – took himself off to the police to report Margaret's disappearance, only to find that she had got there before him, to make some kind of complaint about having been molested in the park. What was very peculiar was her reaction when Brian turned up: 'I don't know this man,' she told the Stockholm constabulary. 'He's nothing to do with me, I've never seen him before in my life.' Brian's half-laughing, disbelieving response – 'Oh, come *on*, Margaret' – only made her persist in her denials, whereupon the police got the idea that *he* was the person who'd been 'molesting' her. They demanded to see his passport, and generally behaved in a threatening and officious way. However, he had the presence of mind to say, 'If you'd like to ring Hotel So-and-So, you'll find that this lady and I are sharing a room.' At this point Margaret burst out laughing; her charade was exploded, though why she'd embarked on it in the first place remained a mystery. Was it to pay him out for having, as she saw it, left her in the lurch, to be subsequently pestered by repellent Swedes? According to Brian, they didn't discuss the incident once it was over;[22] but it stood out in his mind among the instances of Margaret's unpredictability.[23]

Disconcerting though she must have been as a travelling companion, Margaret Swanson continued to hold Brian in thrall. Whatever had happened in Luna Park, he was convinced she wasn't to blame, even though, as he admitted, she probably wasn't sober at the time. The truth was that surly, hidebound Sweden was getting them down. The atmosphere lightened considerably once they'd moved on to Norway and Finland, these areas of Scandinavia being, for some reason, much more congenial to both of them. In Finland they were taken about by a man who worked for *Time* magazine, which proved a pleasant diversion. Then it was back to Warsaw, where the UNRRA mission was being wound up

– and after this, it was understood that Margaret would return to Canada, leaving Brian to his own devices. She at least saw no settled prospects for the two of them together. As for Brian: another stop-gap episode in his life had come to an end; and he was faced, once again, with a very uncertain future.

It wasn't long before he was back in dingy Belfast, at 17, Cliftonville Avenue, staying with his family. In spite of her ecstatic welcome for her favourite son, Eileen Moore was careful to caution her other children not to heed Brian when he'd try to talk them into leaving home, to expand their horizons.[24] (As it happened, Marie-Therese was about to marry a man called Lecky and emigrate with him to New Zealand; Eibhlin and Eilis – the nun – would spend the greater part of their lives in England; and Sean, the youngest son, would eventually follow Brian to Montreal. Seamus, Grainne and Una would stay in the North, in Belfast, Ballymena and Lurgan respectively, and Peggy – Mrs Igoe – would settle in Dublin. The family scattered, willy nilly.) Brian regaled his sisters with rapturous commendations of Dior's New Look, an antidote to wartime austerity, and treated them to an expurgated version of his experiences in Warsaw.

He stayed in Belfast over Christmas and the New Year – though Belfast, as ever, provoked in him an itch to be out of it as fast as he could manage. There was some discussion with his family about what his next step should be. His cousin Brian MacNeill (Niall MacNeill's son) had got a job with an oil company in Bahrain, and for a time it was considered that something similar might have suited Brian himself. But nothing came of this idea.[25] A plan was forming in the back of his head: he knew that Margaret Swanson was still in London, though due at any moment to set sail for Canada; and although she had absolutely vetoed the suggestion that he might join her out there, he still hoped a change of heart would overtake her. He left Belfast for London and made his way to the Canadian Government Office, where he received assurances that a career in journalism would undoubtedly be available to him should he decide to emigrate. He made up his mind; he still had a fair amount of capital saved from his well-paid job with UNRRA. A week after Margaret Swanson had sailed out of England, he sent a cable to the ship on which she was travelling, alerting her to his proposed arrival at her home in Ottawa. Then he caught a flight to Toronto, 'with several hundred other British emigrants'.[26] The time of indecision was over; whatever should happen in the future, he was on his way to a new life.

7

A CITY UNIQUE IN THE WORLD

On the fourth floor of the *Tribune*, the night's business was just beginning. Under fluorescent lights, lit all year around, a few reporters studied the afternoon papers. A police radio blared routine calls in a corner and in the nearby teletype room a jammed machine tintinnabulated incessantly, calling for attention. In the centre slot of a large horseshoe desk a fat man in a woollen cardigan sliced open the afternoon's crop of wire service photographs. He looked up as Coffey approached. 'Yes?'

'May I speak to Mr MacGregor, please?'

'Boy! Take this man to Mr Mac.'

The Luck of Ginger Coffey

'SHE TOLD ME TO get lost,' Brian Moore recalled. 'There I was, on her doorstep – not a welcome sight!' This silly little Englishman, as Margaret Swanson described him to her parents, had trotted after her all the way to Canada – ridiculous! No job, no prospects – 'I was a pathetic figure,' he concluded later, 'without knowing it.' And, 'I was the *last* person she wanted to see.' In fact, Margaret Swanson was about to leave for Washington, where a high-powered job awaited her. She allowed Brian to accompany her as far as Toronto, where they said goodbye – once again – and he was left stranded. After a night in a Salvation Army hostel, he dressed himself 'and went shivering through the snows to that dread place, the Labour Exchange'.[1] The cold was extreme: 'If the immigrant arrived in winter,' he wrote some years later,[2] 'he encountered a cold such as he had probably never known and walked through streets filled with the brown-sugar slush of snow that had been trampled on by thousands of passers-by.'

After filling in forms and waiting for some time, he got to see a Mr Dickey who clearly had no idea what to make of this intractable immigrant who sat there insisting he wanted to be a newspaper reporter and eventually a writer, but unable to offer any practical experience in these areas.[3] The upshot of this interview was that, the following day, Brian was shipped up north, to a construction camp in the furthest reaches of Ontario, as a cost-accounting clerk amassing tallies of caterpillar tractors, earth-movers, dump trucks and so forth, accommodated in a bunk-house and eating his meals in the mess-house alongside the motley lot of dam-builders he'd landed among. It was no closer to a suitable occupation than anything he'd experienced previously. He lived for more than six months in this out-of-the-way place, amid forests and ice floes, getting a taste of Canada in its more extreme manifestations ('Like nothing I'd ever seen before,' he recalled).[4] His co-workers here were mostly young and rugged, and two at least became friends: a Frenchman called Henri, and Art Bulmer, a young ex-table-tennis champion and naval rating from the north of England. It was in the company of the latter that Brian eventually made his way down to Montreal, once they'd had enough of the bush camp and the wilderness of Northern Ontario, and come to the conclusion that Canada was not for them.

Stepping off the overnight bus at the Montreal terminal – according to an article written by Brian Moore for *Holiday* magazine ten years later[5] – they had it in their heads to book themselves a passage on the first ship leaving for Europe, and they started to trudge through the 'thick gruel' of trampled snow with this object in mind, heading towards the docks. (The wintry weather puts their arrival at Montreal towards the end of 1948.) However, the city, with its idiosyncrasies, its bilingualism, its foreign atmosphere, its streetcars and coffee houses, its elegant buildings, began to work its charm on Brian: 'Above us a sign read: *Chiens Chauds* – Hot Dogs. I was falling in love.' And, after being diverted into the Gayety Theatre where the strip-tease artiste Lili St Cyr was offering her famous presentation of Leda and the Swan, they decided it was worth staying on in Montreal for a bit, to see what happened.[6] Art, displaying a proletarian resourcefulness which impressed his companion, bought a newspaper and immediately jabbed his finger at a notice advertising digs. 'Here we are.'

And there they were. For the next four weeks or so they shared a room in Verdun, a basically working-class suburb but with up-and-coming enclaves, and English rather than French in orientation. Their landlady was an English war-bride[7] suffering from a bad case of home-sickness. During this time Art Bulmer found work with an insurance company, and Brian's future began, at last, to assume a more rewarding and appropriate character.

However, he still had quite a way to go. He was twenty-seven when he joined the *Montreal Gazette* as a proofreader, just about the lowliest position the world of journalism could offer. But like the protagonist of his third novel, James Francis ('Ginger') Coffey, he was grateful at the time for the foothold thereby obtained. How it came about was this. His relative-by-marriage Michael Tierney, who didn't fully subscribe to the MacNeill abhorrence of nepotism, wrote him a letter of recommendation which he took in person to the Irish High Commissioner in Ottawa. 'Oh yes,' this person said, 'you're Eoin MacNeill's nephew' – and they talked about this and that. The High Commissioner then wrote to a columnist on the *Gazette* named Gerald FitzGerald ('Fitz'), who took Brian to meet the Managing Editor, coincidentally a Northern Irishman, a Mr Harry Larkin (recalled by Brian without affection). 'Yes, we'll give you a job,' Mr Larkin told him. 'But you need to train first.'

'Train? What do you mean, train?'

'You'll start on the proofreading desk.'

So that was what his grand connections had netted him: a job as a proofreading drudge, alongside a gang of deadbeats and alcoholics. *The Luck of Ginger Coffey* gives the picture:

> The foreman . . . led Coffey across the room to a small, cleared area surrounded by rows of Linotype machines. There, in Dickensian concentration, sat three old men, each facing a pigeon-hole desk, each scanning a galley proof . . .
>
> [Some time later] Coffey . . . sat dumb, drowsy with beer, the glasses multiplying in front of him, the style book forgotten in his pocket. Were they making a joke of him? Was MacGregor tricking him? What was going on? Was it for this he had travelled across half a frozen continent and the whole Atlantic

Ocean? To finish up as a galley slave among the lame, the odd, the halt, the old?

Brian Moore remained for four months at the *Gazette* as a proof-reader, on a wage of about thirty dollars a week. It was a dispiriting time, once the initial euphoria at having secured the job at all wore off. At his lowest moments, it seemed to him that he might be stuck as a 'galley slave' for ever, or, equally miserably, be forced to slink back to Ireland with his tail between his legs, inescapably a ne'er-do-well, the path to achievement barred to him in Montreal, through some fatal weakness in his nature, just as it had been in Belfast. (*Ginger Coffey*, with comic brio, recounts what might have happened had his fortunes spiralled downwards, rather than up-wards, at that moment.) Having left Verdun, he was renting a shabby room in an awful apartment; he had no close friends; he was still hankering after Margaret Swanson, and paying more than he could afford to have flowers delivered each week to her Washington address (this went on for about another three months before he came to his senses and accepted that he never was going to receive any acknowledgement from her). He was living in an alien city, full of people wearing fur caps, heavy boots, snow suits, and dragging children on little sleds behind them. The only thing that kept him going was his conviction that he could make a go of it as a reporter, given the chance. So he went to Mr Larkin and made a fuss, and – unlike Coffey – got himself bumped up into the City Room, where he was an instant success.

Montreal's English-language newspapers were, at the time, the *Gazette*, the *Star*, the midday *Herald* (more of a tabloid), and the weekly *Standard*. None of these was politically or intellectually adventurous – as one ex-employee of the *Gazette* put it, 'most newspaper work was . . . intellectually stultifying, morally degrad-ing and financially unrewarding'.[8] It wasn't long before Brian Moore was in a position to endorse this perception. However, he took to reporting like a country-born sophisticate to the smoke. It was something he was indubitably good at. 'As a reporter, he was enterprising, accurate and – above all – fast,' a colleague recalled, years later. 'He would come into the office at high speed and seemed to start typing while still in the process of sitting down at his desk. He'd have his story finished while the rest of us were still staring blankly at that old Underwood, and adding more sugar to the coffee. Because he was fast he was prolific and the *Gazette* appreciated this. For the puny salary they were paying him, they were getting a lot of words to fill the space between the ads.'[9]

For all its shortcomings – 'It was an old-fashioned, Tory newspaper' – the *Gazette* provided an excellent training for the future novelist. 'I learned a lot,' Brian Moore has conceded; specifically – like Hemingway before him – he learned to be succinct, to make an impact in his opening paragraph and to shape his story in accordance with the five basic journalistic tenets – who, what, why, when and where – the reporter's guiding principles. He learned, by and large, to eschew the poetic touch: 'If you're going to have poetic images they'd better be wonderful – otherwise, you'll just end up with overwriting and lushness.' (He also, at this time, came under the influence of the burgeoning French *nouveau roman*, whose spareness appealed to him.)

The atmosphere of cigarettes, ebullience, a certain waspishness and constant low-level pressure he found incredibly stimulating ('I was sent on a different assignment every day'). At last, his capacities, or some of his capacities, were being exercised to the full. He enjoyed doing features and writing up interviews. Knowing that the copy-editors were sitting there waiting to cut and alter everything, he took a certain pride in making this as difficult for them as possible. A lot of his stuff got through unedited. However, it sometimes happened that his pieces were rewritten as drastically as anyone's. A case in point was a report he did on a political meeting at which the principal speaker was Frank Scott, a prominent figure in Montreal at the time. Scott was a poet, a socialist and a Professor of Law at McGill University, and at this particular meeting he spoke out against the dictator of Quebec, Premier Duplessis, whose period in office would later come to be known as *la Grande Noirceur*, the Great Darkness.[10] Brian was thrilled to hear such revolutionary sentiments as Scott's expressed in public – 'I gave him good coverage, I rushed back and wrote it all up, and took it to the desk, and the deskman said, "What's this?"' Out came the red pencil, while Brian protested, 'But it was a terrific speech.' 'Hmm,' said the deskman, 'Let's see – meeting at so-and-so hall, and the speaker was . . . Just change that to, "The speaker was Frank Scott."' And that was it. It wasn't the *Gazette*'s policy to give coverage to anything remotely controversial: this loomed large, for Brian, among the arguments in favour of resigning from the paper, when the right moment came.

But first he was learning the ropes, getting involved in some significant friendships, and acclimatising himself to a routine that entailed getting up at midday and going to bed around 2 a.m. The *Gazette* was a morning newspaper, and reporters were expected to be in the building by early afternoon, scanning other newspapers for the day's events. Anyone who didn't familiarise himself quickly with the big news stories risked being fired on the spot. (There were no such things as unions to protect staff interests.) Then, it was a matter of working right through until the Ottawa edition came out, around nine or ten at night. After this, they'd all slope off to what Brian Moore has described as 'a newspaperman's bar kind of place', to cash their cheques and eat some kind of inexpensive meal. 'And that was our social life.' And during the afternoons there were tedious events to be covered: Rotary Club lunches and the like. Brian, however, was soon assigned to 'the hotel beat', which meant he got to interview any celebrities who came to town (these included Mae West, whom he judged to be 'a natural' – in other words, a gift to the reporter). Then he became a shipping news reporter, travelling up to a point above Quebec City where a liner could be boarded, and coming back down to Montreal writing frantically in his notebook all the way. He tried to ensure that his stories would have the edge on his competitors', contain some extra ingredient or piece of observation that would lift them above the ruck. 'It was a good training in that way.' He was a fast learner. Indeed, his friend and fellow-reporter from his *Gazette* days, William Weintraub, believed him to be the best reporter that newspaper ever employed.[11]

He met Bill Weintraub in the City Room at the *Gazette* in 1949, and the two became friends immediately and remained friends for life. They had quite a lot in common, the Catholic Belfast surgeon's son and ex-accounts clerk, and the Jewish Montrealer and graduate of McGill University. Both were droll, humorous, quick-witted, sociable, literary, opinionated and moderately left wing, as well as being averse to fools, pretentiousness and kow-towing. The *Gazette* gave them plenty of scope to exercise their bent for mockery. 'We had a lot of fun, actually,' Brian remembered. Whenever he was down at the waterfront on behalf of the *Gazette* (late 1951–early 1952), he and Bill Weintraub would arrange to eat lunch (lamb chops) at a restaurant called The Brokers on St Francis Xavier Street. Both, at the time, were augmenting their incomes by selling stories to *Weekend* magazine at $250 a throw.

On one occasion the two of them were among a group of journalists travelling northwards to write up the launching of a ship or some similar occasion. The party included an ebullient feature writer with the *Montreal Standard*, named Jacqueline Sirois, to whom Brian was introduced by Bill. This would have been in the spring or early summer of 1950, before Bill was sacked[12] by the martinet Larkin ('a heavy-set man with an air of suppressed violence about him').[13] Larkin's obituary, many years later, would note the fact that he had been immortalised (not flatteringly) in not one but *two* works of fiction, Brian Moore's *The Luck of Ginger Coffey* in which he appears as the dread MacGregor, nicknamed Hitler; and William Weintraub's *Why Rock the Boat*, which rechristens him 'Philip L. Butcher'. Larkin it was who told Brian Moore at an early point in his journalistic career: 'Nothing good ever came out of Ireland. Live like pigs over there. You never had it so good, Moore, since you got out here. Wonderful opportunities for advancement here. Stick with this company and you'll get along.'

'I treasure those words,' Brian wrote sardonically to his friend Bill Weintraub in February 1951, Bill having left for Europe and an eight-month stint as a freelance reporter ('Life has been a mad fandango for the past two months'). Brian is writing from the *Gazette* Police Desk, in the gloomy old City Room, where he's on the Graveyard Shift (6 p.m. to 2.30 a.m.). The letter also contains news of his forthcoming marriage to Jacqueline Sirois (née Scully), due to take place at St Anthony's Church ('or is it St Patrick's?' Brian wonders) in St Antoine Street, Montreal, on the 28th of the month. It will be a sacrilegious event, he reports happily, since they are in a state of mortal sin – and the bride, to cap it all, is a divorcee.

Jacqueline – Jackie – Scully had still been married to Bernard Sirois when she and Brian first met, but the marriage was on the rocks, Jackie was unhappy, she and Brian became lovers almost straightaway, and – despite Brian's protests that he was only a catalyst in the worsening situation between her and Sirois – she insisted that a new start, a realignment of affections, offered the best hope to both of them. She was very determined. She was also lively, intelligent, talented, a good sport and a spirited companion, all reasons for Brian to find her attractive, and to envisage, with pleasure, a future in which the two of them would settle into a kind of quotidian content. He had – he said[14] – given up on romantic love since the defection of Margaret Swanson; but the alternative, as he saw it – good-humoured companionship – seemed a reasonable bet. He disliked the unavoidable fuss surrounding the marriage ceremony; having made up his mind, he just wanted to get it over with as quickly as possible. He was twenty-nine years old.

From a Montreal turf accountant named Maxie Shapiro, and for ninety dollars a month, the couple secured a two-bedroom apartment at 1710, Dorchester Street West, and moved in on 15 February. After the Catholic ceremony – 'Jackie got married in the arms of the Church,' her friend Mavis Gallant commented drily in a letter. 'Everyone who writes about it is very amused'[15] – after the ceremony came a honeymoon in Europe, where Brian, back in Paris for the first time since the war, consolidated his love affair with that city. It was (he admitted) the place above all others for which he cherished a romantic nostalgic feeling. In Paris, the Moores met up with some expatriate Montreal friends, including Bill Weintraub and Mavis Gallant. The latter, a Montrealer by birth and ex-colleague of Jackie's at the *Standard*, had turned her back on journalism – and on Canada – for the precarious joys of creative writing, and transported herself to Paris, which became her permanent home. (She was, eventually, to become celebrated as a short-story writer and social commentator.)

Bill was delighted to conduct the newly-weds around a few Parisian high spots, among them an immensely avant-garde restaurant (Le Mouton de Panurge) where the bread rolls served with the soup sometimes came in the shape of penises, women's breasts or genitalia – suitable fare for a honeymoon couple, perhaps, though as Bill commented a long time afterwards, 'It seemed strange as we munched these exotic breadstuffs, to be gossiping about the mundane world of Montreal journalism.'[16] Other venues devoted to exuberant naughtiness included a night-club in Montmartre – Le Ciel – complete with faux-Catholic paraphernalia such as crosses, pulpit, stained-glass windows, mitred archbishop, church pews and waiters dressed as angels, wings and all. The lesbian meeting-place Le Monocle, and the Bal Nègre on Rue Blomet, were other outstanding items on the merrily sacrilegious agenda.

Writing to Alex Cherney, a Montreal friend and former roommate at the Hotel Acropolis,[17] Bill Weintraub described a party held in that same room, in honour of the Moores on their last night in Paris, with copious amounts of vin blanc, Pernod and cognac inducing an uproarious atmosphere, and damage limited to 'a deep cigarette hole burned in the carpet'. Back in Montreal, worn out after all the honeymoon exertions and excursions, Brian was soon regaling Bill with the comments (probably apocryphal) of the hated Larkin: 'How did you find the old country? Bloody awful, eh? I told you when you went away that the finest thing you'd ever see over there was the plane home'; he and Jackie, he reported, were continuing to drink quantities of Pernod, and eating Paris meals with friends like the *Gazette* employee Betty Davidson; and getting on with their careers.

Jackie was much the more successful of the two of them at this time; she was earning $100 a week from the *Standard*, and constantly getting sent off to cover events like the annual American Psychiatrists' Convention in Cincinnati. Jackie – born in 1921 – was the daughter of divorced parents, a French-Canadian mother named Camille Pacquot, and a New Brunswick-Irish father, Frank Scully,[18] who'd become a society doctor and ended up leading a rather louche existence, living beyond his means in the Ritz-Carlton Hotel. Jackie was rather short in stature with cropped brown hair, not beautiful but a considerable livewire, someone who relished being a girl-about-town, downing rye whiskies with the best of them at the Press Club bar in the basement of the Laurentien Hotel, and cutting quite a figure in journalistic circles. One of Jackie's professional triumphs was the story, 'Murder in the Sky',[19] about the trial and conviction of a Quebec City jeweller who'd contrived to kill his wife (along with twenty-two others) by planting a bomb on the Canadian Pacific aeroplane on which she was travelling. This event took place in 1948, and Jackie spent three years researching the background to the crime (dubbed 'Canada's most sensational'); her account of the atrocity, the murderer and his motivation was serialised in four parts in *Weekend* magazine (as the *Standard* became in 1951).

Altogether, Jackie was quite a girl. One story has her ex-husband Bernard Sirois turning up in the middle of a party she was hosting, to collect a radio or something he had left behind, and Jackie flinging the object after him, down a couple of flights of stairs. She was, by all accounts, tremendous fun to be with. Brian was caught up in the whirl of her immense sociability – not that he was lacking in the instinct for conviviality himself. The two of them became known as a party-going, party-giving couple, within a lively and fluctuating circle of friends who included Alex and Gloria Cherney, Bruce and Dorothy Ruddick, Bill Weintraub and – from time to time – Mordecai Richler.

At the start of 1951, the expatriate community in Paris was enriched (briefly) by the presence of nineteen-year-old Mordecai Richler, a Jewish Montrealer and university drop-out committed to free-thinking, literary ambition and moderate lechery. When he and Bill Weintraub were brought together in Paris, at the instigation of Mavis Gallant, an instant rapport sprang up between them, and this resulted in a genial exchange of letters ('P.S. Can you lend me $25?'), once Mordecai (Mordy) had gone on to investigate the possibilities of living very cheaply in Ibiza and other similarly auspicious places. Bill went to stay with him in Ibiza in the summer of 1951, before returning to Montreal and a temporary job on the staff of *Weekend*. More than a year would pass before the two came face-to-face again, but they kept in touch by letter – and this correspondence became a three-way correspondence, which lasted for many years, once Brian Moore had been added to the equation.

Brian and Mordecai, introduced by Bill, met for the first time in 1952, at the bar of the Press Club in Montreal. Mordecai, back home for a short period, had a job in the newsroom of the Canadian Broadcasting Company, while he waited to learn the fate of his novel, *The Acrobats*, which was doing the rounds of publishers. As had happened with Bill and Mordecai, the two literary hopefuls took to one another straightaway, and a state of cheerful fraternising soon ensued, with (as Bill put it) 'long, argumentative dinners in restaurants and in the Moores' apartment'.[20] But it wasn't long before Mordecai Richler's first novel was accepted by an English publisher (André Deutsch), and on the strength of this he resigned from his job with the CBC and returned to London, before going on to Paris and Munich, and then back to London again to work on his second book.

All this time, Brian Moore had continued to write, rewrite and send out short stories; in 1951 the first to be published, 'Sassanach', appeared in the small Canadian magazine *Northern Review*. 'I remember going off to a place called the Honeydew, a kind of coffee shop, with this magazine and opening it up – and there was my name! It was amazing, I was just so chuffed; it was fantastic!' 'Sassanach' is about a street performer in Belfast, a Cockney Englishman whose gyrations hold the crowd's attention until the point when the hat starts going around, when everyone melts away. Brian Moore referred to himself as having cast a cold Northern Irish eye on this tiny event, remembered from his childhood; and to see the story in print, in front of him, reinforced his conviction that a literary future might still remain a possibility.

Though life as a *Gazette* reporter suited him better than anything he'd experienced up until that time, it was by no means satisfactory in terms of livelihood or reputation. And, no sooner had he established himself as a crack reporter, than he began to think about moving on to something even more advantageous. 'I mean – I didn't want to be thirty-five years old, and the City Editor instructing me to get out and cover such-and-such a convention, or record the repellent views of some brash businessman or industrialist.' Money was, as ever, the sticking-point. However, in 1950, he had found a stop-gap means of subsidising his literary ambitions. As had happened before – and would happen again – he was spurred on by the inadequate credentials or poor performance of some contemporary to do better himself.[21] An acquaintance named Ronald Cooke had written a thriller which had earned him an outright payment of $3,000 from Harlequin Books. Brian read the thing, found it truly deplorable and immediately understood that something similar could be knocked out by himself, in a matter of weeks. The result was a couple of pulp paperbacks – *Wreath for a Redhead* and *The Executioners* – 'poor clones of Chandler and Dashiell Hammett', as he put it himself, both of which Harlequin Books of Canada were happy to accept. They came out under his own name in 1951, within a few months of each other, and shortly after his marriage to Jackie Sirois. Her parents weren't fearfully impressed. 'Jackie's mother sees no reason why I should have put all that disgusting sex into *Wreath for a Redhead*. Jackie's stepfather says: In certain questionable French novels I have read about men tearing women's clothes off. Now where would Brian have read a thing like that.'[22]

Both these lurid-looking novels are set in Montreal: the first concerns an enigmatic redhead – the eponymous corpse – encountered on a train by a sailor, John Riordan, at the start of what proves to be an eventful shore-leave. (The American edition, published two years later by Pyramid Books, is retitled *Sailor's Leave*.) The complications and predicaments that ensue suggest that Brian Moore had made himself thoroughly familiar with the requirements of the 'sub-Chandleresque' mode he was appropriating, however much this went against the grain ('I *hate* detective stories, I *hate* them, those books my father read, you know, like *Flowers for the Judge* and all that stuff, I *hated* it'). *The Executioners* is even more of a plot-driven farrago, furnished with hired gunmen, secret police, an Eastern Bloc statesman on the run, and an upright hero who wins through to victory and romance. Well, it seemed Brian Moore could do this sort of thing standing on his head; but it was a skill that embarrassed him, and which he disowned as far as possible in later years. He must also have felt that, by indulging this – to him – worrying facility in synthetic plot-making, he was somehow eroding his genuine abilities, and that a price would be exacted, in some form or other, for what he could only view as literary prostitution. The price, in fact, turned out to be guilt and embarrassment over the wretched thrillers; but, at the time, with his practical side in the ascendant, he coolly assessed the available means of achieving his larger ambitions, and acted accordingly. If it meant writing sentences like the following – 'A man came in. A fat, middle-aged man. He wore a blue, double-breasted suit and a brown hat. His nose was squashed flat against his cheeks. His right hand motioned me to stay quiet. I did. In his left hand was a gun'[23] – well, he would write them, with as much conviction as he could muster. It was no good taking a superior attitude while he was doing it, since this would have distorted the narrative tone. But the impersonation wasn't effected painlessly.

He wasn't the only author driven to this expedient to boost his income: Gore Vidal was doing the same thing, 'under the name of

Joseph Fox' (Brian means Edgar Box). 'Latest offering' (1954): *Death in the Fifth Position*.' At one point, Brian kindly wrote out a fifteen-page synopsis of a typical 'Gold Medal'[24] thriller to encourage the chronically hard-up Mordecai Richler to try his hand at the genre; however, he never got around to doing so. Brian himself turned out seven of the potboilers, three under the name of Bernard Mara, and two as Michael Bryan, before circumstances enabled him to draw a line under this – as he saw it – discreditable portion of his output. Actually, they are all perfectly efficient and enjoyable exercises in production-line intrigue (even if some of them come complete with covers featuring impossibly succulent-looking women). Quests, disappearances, assassination plots, colourful settings, resourceful, deracinated heroes and upbeat endings: all these ingredients of the mid-century thriller genre the adept storyteller took in his stride. 'Bernard Mara' came into being in 1954, the name chosen 'because it couldn't possibly be mispronounced in any language'.[25] *French for Murder*, the first Mara novel, was followed by two others, all published by Fawcett in New York.[26] Fawcett's 'Gold Medal' division, under the direction of Mr Knoxburger and Mr Taylor ('high-profile American editors', according to Brian), was so pleased with these efforts that an invitation went out summoning the author to Gold Medal's New York offices. Clearly, on the strength of the fiction, they expected to see a Humphrey Bogart-type figure, complete with trench coat and American accent; and when (as Brian has it) 'this wee fat Belfast-man in a Brooks Brothers suit walked into their office claiming to be Bernard Mara' a moment of total stupefaction followed. However, they quickly gathered their wits and swept him out for lunch, an occasion made memorable for him by a phrase used by Mr Knoxburger (or Mr Taylor). He'd politely enquired what their current projects were, and been told they were planning to fly down to Texas in an Air Force combat jet to attend a Western Writers' Conference. 'And we're going to cut one out of the herd.'

'We're going to cut one out of the herd.' This expression was greatly relished by Brian, as was the hype and hullabaloo surrounding commercial paperback publishing, an area he was increasingly anxious to remove himself from. By this time (1956 or 57) he was in a position to turn down offers from Gold Medal Books, or any equivalent firm, having had a considerable *succès d'estime* with his first serious full-length work of fiction, *Judith Hearne*.

Before this novel could be written he had to take the courageous step of resigning from the *Gazette*, which he did in 1952, some three years after joining the paper. He was then dependent on his income from writing the thrillers, occasional short stories – 'awful stories', he called them – and articles (hack work) and Jackie's salary from *Weekend* magazine. It was enough to keep them going. By now the Moores had moved to a flat at 4525 Ste Catherine Street West (on a site later occupied by the Reader's Digest Building), and were enjoying an animated, if precarious, way of life. All the time Brian was planning a novel, considering first one possibility and then another, before fixing finally on the germ of an idea which had come to him in 1946,[27] been abandoned and then returned to a couple of years later, when it evolved into the story, 'A Friend of the Family' (one of his early literary stories which proved unsaleable). In the earliest version, the protagonist is referred to interchangeably as Miss Keogh and Miss Hearne, the family she visits is called Brannigan, and the *paterfamilias* – Professor Brannigan – is irritated by the old maid's implication 'that she and he had been partners in an old romantic friendship'. For Professor Brannigan's daughters, Miss Keogh/Hearne stands as 'a grim and terrible reminder of what happened to girls who did not get married and in moments of depression they would see themselves as versions of Miss Hearne, old, neglected, living in rooms, being asked out to Sunday dinner and on Christmas day by people who were sorry for you, living on small annuities and devoting one's time to pious good works'.[28] Version two is set in Dublin, and although secret drinking comes into the picture, it doesn't precipitate a crisis of nerves or anything of that sort. Something more was clearly called for to strengthen Judith Hearne's impact; and in the early summer of 1953, Brian Moore took himself out of Montreal to a cabin in the Laurentian Mountains of Quebec,[29] at a place called Fourteen Island Lake, to see if he couldn't succeed in hammering out a compelling narrative from the bare bones of the situation that had been humming away at the back of his imagination for years.

'It was a lonely and somewhat frightening decision,' Brian

Moore claimed, looking back.[30] 'I was hard up for money . . . I'd had reason over the years of exile to question every belief I had formerly held. I had few friends and many doubts. In exile, in a summer cabin . . . I began to make the pilgrimage back in my own mind to the house I had been born in, to the people I had known as a boy.' He goes on: 'And in that first novel I discovered, partly because of my own situation, a subject which was central to much of my early writing. It is loneliness . . .' It was indeed a risky decision (though it paid off), but what this account omits to mention is the existence of a supportive wife and a great many friends, some of whom would drive up to Fourteen Island Lake at the weekends, providing a valuable and boisterous antidote to the midweek isolation. 'There'd be a lot of drinking, cooking meals and going out and so forth – and then I'd be left alone from Monday to Thursday.' With both his social and reclusive instincts satisfied, then, and in the peaceful lakeside setting, Brian got on more swiftly and swimmingly than he ever managed again, as the character of his heroine diverged from that of the tedious, remembered Sunday visitor at Clifton Street, and took on a vigorous fictional life.

Judith Hearne was not the only crucial area of gestation during the summer months of 1953: Jackie was pregnant. This, according to Brian, had not been on the cards at the time of their marriage, when they'd agreed between themselves, in a civilised manner, that, 'if things didn't work out', there'd be nothing to stop them parting amicably. Jackie's first marriage had been childless, very much to her dismay; she'd confided to Brian that she believed herself to be infertile, since no precautions had been taken to stop her conceiving. It was no big deal as far as he was concerned; having grown up in a family of nine, he had no particular yen to be a parent himself. (No doubt the presence in his home of five younger siblings had helped to disabuse him of any romantic notions about the business of procreation, as well as getting any quasi-paternal leanings he might have nourished out of his system.)

However – it happened that Jackie was sent by *Weekend* magazine to interview a leading gynaecologist, and before she left his office she'd had the cause of her own problem identified: a tilted uterus. Once that was put right, it was only a matter of weeks before she conceived. Brian was half pleased, when it came to the bit, and half filled with trepidation, while Jackie was wholly delighted. The news didn't interfere with Brian's plans to get out of Montreal for a bit, to write undisturbed when the fancy took him, in the middle of the night, at six in the morning or whenever. Except at weekends, he ate out of tins, replenishing his stock at a village store to which he'd ride on a bicycle (he didn't own a car or drive at the time). In the afternoons he would swim, then get back to the book. The first half of *Judith Hearne* was written, he said, in a kind of trance. Outside his cabin windows were the glorious Laurentian Mountains but he barely noticed them; in his head he was back in miserable Belfast, but the misery and the provincial accoutrements had gained an extraordinary pungency in the course of his effort to recreate them: the rain pattering on the windows, 'growing heavier, soft persistent Irish rain, coming up Belfast Lough, caught in the shadow of Cave Hill. It settled on the city, a night blanket of wetness.'[31]

And then a shocking accident occurred. Brian had met some people who owned a holiday home nearby, and they allowed him to borrow their rowing boat, which enabled him to get to the other side of Fourteen Island Lake where he would swim and relax in the sunshine, going over the morning's work in his head. One day – 'it was very hot' – he was swimming idly with the towing rope wrapped around his hand, when suddenly, out of the narrow entrance to another lake, 'I saw coming roaring towards me an enormous, apparently unmanned, motor boat.' There was no time to take any evasive action; he was hidden from view by the boat he was towing, and the next minute the motor boat had smashed into the rowing boat, hitting Brian on the head and driving him under. 'For some reason, God knows why, I didn't lose consciousness. If I had I'd be dead.' He came to the surface with blood pouring out of him; the motor boat had slewed round and taken off, under the impression that what had been struck was an empty vessel. It turned out that the person in charge of the runaway boat was an unemployed silk-stockings salesman, who had a two-year-old child on board with him; looking out for some need of the child's, he lost control of the boat, failed to observe the swimmer he was about to crash into, and nearly deprived literature of one of its future luminaries.

Fortunately there were some people on the other side of the lake who heard the crash and saw what had happened; they jumped, aghast, into their motor boat and got Brian out, then drove him – by now unconscious – twenty miles or so to a place called St Jerome, where a doctor pronounced him terribly injured, beyond his capacity to deal with; so he was transferred to an ambulance and rushed down to Montreal. Montreal, at the time, as it happened, was home to an extremely sophisticated neurosurgical centre,[32] under the direction of a Dr Wilder Penfield; and the prompt care that Brian received here, particularly from a doctor named William Cone, undoubtedly saved his life and his faculties. His skull was fractured in four places when he was wheeled into an observation ward containing the hospital's most serious accident cases (including a boy who'd been struck by a motorbike and lost an arm and a leg); he was wearing nothing but a pair of swimming trunks and had no means of identification on him, and it was some time before he came round sufficiently to tell the hospital staff who he was. His pregnant wife then had to be sent for (she was in Quebec on a journalistic assignment when news of the accident was relayed to her); and, after a week or so, friends were able to visit him, including Bill Weintraub who remembers him sitting up in his hospital bed with his head swathed in bandages, joking about his indestructibility.

Brian Moore's recovery was extraordinary, considering the seriousness of his injuries; he was left with hearing slightly impaired in one ear, but no other damage that he was aware of. It took about six weeks for him to get back to normal; in the first days after the accident he found it impossible to read, and as for writing – if he tried to write at all, he produced only gibberish. He was kept under close observation for about three weeks, Dr Cone – wisely, in Brian's view – having decided to keep treatment to a minimum, and to let the recovery proceed at a natural pace. Brian was told a gruesomely humorous name for his condition: Railway Head. The term derived from patients who'd survived collisions with trains, or some equivalent impact.

Like most other things that had happened to him, the near-death experience was filed away by the thrifty novelist in a recess of his consciousness, to be available for retrieval at the appropriate juncture.[33] The most urgent matter, though, once he was himself, or almost himself, again, was to finish the novel – the accident having alerted him to the fact that, as he expressed it often enough, he 'wasn't going to be around for ever'; and if he was going to make his mark on the world of literature, he had better get on with it. He was thirty-two years old. The writing of *Judith Hearne* continued, only now it required a slightly more laboured approach to get the same effect of fluency and high pressure. There were interruptions too: to make up, financially, for the time lost, he was forced to turn his hand to another thriller (the first of the three Bernard Mara titles), which was placed by his agent, Willis Kingsley Wing, with Fawcett in New York, and published in May 1954 under the Gold Medal imprint.

In the four years or so since he first set foot on the icy pavements of down-town Montreal, Brian Moore's life had been subject to some extreme vicissitudes; but what gradually became clear was the fact that the city suited him, or at any rate provided the conditions in which his talents could expand and flourish. He ceased to be hopelessly at odds with his environment. Indeed, the one-time failure at maths had become a considerable success, even if his major achievements were still in front of him. Ambition, boldness, resourcefulness, a survivor's instincts: he had proved to himself, and others, that these were qualities he possessed in abundance. He was also an amiable husband and – eventually – father, and a witty, discriminating and generous friend – even if these aspects of his personality conflicted somewhat with his perception of himself as the complete outsider, an image he returned to over and over.[34] It's true, of course, that he always resisted attempts by journalists and others to assign him to any literary movement or clique, relishing the contradictions that – for him – underscored his independence. First as an Irishman living in Canada, and later as a Canadian citizen who made his home on America's Pacific Coast, he evaded categorisation by nationality, or affinity. But for a time, at least, in the 1950s, he was happy to be counted among a group of 'creative Montrealers':[35] Mordecai Richler, Bill Weintraub, Hugh MacLennan, Frank Scott, Mavis Gallant and the rest of them.

8

CREATIVE MONTREALERS

To talk of extra-island and extra-peninsular matters, I have not heard from the young authorman[1] but when I last saw him he was waiting with great hopes of getting an 'obscene' review in one of the big dailies which would make his opus a resounding success. For my own part I have heard nothing from either side of the Atlantic, a fact I find curiously undepressing. I don't understand this, but it seemed to me that the minute the book was out of my hands all my interest in it and hopes for it disappeared. This is not wholly true as I would be very disappointed if it is not published. But the practice in waiting for other things has developed a tolerance or an indifference in me towards this.

Letter to William Weintraub, 20 April 1954

BRIAN MOORE BECAME A Canadian citizen in November 1953, shortly before the birth of his son Michael[2] on the 24th of the month: this was turning his back on Belfast with a vengeance, assuming a new identity to accord with his commitment to Canada (for the time being). However, his first two novels dealt with topics from his childhood – his family home and his schooling – albeit obliquely. The O'Neills in *Judith Hearne*, the family doggedly visited by the eponymous heroine on Sundays and on Christmas day, are of course the Moores, cut down to four children but otherwise unmodified, down to the tortoiseshell monocle before the father's beady eye. Two of his siblings' actual names, Shaun and Una (the first spelt differently), are bestowed by the author on the children of the family who chafe under the obligation to make themselves agreeable to the excruciating bore with her meagre experience of life's excitements and disheartening signature tune, 'It's only me!'

'It's only me!' Shaun cried, in a high-pitched, feminine voice. Una and Kevin echoed it. 'It's only me! It's only me!'

Professor O'Neill stood up hurriedly, gathering the *Sunday Times*, his pipe, matches and tobacco pouch. 'I'll be in my study if you want me.'

Shaun bounced up from the sofa, big-boned, adolescent. 'I'll come with you, Daddy.'

'You'll stay here, sir,' Professor O'Neill said. 'Stay for half an hour at least, to help your mother.' He looked at his son and raised his hand against an unspoken protest. 'Now, that's enough. No nonsense.'

The O'Neills' maid was coming upstairs as the professor left the drawing-room. 'It's Miss Hearne, sir.'

The highlight of her week is the nadir of theirs. Why, you might ask, as a heroine for this unusual young man's novel, Miss Judith Hearne? Or, to go back to origins, why Mary Judith Keogh, the ex-convent girl who continued to sign her letters, M. J. Keogh, Enfant de Marie? Well, Brian Moore made no secret of having consciously turned his back on the standard Irish *Bildungsroman*,[3] the kind of novel that ends with the hero or heroine on the verge of a new life elsewhere, getting the hell out of the godforsaken country. In the wake of Joyce's Stephen Dedalus, indeed, this expedient was no longer an option for the properly self-conscious Irish writer, desirous of finding an individual voice, and skirting a potentially overwhelming influence. (It's true that Miss Hearne has elements of Joyce's Maria, in the story of that title in *Dubliners*; but the whole tone and drift of the novel establishes it as a work without obvious precedent.[4]) Just as (as he reported) he'd had 'to exorcise Heming-way through a series of rejection slips',[5] Brian Moore needed to be wary of the even more dangerously enticing example of his most famous literary countryman.[6] To make matters worse, he had it in his head to write about 'a crisis of faith' ('my material'); but then he began to think: what if such a state should overtake, not a young ferocious intellectual in the Stephen Dedalus mould, but an un-remarkable person, a sodality lady, say, 'a lady much like the ladies

I'd seen in our drawing-room at home as a child taking tea with my mother'.[7] It was time for a reworking and expansion of the 'Sunday Visitor' theme. Mary Judith Keogh, with her red raincoat and straw hat decorated with a bunch of cherries, and her 'dear aunt', plus the comment she once uttered in Brian's hearing, to the effect that such-and-such a man was her 'brother-in-law who was to have been'[8] (meaning she'd once been engaged under a misapprehension, thinking the man in question had money, while he thought the same about her: and when it transpired that neither of them had a penny to their names, the engagement fell through) – these fragments made a starting-point for a piquant and original creative enterprise.

Having fixed on Miss Keogh, Brian consulted one of his sisters about this lady's characteristics – most of which he then proceeded to jettison, in the interests of his evolving plot. Relatives who subsequently approached the book anticipating an unadulterated portrayal of their old Clifton Street acquaintance were bemused and disappointed – before the narrative momentum began to carry them along. Mary Judith Keogh was actually rather a stylish woman, according to Brian's cousin Eilis McDowell,[9] and 'a friend to all the family'. All of which was totally irrelevant, indeed, as far as the novelist's purpose was concerned: he had his unattractive heroine, a failed music teacher in her early forties, eking out a dismal existence in furnished rooms, bolstering herself up with delusions of continuing respectability and religious observances, setting her sights at her current landlady's boorish brother, a returned American and one-time hotel doorman, only to find that even he, like every man before him, is unable to view her in any remotely romantic light. After this final emotional let-down, come the intensified drinking bouts and episode of blasphemy, as every pretension and every refuge is stripped away from poor Judy Hearne. Actually, the crisis of faith is the least satisfactory part of the novel; you feel it is somehow manufactured to add point and drama to the plot, whereas the ordinary miseries of the protagonist, the boarding-house life, the contrast with the domestic warmth of the affluent O'Neills, the men's talk in pubs, the rainy atmosphere of the uninspiring city – all these ring wonderfully true. The real point of the story is the importance (to its heroine) of being genteel, and the moral perplexities attending the loss of gentility.

Judith Hearne's is a thoroughly dispiriting life, presented with redeeming vigour and dispassion. Brian Moore, with this first novel, is observant without being satirical, imaginative without displaying, or soliciting, undue sympathy for his central character. Miss Hearne isn't likeable, but her predicament is riveting – because of its implications for Irish society in general, with its upholding of suburban values and its arid Catholicism; and because it's delineated with such confidence. It is, of course, significant that each of Brian Moore's three early Belfast novels should be centred on a different kind of failure, social in *Judith Hearne*, sexual in *The Feast of Lupercal* and intellectual in *The Emperor of Ice Cream*; Belfast, after all, was the place where he himself was branded a failure, a boy unable to pass exams, charm girls, or fit in with conventional social expectations. But it's not in any sense a matter of exacting revenge for remembered mistreatment; rather, he puts his finger on the different kinds of backwardness and malaise afflicting his birthplace. He showed himself straightaway to be a compelling social critic.

One or two of Brian Moore's relatives[10] considered it brave of him to put himself into *Judith Hearne*, in the form – as it seemed to them – of Bernard Rice, the landlady's son, a fat mother's boy and would-be poet, anti-religious but a bit of a hypocrite, and given to unscrupulous machinations. It's true that Bernard is the mouth-piece for a few of the author's opinions, but that's as far as any attempt at self-portrayal goes. Young Shaun O'Neill is more akin to Brian (though his is only a walk-on part). And, although Judith Hearne herself 'is not me – very much not me!', according to Brian Moore, albeit a mite disingenuously, there were qualities and experiences they had in common. Being 'lonely and not good-looking' were two he specified. Well, one should keep in mind Flaubert's famous assertion, '*Madame Bovary – c'est moi*', to get at the underlying point he is making.

Judith Hearne was completed by the end of 1953 and dispatched to a few friends whose response was enthusiastic, even if one or two suggested the odd tiny amendment.[11] It then went to Brian Moore's American agent, Willis Kingsley Wing,[12] who began sending it out to publishers. In the meantime, Mordecai Richler, whose own first novel *The Acrobats* had come out in England with the firm of

André Deutsch, persuaded his publishers to take a look at his friend's work. Brian had not heard from them, or from Wing, by the time he left Montreal in March 1954, bound first of all for New York where he boarded the *Maasdam en route* to Ireland, England and Spain. He notified Wing of his intention to be away from home until the middle of June.

He was heading for Spain, where, he believed, one could live cheaply, to get going on a couple of novels, the second 'proper' novel, and another thriller to pay the bills. (It's also probable that he was removing himself from the vicinity of a four-month-old baby and consequent disturbance.) But first came London, followed by a fleeting visit to Cliftonville Avenue in Belfast – his first time home since he'd emigrated to Canada. Once there, he found himself surrounded by middle-class comforts: everyone owned a car, there was an abundance of good food, drinks, fivers, wine for dinner. He, in the bosom of his family – as he reported in one of his exuberant letters to Bill Weintraub – 'was an American freak, a bit of a failure, the arty fella off to Spain on ha'pence'. The next minute he was back in London where the constantly impoverished Mordecai Richler and his wife-to-be Cathy Boudreau regarded him as 'the rich friend who could take a luxurious holiday [they] could never afford'. Between these two conflicting views of him, Brian felt somewhat disorientated. 'I wasn't at home in either place. Perhaps in some strange way I've found a synthesis of both in Montreal. Or,' he went on, terrified as ever of the least tinge of pomposity, 'does that sound like Fitz? I don't mean it to be Fitzian.'[13]

Before he left London Brian received a mysterious telephone call from his brother Seamus in Belfast; Seamus had something on his mind, a matter of such urgency that it couldn't possibly be resolved over the telephone but demanded an immediate face-to-face confrontation. Seamus was therefore on his way to catch a flight. Some hours later he erupted into the hotel where Brian (rather bemused) was staying, announcing that he had just one question to put to his brother, and this was it: 'Have you had the child baptised?'[14] On receiving an answer in the negative (in fact Michael Moore had been registered by his non-religious parents as 'something like the 780th pagan in Montreal' since the city was founded), Seamus whirled around in a state of Catholic dudgeon and took himself straight back to Belfast. This pair of brothers, the devout GP and the atheistic author, were never exactly kindred spirits; however, family feeling (to an extent) overcame their temperamental differences, and for most of their lives they remained on perfectly amicable, though distant, terms (tempered, for each of them, by a sardonic attitude towards the other).

London, at this period, presented itself to Brian Moore as a jumble of pubs through which he was conducted by Mordecai Richler and others ('all very jolly, very British'). Mordecai (Mort) was very much at home in Soho, having grown his hair quite long and taken to wearing grubby corduroys. This was the time of the flourishing of Fitzrovia. And certain authors loosely connected to the group which would come to be known as 'the Movement' had recently published, or were about to publish, their first novels: Kingsley Amis, Iris Murdoch, John Wain. A kind of creative philistinism, in the sense of anti-pretentiousness, was in the air, and this was something to which Brian Moore was naturally attuned; though in him it took a peculiarly Northern Irish form. An outlook inimical to preciousness in any sense, a matter-of-fact manner, a fascination with wrong-headed values, and the ways in which lives are altered because of them: these were characteristics he shared with the Movement authors. He was still at the stage in his career when his narratives were fuelled by exasperation – a productive exasperation, in his case. He had certain strong irritants to get out of his system.

At the same time, he was immensely drawn to the trappings of 'bourgeois' living, and mildly deplored the mild bohemianism of the Richler set-up in London. A highlight of his London stay was the time he spent at Brown's Hotel in Albemarle Street, as the guest of his old friend from his Warsaw days, John Vachon – 'tea at Brown's in the main lobby with John used to be a fine ritual'.[15] He did not introduce Mort to Brown's, bastion of generals and old Etonians, feeling it would not be fitting. And, along with his delight in everyday formalities and luxuries – the silver tea service, the fresh bed linen – went a willingness to subscribe to certain bourgeois values, such as monogamy. This was not, indeed, a legacy from his Catholic upbringing, but rather an instinctive repudiation of any kind of avoidable disorder. Despite the predictions of jocular male friends, sexual adventure was very much *not* on the cards as far as this European trip was concerned.

In the past, Brian Moore explained in a letter to Bill Weintraub, the whole experience of being or travelling abroad had been coloured by the presence of a significant woman, or the possibility of meeting one at the next stop, or even in the next café: but not any more. Since he'd got used to the intimacies of the married state, his current – temporary – reversion to bachelorhood had entailed an adjustment he found disagreeable, and which no episode of mere sexual diversion could assuage. His friends were all wrong: things would look up immeasurably as soon as Jackie was able to join him. (She, in the meantime, was dashing all over Canada on a succession of photostories – leaving the child with her mother.) As it was, with every woman he met, he felt a compulsion to make it clear straightaway that he was married, and to speak well of his wife.[16]

At the beginning of April, Brian Moore reached Barcelona, where it was raining and continued to rain. He put up at the Hotel Viena. Rain, and impending religious festivities (Palm Sunday), led him to book a flight immediately to Palma ('A small stone town, hot and not interesting,' according to the girl in the travel agency). However, before he left Barcelona he made time to visit the cathedral, and then went wandering among museums, courtyards, small streets, all 'very twelfth-century' and entrancing for the tourist. In Palma, he settled into another cheap hotel, the Suizo, and tried to get going on his latest potboiler (the second Bernard Mara title, published in 1955 as *A Bullet for My Lady*). 'Action, authenticity, violence, pace, sex and the neurotic wisecrack: all these elements must be kept in a firm simmer on the surface of things.' By 23 April he had hammered out the first draft of the first four chapters, despite temptations to idleness such as sitting outside cafés in the sunshine, getting bitten by mosquitoes and drinking wine, Cognac, Pernod and Cinzano (not all at the same time, one hopes). He also developed an enthusiasm for bullfighting, an *afición* shared by Jackie when she joined him in Spain on 1 May. 'We took a cab seventeen miles to Palma last Sunday and had him wait while we watched some good *novilladas*,' he wrote on

18 May from Camp del Mar. And he adds: 'Ernest Hem. is in Madrid now in pink pyjamas for the San Isidro fights.'[17]

Around this time, intruding on the Spanish idyll, came dismaying news from New York: Putnams had rejected *Judith Hearne*, on the grounds that the central character 'is just not strong enough or interesting enough to support the weight of the novel'.[18] It was the first of many similar assessments. Also Michael Horniman of A.P. Watt, Brian Moore's new London agent, after reading the book, sent off a letter expressing a lukewarm response – though, he said, he was willing to offer it to likely British publishers, despite the fact that 'in the present state of the market our prospects of success are not as good as I could wish'.[19]

However, there were people prepared to do battle on behalf of this novel, and one of these was Diana Athill of André Deutsch. When Deutsch received the manuscript, with Mordecai Richler's recommendation, they sent it out to one of their most trusted readers, Laurie Lee.[20] Lee found himself in a state of some perplexity over this manuscript, being both repelled by its 'extreme joylessness', and filled with admiration for the quality of the writing, and the author's technical expertise. The first verdict had the effect of making André Deutsch inclined to turn the book down – whereupon his co-director, Diana Athill, started screaming at him, 'But you're *mad*!'[21] She, from the start, had no doubt whatsoever 'that a man who can write so well and has such a power of creating character is a man we ought to hang on to';[22] and fortunately, after some toing and froing, it was her view that prevailed – though not before a second report from Laurie Lee (16 July 1954) had addressed some specific small defects of the book (for example, 'the picture of Bernard is so effectively gross, must his flies be unbuttoned as well?'). The reader also commended the set of interior monologues (Chapter Six), the reflections of Miss Hearne's fellow-lodgers at the Camden Street boarding-house – 'these soliloquies are good, but heavens what a crew' – though in time Brian Moore would come to regret the use of this device. Laurie Lee, despite his personal distaste for the novel, reiterated his basic opinion – 'As an exercise in creative imagination it remains a little work of art and I don't really see how it can be improved.' After that, there was no further room for argument. Deutsch's letter containing an offer for *Judith Hearne* reached Brian Moore in Paris, where he and Jackie spent the first week of June (after having had a jolly time in Madrid). The advance – £100 – was hardly munificent but he was happy to accept it. Deutsch's autumn catalogue announced a publication date of March 1955.

In his first letter to his English publishers, written when he was back in Montreal, Brian Moore defended his literary rationale: 'I make no apology for its being about an uninteresting woman. Miss Hearne is meant to bore and irritate the reader at times. Real people do. There's far too much of a vogue at the moment for books about one-eyed men, whores and other assorted weirdies – for phoney sensationalism – which I feel has little or nothing to do with life as it is lived by most of us.'[23] (He kept quiet about the fact that he himself was busy contributing to the 'phoney sensationalist' genre, albeit out of financial necessity.) The acceptance of the novel in England encouraged him to believe that America would quickly follow suit; but in fact American publishers – including Alfred Knopf – continued to reject the book in droves.[24] 'Too depressing . . . too depressing . . .' went the dismal chorus.

Then *Judith Hearne* came out in England (actually in May 1955) to an outburst of enthusiasm, and within a couple of weeks Willis Kingsley Wing was inundated with calls from American publishers – many of whom had already received the book once, and turned it down. As it happened, first in the field was Seymour Lawrence of the Atlantic Monthly Press,[25] who had been in England and read the reviews as they appeared. On his return to America, he asked to see the book and immediately made an offer for it. 'Sam Lawrence says that although the terms are modest, their interest in your future as well as your present is very keen indeed, and I believe this,' Wing wrote.[26] Brian was convinced. 'I am an Atlantic man now,' he gleefully informed Bill Weintraub.[27] 'I join the Sitwells and publish from Boston.'

Two days after he'd become an Atlantic/Little Brown author, Brian was summoned to lunch with the great Alfred Knopf at the Mount Royal Hotel in Montreal. There could only be one reason for this meeting, and in due course – over lunch – the subject of Brian's novel was raised. Mr Knopf had, he said, heard good reports of this book – had even read it himself and found it quite interesting, and had now decided it was something that could, with profit, be brought out under the Knopf imprint. Brian then had the joyous experience of being able to counter this less than over-whelming proposal: 'Well,' he announced. 'In the first place you saw it six months ago and turned it down, and in the second place, it's going to be published in six months' time by the Atlantic Monthly Press. I'm sorry no one saw fit to tell you this.' After which, he remembered, coffee was called for pretty quickly. He regarded this incident as a highlight of his early writing career.

A couple of months earlier, when the first batch of English reviews had reached him in a large envelope from Deutsch, he had carried them off in fear and trembling to Westmount Park, where he sat down on a bench to leaf through them. The first his eye fell on – from the *New Statesman* – hailed the appear-ance of two young novelists, Françoise Sagan and Brian Moore, and amused him by seeming to suggest they were both the same age (i.e. eighteen). To his considerable relief the reviews were nearly all favourable, and after a bit he became quite blasé about this, not understanding (he said later) just how rare it was for an unknown novelist to be accorded such a glowing recep-tion. John Betjeman in the *Daily Telegraph*, Stevie Smith in the *Observer* . . . The 'dreary and static'[28] verdict, it seemed, had not been prophetic of how critics and the reading public would react to *Judith Hearne*.

What was possibly the worst of the early reviews – in the *Irish Independent* (2 July 1955) – did, however, refer to 'this drab story'; and for good measure it taxed the author with cruelty and crudity, and sneered at his decision to present 'a group of human derelicts and [reveal] their follies, their weaknesses and their vices'. (Well, this was Ireland, the country he'd fled from – what else could he expect?) The 'crudity' charge echoed a complaint contained in a letter to Brian from his mother[29] written the previous month; she'd have liked the book better, she said, if he had omitted 'the part about Bernie and the maid also Mr Madden in some of his moods'. She advised him, in future, to keep the 'sex parts' for his Bernard Mara novels. 'You have a good imagination,' Eileen Moore scolded her wayward son, 'and could write books anyone could read.

Perhaps you will think me rather hard and critical, but this is exactly what I feel no matter what anyone thinks.' (One odd comment, 'I am glad to find you were kind to the Church and clergy', makes one wonder whether Mrs Moore had really read the novel with proper attention.) There's a bit of a conflict here between maternal pride and Belfast respectability. Getting a copy of *Judith Hearne* off to her daughter the nun, Eileen Moore first sat down with a pair of scissors and excised from the novel every item of sexual explicitness and everything else she held to be in dubious taste. It must have been quite difficult for Eilis, when she received the copy, to make head or tail of her own private expurgated version of her brother's book.

Fan letters started arriving in the post for Brian Moore, from (among others) Arthur J. Roth, Gisele Freund and Monica Dickens ('I do want to congratulate you on your touching, comic, devastatingly true book') along with other, less welcome, communications. A pamphlet of the Catholic Truth Society arrived from Dublin via André Deutsch – 'The message tells us what Christ is – what Christ gives.' The Censorship Board of the Irish Republic then proceeded in August 1955 to ban *Judith Hearne* on the grounds of general indecency,[30] and thereby added Brian Moore's name to a list of distinguished authors who had suffered the same treatment, including Beckett, Sean O'Faolain, Frank O'Connor *et al.* (though not James Joyce, who slipped through this particular net). It didn't help his sales figures, though, that the book was unavailable in Southern Ireland just when interest in it was at its peak; and something similar happened when it came out in America in the following year, though for different reasons. The influential Orville Prescott[31] of *The New York Times* gave the book a rave review; and, Brian Moore said, 'I was launched!' Except that, unfortunately, Atlantic Monthly Press – not anticipating any great demand – had had a first print-run of only 3,500 copies, and, by the time they got out a second edition, interest had evaporated somewhat. So – 'it never was a bestseller'. On the other hand, it continued to be a steady seller, eventually achieving 'classic' status as its heroine became absorbed into a communal store of Belfast archetypes. 'Judith Hearne is alive and well and living in Camden Street'[32] proclaimed a piece of graffito of the 1980s, on a wall near the scene of Miss Hearne's tribulations – though whether in a spirit of protest over the changelessness of things, or out of some kind of feminist assertion, it is hard to say.

No other novel of Brian Moore's was ever written as easily as *Judith Hearne*. His work diaries document extraordinary feats of concentration and perseverance, as each work of fiction went through numerous drafts, suffered radical restructuring or was abandoned altogether, as happened with *Judith Hearne*'s immediate – proposed – successor. This story about the return home of an expatriate Irishman named Michael Russell simply couldn't be got to work, in the author's view, and so, after a great deal of hard labour had gone into it, it was scrapped. What actually became the second Moore novel, *The Feast of Lupercal*, was under way by November 1955. 'My new book is 85 pages at the moment,' Brian wrote to Bill Weintraub. 'It is about a man called Mr Devine. He is a schoolteacher. I am working full time on it but it goes exceeding slow.'[33]

Mr Devine may have been progressing at a snail's pace, but this was not the case with three further thrillers, knocked out at high speed during the spring and summer months of 1955. It was worth the effort. After this final feat of writing to a formula, Brian Moore was free to cease his production of potboilers. In the middle of composing *This Gun for Gloria* (his last Bernard Mara title), which is set in post-war, back-street Paris, and deals once more with drug-peddling, he turned out another couple of adventure stories, *Intent to Kill*, which concerns the attempted assassination of a South American president receiving treatment in a Montreal hospital, and *Murder in Majorca*, which is centred on a diamond-smuggling racket, with an attractive young woman implicated in the business, and a footloose American photo-journalist as hero. The last two, published in 1956 and '57 respectively, came out under a new pseudonym – 'Michael Bryan' – and with a new publisher, Dell in the US and Eyre and Spottiswoode in England. The Dell print-run for *Intent to Kill* was a stupendous 205,000 – and when the publishers became aware of the success of *Judith Hearne* they wanted Brian to come out in the open and allow the book to be issued under his proper name. But he put his foot down. The pseudonymous thrillers, however, are all perfectly competent and readable, if not written with the full engagement of the author (for whom they came under the heading of 'commercial writing I'm not too proud of') – 'just a lark, really', according to his old friend and sparring-partner Mordecai Richler,[34] who professed himself at a loss to understand why Brian had become so touchy about these early moneyspinners, once his prominence as a serious novelist was established.

Another boost to his confidence came in April 1956, when Penguin Books bought the paperback rights to *Judith Hearne*, a transaction summed up by Brian in an imaginary newspaper head-line: 'PENGUINS PICK SICK OLD CHICK.' On the morning he heard this news, he'd gone with Jackie to watch twenty abstract painters being photographed with their work on the steps of McGill (for a feature in *Weekend*). It made a good show, he decided, being as ever in favour of the avant-garde. All in all, it was a time of jaunty spirits. When Brian wrote about Montreal's 'social round' continuing to swing 'in its ever sickening circle of futile failure',[35] he didn't mean it in the least.

By October 1955, Brian Moore was a husband and father, solvent, and something of a literary success. The next obvious step was to put down roots, and so, for $15,500 ($7,500 down and a mortgage of 5 per cent), a house on Lansdowne Avenue, in the Westmount district of Montreal, was duly acquired: 'Seven rooms, plus base-ment. Living-room, dining-room, large hall, kitchen, pantry . . . Plus garden,' he reported to Bill Weintraub. 'Had new roof put on for $300 and had painters (German) do whole house, much white and grey. Moving next week.' Jackie's mother, he adds, has pitched in with 'some expensive Bronzini stuff, sofa and chairs'. As well as conveying a natural jubilation, he can't help striking a note of self-mockery as he contemplates his arrival among the bourgeoisie: 'Possessions! *Imaginez vous*, that you are sitting in a house, all of the inside painted white, bamboo lamp in dining-room overlooking garden . . . Everything of the best, man. I mean it isn't real. I look and I say what am I doing here . . .' Bill Weintraub soon had a chance to judge the new house for himself. A great many evenings were spent there, over the next few years, with Bill, Brian and others assembled by the window of the front room at Lansdowne Avenue, huge tumblers of gin-and-vermouth constantly in their hands ('We all drank a lot more in those days').

One of the people constantly about the place was Brian's younger brother Sean, who had his own room at Lansdowne Avenue for a time. Sean, who had followed the family tradition and obtained a degree in medicine from Queen's University, Belfast, had arrived in Montreal in 1951. Brian was covering the waterfront beat for the *Gazette* at the time, and had arranged Sean's outward passage on a freighter (on which he was one of only ten passengers). It was quite an eventful trip: the freighter ran into the tail-end of a hurricane, and was delayed by seven days. It was also fateful: Sean, who had come for a three-week holiday, stayed on in Canada, in Montreal (apart from a thirteen-year stint in Ontario), for the rest of his life. He looked around, noted that the country had a great need of doctors, and – when he thought about it – found the prospect of staying on considerably more appealing than that of returning to Belfast, where – as he put it – he'd have been forced into the position of playing a role, being a Catholic doctor in a Catholic community ('There's no question of switching sides there, you're either one side or the other').[36] After sending out a number of letters, Sean was summoned to an interview with a man called Dr Lyman Duff, holder of the Chair of Pathology at McGill University. Dr Duff, as it happened, was a friend of the Professor of Pathology in Belfast, John Henry Biggert, from whom Sean (a prizewinner like his father) had a letter of strong recommendation. The upshot was that he was offered, and accepted, a year's postgraduate work at McGill.[37] So – as with Brian, who'd come to Canada on a whim – Sean's entire life and career were shaped almost accidentally, by a conjunction of felicitous circumstances.

A considerable attachment had sprung up between the Moore brothers; and when one of Brian and Jackie Moore's social circle, Bruce Ruddick (a psychoanalyst), made some off-hand comment about Sean Moore's supposed sexual activities, quoting one of his patients, Brian flew off the handle, accused Ruddick of professional indiscretion and incompetence, added that he didn't like his fat face anyway, and ordered him from the house. 'A monumentally boring row', Brian described the incident. Things were later patched up, in a way, after Ruddick's wife (a painter) had rung up in tears; but relations 'are not and never will be the same between Belvedere and Lansdowne'. It was always a characteristic of Brian's that he would 'take a scunner' at this one or that one (in the pungent Northern

Irish phrase, meaning a sudden dislike or aversion to, a phrase to which he was still resorting late in life); but clearly he had good cause in this instance. 'My brother dearer is by far than you, sir.'

As soon as Brian and Jackie's son Michael was old enough (two years and ten months) he was sent to a private infants' school in Montreal, St George's – 'My boy's gonna get himself an education like I never did' – where he found himself cast as the Infant Jesus in his first Christmas play. Michael's first five years were spent in the city, and he has memories of a secure childhood, with a father who seemed 'an immensely powerful person'[38] (just as Brian Moore's father must once have seemed to him), pretty strict in a European way, unlike his friends' North American fathers who took a more free-and-easy attitude to their offspring. There were winters spent tobogganing on the hilly, snow-covered streets of Westmount, and blazing summers in the garden at Lansdowne Avenue . . . 'Little fellers are great',[39] Brian wrote to Mordecai Richler in 1954, recommending fatherhood to his friend. However, as a general rule, at that period, he kept off the subject in his letters. 'You never mention young Mike,' Bill Weintraub complained. 'How is he? I almost bought him a little Hunsuit, with leather pants, in Germany, but decided finally that it was repulsive.'[40] Brian took this stricture to heart and began to include references to Michael in his letters. Bill would have been interested to read that the two-year-old could identify his picture, along with works by Picasso, Klee and Roualt, and pictures of Joyce, Proust, Gide, Dostoevsky, Flaubert, Yeats and O'Casey. This party trick was taught him by his father, and went over 'pretty good' with visitors.

Early in 1956, a domestic crisis arose when the Moores lost their childminder Elfriede, who had to go into hospital to have a hysterectomy; however, the gap was quickly filled by a German couple, a factory worker and his wife who moved into the basement and took over Elfriede's role. 'It was hell while we had no domestic, believe me. HELL,' Brian told Mordecai Richler.[41] But otherwise, life seemed pretty agreeable, on the whole. There are two characteristic photographs of Brian Moore from the late 1950s. One shows him and Bill Weintraub in comically lugubrious mode: seated at a table, surrounded by innumerable bottles and glasses, elbows on the table and hands on cheeks, facing the camera head-on, and with regret for over-indulgence stamped all over their faces . . . The other, by Sam Tata – it appeared in *Holiday* magazine in 1958 – has Brian at home with his dog Bonnie (an intelligent-looking terrier), seated on his expensive sofa, surrounded by books and avant-garde prints, and looking, after all the years of perplexity and precariousness, pretty sleek and contented.

9

LITRY GOSSIP

I think it's terribly phoney to make statements about your work. Dorothy Parker once said something about success being 'the seat of the pants glued to the seat of the chair'. I write by sitting down and sweating. I'm very happy once I get started – it's the getting started that's difficult. I think Canada was the country where I got a chance to do it . . . Here, unlike Europe, any young person can save enough money to do some serious writing . . . A writer's big worry is whether he's going to last; very few make a living at it. Most artistic people feel strongly for or against something. Gauguin once said, 'Every artist is obsessed, and this is our revenge.'

Brian Moore, Interview in *Holiday* magazine, 1958

BY THE START OF 1956 Brian Moore had completed the first draft of what became *The Feast of Lupercal*, and then quickly got going on draft no. two – though, as he said, he'd already rewritten each page so many times that it might be more accurate to call it the fourteenth draft. This was in the intervals of enjoying a very jolly social life, with women sitting close beside him at the dinner table, telling him over and over in intimate tones what a great genius he was, and how the Canadian Ambassador to Australia 'just loved' *Judith Hearne*.[1] He lapped up this sort of stuff, indeed, but also took a self-mocking attitude to it: his letters throughout this period, particularly those to Bill Weintraub, show him to be in extremely exuberant spirits, despite suffering from stomach ulcers – a recurrent health problem – and worrying about his figure ('I note with disdain your arrival at the weight of 161 pounds. You must look terribly slight and unimportant,' Bill Weintraub joked).[2] 1956 –

annus mirabilis – was the year in which Brian had three novels published, under three different names. *Intent to Kill*, by Michael Bryan, came out on 9 February, Bernard Mara's *This Gun for Gloria* on 29 March, and the US edition of *Judith Hearne* (retitled *The Lonely Passion of Judith Hearne*) on 12 June. The first of these caused some consternation at the Montreal Neurological Institute (as reported to Brian by his brother Sean), where everyone suspected everyone else of having written the thing, since it was clearly 'an inside job'; and a lot of joking occurred on the subject of the 'nefarious doings' that went on there, blackmail and assassination and what have you.

Brian had written to André Deutsch, on his authors' publicity form, that he was 'Jesuit-educated' (this was not true, of course, but it was a way of summing up his schooling in terms that an outsider would understand immediately), describing himself as 'a sort of Graham Greene running the other way'. He admired Greene, and his admiration was soon reciprocated, as the older novelist became an enthusiast of Brian Moore's work. In fact, in the end, the tag 'Graham Greene's favourite living novelist' became something of an embarrassment, through its overuse by literary publicists; but certainly, at the start of his career, Brian was thankful for the Graham Greene seal of approval. '*Judith Hearne* seemed to me to be one of the best first novels I have ever read and this [*Lupercal*] is certainly one of the best second novels – always a more difficult feat. There is a quality of realism in Mr Moore's writing which gives the reader a kind of absolute confidence – there will be no intrusion of the author, no character will ever put a foot wrong,' Greene wrote to Seymour Lawrence at the Atlantic Monthly Press, in June 1957.[3] Later that year, finding himself about to visit Montreal, Greene asked his hosts to find out if Brian was still living there; if he was (Greene said), he'd like to invite him out for dinner. The unfortunate thing – according to Brian – was that, on the day of Graham Greene's arrival, *he* was due to attend a PEN Club Luncheon as Guest of Honour. The previous year, he'd been invited to become a member of PEN, and refused, 'Because I hate clubs and now . . . they are coming around with the guest of honour treatment. And would I speak? And if I *do* speak, then it might be reported in the local paper and Mr Greene might read it and somehow that would make me seem the sort of person who is always speaking at functions . . .'[4]

You feel he is poking fun at himself for worrying excessively about the sort of impression he will make on the famous elder novelist; but it is a worry nevertheless. However, things went splendidly when the two did meet; no illusions were shattered; and some years later,[5] Graham Greene was still expressing the 'sense of pleasure and exhilaration' he always derived from reading a Brian Moore novel. (By this time – 1966 – the two writers had become, if not exactly friends, at least affable acquaintances; Greene refers nostalgically to an evening they spent together in Montreal[6] at an 'amusing strip-tease joint which has since been closed down!'.) In 1956 Brian mentions having read an article by Laurie Lee in *Encounter* magazine describing a trip to Warsaw – and there, 'in my hotel . . . was old Graham Greene reading a book and having vodka for breakfast'.[7]

At this time, the whole of literary Montreal seemed to be taken up with grants and fellowships. 'By God . . . I am the greatest fellowship expert alive,' Brian reported to Bill Weintraub,[8] 'being the chap who did all the research and then funked sitting for it. Anyway it is great fun writing other people's applications . . .' (This recalls his schoolboy practice of writing other boys' essays.) He may have 'funked' putting in an application for funding – but awards were about to be showered on him, without any extra effort at all on his part. Through Collins of Canada he learnt, early in March, that *Judith Hearne* had won the Beta Sigma Phi award for the best first novel by a Canadian author published in 1955 ('the important thing about this prize is that it is for $1,000').[9] Hard on the heels of this, from André Deutsch, came the news that the novel had also been awarded the 1955 Authors' Club prize (chosen by C.S. Forester of Hornblower fame). The award was not worth much in monetary terms but carried a good deal of prestige; and Brian was urged by his publisher to attend the presentation dinner at the Authors' Club in London on 16 May. After thinking it over, and with the encouragement of his mother-in-law, who stumped up the plane fare, he agreed to be present to receive his silver quill. In the meantime, negotiations were going on with Dan Petrie to mount a Theatre Guild production of *Judith Hearne*, with Shirley Booth in the title role; paperback rights were sold to Penguin; Brian was flown to Toronto to appear on a television show on a national network; and then he was offered a $30,000 advance to write a biography of the Canadian steel magnate and multimillionaire Sir James Hamet Dunn, whom – unfortunately – he considered to be the world's greatest bastard. 'My father's Catholic conscience fought with Greed'; but really, greed didn't stand a chance. 'I gave it up and am glad: I hate to think that money can buy everything, and hate, more than that, the idea of giving up two years of my life to being Lady Dunn's lapdog and writing a shameful eulogy . . .'[10] It was never a serious temptation for him. By this date – April – the second draft of the second 'serious' novel was on his desk in front of him, and he just wanted time to apply the usual 'spit and polish' to it, before submitting it to various critical gazes.

Part of the polishing process entailed revisiting Belfast to check certain facts and subject himself to a new dose of the atmosphere pervading the book. He therefore arranged to fit this detour (five or six days) into his European trip. He left Montreal for London on 11 May, duly attended the Authors' Club of Great Britain's Presentation Dinner, at last met his publishers face to face (introduced by Mordecai Richler), and accepted an invitation from Diana Athill to dine at her North London home. (That was the occasion when he announced, very firmly, that he was fond of his wife; it amused Diana Athill to think that he might suspect her, this young woman publisher, of trying to get off with him.) The whole trip lasted about three weeks, during which time he saw friends such as Bill Weintraub, now married to physiologist Bernice Grafstein, and back in London for the moment working for the National Film Board, while his wife held a fellowship at University College. Brian also managed to put in a few days in Paris (still his favourite city).

It was his favourite city because it was in many ways the opposite of Belfast: elegant, exciting, cosmopolitan and urbane. Brian Moore spoke often about his bitterness towards his birthplace – 'bitterness against the Catholic Church . . . against the bigotry in Northern Ireland, my feelings about the narrowness of life there . . .' – and his first two novels owe their existence, at least in part, to an attempt to write this bitterness out of his system. (Paul Pickerl, reviewing *Judith Hearne* for *Harpers* in the summer of 1956, remarked drily that 'the picture of Belfast suggests that all of us who live somewhere else have something to be thankful for'.) Hopelessness, bad weather and self-perpetuating forms of repression: these aspects of Belfast wouldn't leave him alone until he'd thoroughly denounced them for all to read, and he went about the business with energy and aplomb. By September, after four complete rewrites (with extraordinary feats of typewriting undertaken by Jackie), he had a version of *Lupercal* he was reasonably satisfied with; and an arrangement was entered into whereby his American publisher Seymour Lawrence would come from Boston to Lansdowne Avenue for a couple of days to read the typescript and deliver his verdict. At the same time the final – 60,000-word – potboiler, then called *Free Ride Home* though it appeared in print as *Murder in Majorca*, was ready for a different publisher. This book is 'set in the by now tired locale of the Balearics on which as you will recall I once spent three weeks and wrote two novels on', Brian told Bill Weintraub. 'Do not look for depth of local observation in this opus.'[11] (In 1958, the 'Mystery Writers of America' tried to get 'Michael Bryan' to join them – an invitation at which Brian Moore turned up his nose.)

The long-running saga of the attempts to dramatise *Judith Hearne* was already under way. Brian – who wanted to write novels, not plays – had doggedly turned out an adaptation which failed to satisfy New Yorker Dan Petrie. He was pretty fed up about this, but agreed to continue working on the thing. 'I am crushed, all washed up,' he told Bill Weintraub. 'I have now reached the stage of my final exams and have failed once more. Ten amateur critics in New York have read my play and not one liked it.'[12] Over the years, in fact, the book would attract the attention of stage and film producers, from José Quintero to John Huston, who rushed to take out options on it every time it became available, envisaging the enlistment of leading actresses such as Katharine Hepburn, Shirley MacLaine, Helen Hayes, Peggy Ashcroft, and Siobhan McKenna (all of whom expressed interest), before being defeated by technical, financial and casting problems. To offset this first theatrical disappointment, however, came the news of *Lupercal*'s acceptance by the board of Atlantic Monthly, and Seymour Lawrence's personal enthusiasm for the novel. 'I could not put the book down, and I often found myself wrenched as I read of Devine's valiant attempts, his self-doubts and his humiliations.'[13]

The US publication date was set for June 1957 (it was later

brought forward to April). In the meantime, the manuscript went off to Deutsch in London, and Diana Athill's first reaction was conveyed to Brian Moore in a letter from Mordecai Richler – 'Diana thinks yr new novel is excellent, better told than Judith Hearne, but crueller, less compassionate. She doesn't "like" it as much.'[14] In fact, she was angry with Brian for having sent the novel to the Atlantic Monthly Press, a full two months before Deutsch – 'yr original big backer'[15] – got a look at it; and André Deutsch himself was up in arms over the question of Canadian rights, which he felt his firm should have been invited to bid for. These troubles and annoyances, the downside of life for any halfway successful author, simmered on for some months before being more or less amicably resolved. (Brian quite rightly believed that such disputes were a matter for his agent Wing to deal with, not himself.) 'Anyway, now we have all counted ten before we speak,' Diana Athill wrote at the start of 1957, 'and I can tell you now how much I admire the book . . .'[16] It was full of strong stuff. She went on to confess to being overpowered by the horror of it all, particularly the scene in which the celibate schoolmaster of thirty-seven is attempting to discard his virginity. 'He approached the bed like a man condemned.' 'You really are my best critic,' Brian told her[17] – though he also professed himself 'delighted' by the comment of one of Seymour Lawrence's readers (a woman) who observed that 'the whole book is a great image of the sterility being imposed on the people of Ireland'.[18] Well, it's a more perceptive remark than that of the reviewer who claimed that Brian Moore had identified Judith Hearne with the lost cause of Ireland.

It's surprising that Diana Athill and others considered Diarmuid Devine in *Lupercal* less likeable than Judith Hearne, who really isn't likeable at all. Devine is supposed to have been treated more 'sadistically' by the author of the novel than his predecessor was; Brian Moore didn't deny this, but pointed out that the cards are not so heavily stacked against the schoolmaster: having greater resources, he must therefore bear greater responsibility for making a muddle of things, for being ineffectual, hidebound and pusillanimous. This is true – however, Devine should be viewed as an illustrative figure, illustrating the author's case against the role of the Church in education, which he does to perfection, as well as being a fully realised, vibrant and believable character in the novel; and it's not out of some kind of sadistic impulse that Brian Moore inflicts a series of blows and humiliations on poor, weak-willed, shilly-shallying Dev, but simply to show up the frightfulness of the system he – the author – is inveighing against. *The Feast of Lupercal* (which is dedicated to his mother, since he believed, rightly, that she wouldn't be alive to see another book of his in print) is in fact an advance on *Judith Hearne*: it is less contrived, contains no tabernacle-bashing or other melodrama, and shows an enhanced narrative confidence. Brian Moore was well aware of this, and it always rankled slightly that the book was overshadowed by its predecessor – a common enough fate of second novels – and that the critical response fell short of what might have been expected. It wasn't that the novel received tremendously bad reviews or anything – well, aside from the odd stinker such as the one by Penelope Mortimer in the *Sunday Times* – just that some of its virtues were overlooked. If he'd been asked, late in life, to nominate the best passage he ever wrote, Brian Moore (as he often said) would have singled out the closing scene of *Lupercal*:

> Beside him, in the avenue, a horse and cart waited idle, as their owner offered wood blocks by the bag at a front door across the way. The horse's head moved like a mine detector along the gutter, reins slack over the strong back. Mr Devine watching as Una turned the corner, absently put out his hand and fondled the horse's neck. The powerful muscles fluttered at his unexpected touch and the horse swung its head up, looking wildly down the avenue in the narrow focus of its blinkers. Horse and man looked down the avenue, and there was no one there. The horse, harnessed, dumb, lowered its head once more. The man went back into the house.

The Belfast of *Lupercal* exudes an overcast atmosphere: on the opening page, we find a school bell 'echoing across wet playing fields to die in the faraway mists over Belfast Lough'. The playing fields are those of Brian Moore's old school St Malachy's, but the school itself is shifted a good way up the Antrim Road, to the suburb of Glengormley. Ardath College – as it is called – true to life, is staffed by priests and lay teachers all skilled in sarcasm, and in administering whacks.

The story is centred on Mr Devine's – Dev's – ineptitude when it comes to sexual relations: 'He never had much luck with girls.' (He's a kind of urban, and indeed more urbane, counterpart to Patrick Maguire in Patrick Kavanagh's poem, 'The Great Hunger'.) This misfortune, as Dev sees it, is an effect of education in Ireland; he is himself a product of Ardath College. 'He had been a boarder at this very school, shut off from girls until he was almost a grown man.' Now his own pupils are undergoing the same incapacitating process: 'No wonder these boys weren't fit to go out with girls when they left school. It was a matter of ignorance, pure and simple.' Dev is no reformist, however; this awareness amounts to just another instance of the exasperation engendered in anyone even reasonably thoughtful by Belfast society with all its short-comings.

Exasperation is the driving force in Brian Moore's Belfast novels, an exasperation that extends even to the appearance of the place – its workers' houses look as mean and drab as ever they did to the earlier novelist Forrest Reid,[19] its grander buildings smack of gracelessness and mediocrity. And that's just for starters. His removal from the place never tempered Brian Moore's attitude towards it; to return there was for him a form of penance, which isn't to say that the process of deracination ever became absolute. The lure of the homeland remained, in however askew or ambivalent a form; and this force was tied up with the need to criticise perceived enormities, such as Catholic education. In *Lupercal*, Mr Devine's views on education coincide basically with the author's; but we may be sure that that is the limit of the correspondence between them. Poor Dev, who is well-meaning and efficient in a good many areas, is lumbered with insufficient libido, because of his temperament, social unease and the requirements of his religion. What happens? He gets himself into a pickle with a silly young girl, a Dublin Protestant, which complicates matters, though not very much. Una Clarke is the niece of a colleague of Dev's at Ardath College, Tim Heron, and she's been packed off to Belfast following some contretemps in Dublin involving a married man, a business that seems to have more substance in her head than anywhere else.

One of the things that contributes to banefulness in Northern Ireland is relations between the sexes, with misogyny well to the fore: this is another of Brian Moore's perceptions. In *Lupercal*, a member of the Ardath College staff, obnoxious young Tony Moloney, confides to Dev his assessment of Una Clarke: 'Hot stuff . . . I have a pal in Dublin used to take her sister out. He had a rare time of it.' As a piece of social observation on the part of the author, Moloney's remark is funny and telling and pinpoints an attitude to be decried. In his treatment of social abuses, Brian Moore is always deadpan and unimpassioned. His intention is to show things as they are, and moral protest, if it comes into the picture, is very subtly conveyed. He steers well clear of overstatement, or indeed any kind of evaluative statement. Here are the facts, he seems to be saying: now it's up to you, the reader, to form your own conclusions.

Peaceful Devine, the Ardath schoolmaster, is intimidated by women rather than bearing any animosity towards them; he and Una Clarke are a pair of innocents. So innocent are they, in fact, that each suspects the other of being vastly experienced: she because of Dev's great age, he because he's listened to insinuations like Moloney's. At the height of the action comes a frightful evening, with Una somehow ensconced in Dev's untidy basement flat: 'It was like an old pensioner's place: a disgrace. He was too ashamed even to make an excuse for it.' Matters quickly get out of hand, culminating in an episode even more nightmarish (because more mundane) than the one concerning the drunken assault by Judith Hearne on a tabernacle in a church. Brian Moore, at least at this stage, was a purely straightforward writer, and although Dev's predicament has all the ingredients of comedy – dirty old slippers in a cardboard box a few inches away from Una's head as she lies on the hearth-rug, the long white combinations worn by Dev, the hysteria that overtakes the hapless schoolmaster as he anticipates exposure to ridicule – it isn't presented comically, even at a subterranean level. 'Oh God, this is awful. Awful!'

The reality of the business is too much for Dev, who is used to experiencing sex in the head: 'He approached the bed like a man condemned.' Few accounts of embarrassing situations reach this pitch of excruciation. Everything that can go wrong, goes wrong. Some serious distortion has occurred in the schoolmaster's faculty for arousal. 'It was a matter of ignorance, pure and simple.' Some time later, we find Dev bitterly imagining the words of penitence he will offer the priest in Confession: 'Do not worry about that sin, Father. Tried it once and didn't like it.'

After the failure to sin, comes a full measure of atonement. Una, in a moment of pique, informs poor Dev (who wants to marry her) that he'd betray his own mother to avoid a row. Intolerable pressures are put upon him. His landlady asks him to leave. His job is in jeopardy. Una's uncle, Tim Heron, lashes out at Dev with a cane in a football field. It isn't funny, the spectacle of one over-wrought schoolmaster, gown awry, slashing away at another who has fallen to his knees. It isn't funny; but the author does have a sense of the absurd, and it finds an outlet. The Ardath boys get wind of the association between Dev and Una Clarke, and a ribald rhyme, specially written for the occasion, appears on the wall of a school lavatory. It contains the phrase 'and pulled her drawers down'. Outraged Dev, in company with another master, has to scrub the thing off before the Dean should see it. Later, 'as he stared back across the rain-washed yard, he seemed to hear three hundred boyish voices chanting in eerie unison . . . *drawers down, drawers down*'.

Dev loses Una, but keeps his job; the school President, who'd earlier seemed to be losing his grip on things, sees to it that the business is smoothed over. This action is taken for the good of the school. The system keeps Mr Devine, who has had his fling and made a sorry mess of it. 'Tried it once and didn't like it.'

Brian Moore was surprised to find that certain critics took the headmaster of Ardath College, Dr Keogh, as 'a kind old man', when he was actually meant to stand for authoritarianism at its most virulent. 'He is the person I think one should be most frightened of.'[20] This character bears some physical resemblance to Brian Moore's old headmaster Dr Hendley, but, he insisted, no resemblance in any other respect. Agitated about possible libel action on the part of St Malachy's, he got his brother Seamus to check the manuscript for characteristics inadvertently drawn from life. There was nothing to worry about, Seamus concluded. And, 'I cannot see the Diocesan authorities marching into court to an-nounce that *that* cap fits them,' Brian assured Seymour Lawrence,[21] a point on which he was proved right, even though, as he'd anticipated, it quickly became an open secret in Belfast that Ardath and St Malachy's were one and the same. Looking back on his own awful school life, whose atmosphere is so astringently reproduced in the novel, Brian Moore is often very funny. For years after he'd left the place, he claimed, he still went on suffering nightmares on account of his schooldays, however much he'd chivvy himself in the dreams, ' "Listen, I'm married, I'm thirty years old, I have a wife and child, I'm wearing a Brooks Brothers suit, I live in Canada. Leave me alone. You shouldn't be caning me." And he'd say, "Out with your hand," and cane me. And then I used the caning incident in the novel and never had the dream again.'[22] *Lupercal* came out in England in February 1958, got a good boost from the BBC Third Programme and was generally pretty well received, with the edition of 3,500 selling out fast, as Diana Athill reported to Brian.

In the autumn of 1956 Brian followed with interest the unfolding of events in Europe and the Middle East. First came the anti-Soviet uprising in Hungary (quickly suppressed), and then the Suez Crisis, with Sir Anthony Eden dispatching troops to Egypt in an attempt to safeguard a British trade route, in what amounted to a misguided gesture of old-fashioned imperialism. 'The unspoken question here is Israel's part in all this,' Brian wrote excitedly from Montreal to Bill Weintraub in London. 'Liberal opinion is too polite to say it, but generally people – including me – think the Israelis are fools and possibly scoundrels . . . A point forgotten by almost everyone is my small Irish one. Egypt is Nasser's country – he is a hero to his people, he ousted the monarchy, he blustered but at least he freed his country from foreign rule . . . It's his country, for heaven's sake, it's his canal . . .'[23] (It was Nasser's plan to nationalise the Suez Canal that had precipitated the crisis.) 'Eden must go,' Brian declared, a slogan reiterated a bit less vehemently by his friend in his response to Brian's letter. 'Yes, Eden Must Go.' Bill was less inclined to accord wholehearted credit to Nasser, bearing in mind the Arab raids into Israeli territory, and other factors contributing to the worsening situation. 'Being Irish,' he told Brian, 'you seem to give 95 marks to anybody who kicks out the British, but I only give 60. I'd give him the other 35 if he let his people vote, and bought the poor bastards food and medicine with their cotton crop rather than bombers to "defend" them from a country that has never stopped asking him for a peace treaty.'[24] Atavistic promptings, indeed, had led Brian to equate (at some level) the indigenous Arabs with the native Northern Irish at the time of the Plantation, and the Israelis with the English and Scottish planters imposed from outside – imposed, moreover, by 'Perfidious Albion'. This portion of the Moore/Weintraub correspondence shows a couple of well-informed young liberals who were more or less in agreement over this issue, but not totally. However, by Christmas, things had simmered down sufficiently (as Bill has it) to allow 'our letters [to get back] to the usual topics, like money, publishers, editors, agents, and – of course – how stressful our work was, poor drudges that we were'.[25]

Towards the end of 1956, and again in February 1957, Brian Moore was in New York working on yet another version of his playscript with Dan Petrie of the Theatre Guild, staying at the Park Sheraton (courtesy of *Weekend* magazine) and gaining an insight into theatrical goings-on in the city, as well as enjoying a strip-tease act performed 'to great jazz'. At one point he meets the Irish actress Siobhan McKenna and goes with her to the Park Avenue home of some Irish-American grocery-store tycoons. 'She entered this world of white-gloved footmen, Edwardian maids, women in black and pearls dressed in her fifty-shilling Dublin tweed suit, ankle socks and flat brogues – a great performance. She's quite an astonishing girl. An ego as big as the Ritz but weird and bright and drunken and charming.'[26] Over the Christmas season, he'd had a pretty hectic round of party-going at home in Montreal, while the snow came down in buckets and the temperature dropped to 15 below. Bill Weintraub, as usual, was the recipient of Brian's exuberant account of how he had drunkenly misbehaved, going round fondling bottoms and kissing girls, all in full view of Jackie, who 'stayed sober so that she would be able to tell me in detail the next day how disgusting I was'.[27] ('Your social gyrations dazzle me,' Bill mocked.) At one gathering he is introduced to the English author of *Testament of Youth*, Vera Brittain, and her husband Professor Catlin, and isn't greatly taken with either of them: Catlin speaks donnishly and wears a three-foot-high collar, while she is described as 'a small mousy lady with Cockney accent who has published 22 books'. More enjoyable is a 'fine party' in Toronto at the home of Bob Weaver of CBC Radio, with guests including Kildare Dobbs, Morley Callaghan and Jack McClelland. In the meantime, *Judith Hearne*, continuing to sweep all before it, won $800 in a Canadian Provincial Government literary contest.

Around this time there was some talk of an Italian trip for the Moore family in the coming summer, despite the large expense occasioned by having had renovations carried out to the basement at Lansdowne Avenue, and Brian's continuing struggles – unremunerated – with his playscript. However, in the event, they spent the summer months in Villefranche in the South of France, first at the Hotel Welcome and then in a rented villa, where friends arrived in droves to visit or stay with them. Sean Moore was there in July, then Bill and Bernice Weintraub. Mavis Gallant motored over from Menton, the Richlers came – though relations between Brian and Mordecai, now referred to in letters to Bill Weintraub as 'the Bard', cooled off a bit after the former steeled himself to express his true opinion of his friend's latest opus ('stinks . . . full of crap . . . poor writing . . . coincidences') – Giselle Freund came from Cannes to take Brian's photograph. Diana Athill of Deutsch, who was also in the area, came to Villefranche a couple of times in the intervals of travelling around the coast, and struck an immediate rapport with Jackie Moore, whose hospitality, high spirits and wit she wholeheartedly applauded. 'She was a person who responded to life so keenly that when you were with her you enjoyed things more . . . Once I'd got to know them as a couple, I used to ask myself sometimes, which of them do I like best? It was hard to decide. I enjoyed being with Jackie, and I enjoyed being with Brian – he because he was always interesting, talking about writing and everything else, Jackie because she was always such fun.'[28] (That year, 1957, was an eventful one for Jackie; her mother died in May, and in September she decided to give up her job at *Weekend* magazine and become freelance.)

A pleasant, 'if expensive',[29] family reunion took place in August, when Brian's sister Eibhlin brought their mother down to Villefranche for a short holiday. (Earlier, Brian had dashed off from the South of France to spend a couple of days in Dublin and Belfast.) By this time Eileen Moore was crippled with arthritis and had to be brought off the plane at Nice in a wheelchair. Brian was always glad he'd organised the trip, since it was the last time he saw his mother in a reasonable state of health (arthritis notwithstanding). A couple of months later – after the Moores were back in Montreal, having returned via Paris where they met up with Seymour Lawrence and his wife – word came from Belfast that Eileen McFadden Moore had suffered a heart attack and wasn't expected to recover. What had happened was this: after the Villefranche trip, she'd gone to Dublin to visit her daughter Peggy (Mrs Igoe), and stayed on there to avoid an outbreak of Asian flu that was afflicting Belfast. She'd only been back in Cliftonville Avenue a week or so when the heart attack occurred. Brian immediately caught a flight to Glasgow, where, he was told, he'd be able to pick up a connection for Belfast – and at Glasgow Airport he bumped into his brother Sean, who'd arrived from New York on the same mission. Sean, who had married Cynthia Balch of New Brunswick, had been honeymooning on the coast of Maine when news of their mother's illness reached him, and he too had been advised that the quickest way to Belfast was via Glasgow. The brothers hardly had time to marvel at the coincidence of their meeting like that, before they were back in North Belfast where Eileen Moore had rallied sufficiently to be able to joke that it would be a terrible shame if the two of them had come all that way, only to have her let them down by failing to die. In fact, that was exactly what happened. The death occurred on 17 November, a week after they'd returned to Canada, believing her to be more or less on the mend. Eibhlin, who was staying in the house, was wakened in the night by the frantic ringing of the invalid's bell, rushed downstairs and found her mother struggling for breath, unable to do anything but gasp out a request for Seamus and a priest. It was a fraught night: she died at 9.55 a.m. the following morning. Brian and Sean, who had taken their leave of their mother, decided there was no point in returning yet again to attend the funeral, which took place without them, though it was otherwise exceptionally well attended. His Lordship the Most Reverend Dr Daniel Mageean, Bishop of Down and Connor, presided over the obsequies – the *Irish News* reported – and innumerable relatives, clergy, 'representatives of the medical and legal professions', Cross and Passion and Mercy nuns were among the mourners. The interment took place at Crebilly, Ballymena, in the place reserved for Eileen McFadden Moore alongside her husband Dr Moore.

*   *   *

It was a very Catholic affair. Eileen Moore had been 'a very religious woman', according to her son Sean;[30] and other relatives would go along with this. (Odd, though, that she should describe her youngest daughter's determination to become a nun as the hardest burden she'd ever had to bear, after the death of Dr Moore.[31]) Eilis Moore, Sister Anne, declared in 1993[32] that Brian's imagination had been running away with him when he attributed to their mother a moment of scepticism, or – if you like – a sudden revelation of the truth about humanity: that there is, in fact, no afterlife. This is supposed to have taken place on her deathbed, and – he claimed – many years later, supplied a title and a theme for his novel No Other Life. In that novel, the central character, a priest, visits his mother as she lies dying, and receives from her a final message: '"Do you remember when you were a little boy and did something bad? I would say to you, 'Remember, Paul, the man upstairs is watching you.' I was wrong to tell you that . . . There is no one watching over us. Last week, when I knew I was dying, I saw the truth . . . There is no other life."' 'The man upstairs', a way of desolemnising devoutness at the same time as upholding it, was indeed an expression of Eileen Moore's; but as far as the import of this deathbed assertion is concerned – well, whatever Eileen Moore may have said to Brian in her final days, it seems unlikely that she'd have jettisoned a lifetime's piety at this crucial juncture; and, indeed, her final call for a priest to administer the last rites indicates that she did not. But Brian may not have been altogether wrong to point up a potentially free-thinking streak in his mother; she was, by all accounts, a worldly, gossipy, sharp-tongued, smart and authoritative woman, and in other circumstances might, off her own bat, have reached a conclusion not dissimilar from that of Paul Michel's mother in No Other Life. Eileen Moore, her son insisted, was a far more sophisticated woman than the character Mrs Tierney in An Answer From Limbo, who is generally held to be imported more or less directly from life, and kitted out with some recognisable priorities and preoccupations of Mrs Moore. Mrs Tierney (as we shall see) embodies the kind of stuffy, provincial and pigheaded Catholicism that Brian Moore had always found himself up against.

There may be a very simple explanation for the novelist's impulse to endow his mother with last-minute religious misgivings. Just as certain members of his family liked to claim that *his* atheism was a kind of affectation (or aberration), and that Church teaching actually struck much deeper than he cared to admit – so he was always on the look-out for signs of back-sliding, actual or potential, in *them*. His mother may have said or done something along these lines that enabled him to enlarge on it.

The novel that became *The Luck of Ginger Coffey* (originally called *The Mirror Man*) was under way when an invitation arrived for Brian Moore to spend a couple of months at the Writers' Retreat at Yaddo in New York State, and he was glad of the opportunity – in accordance with his usual practice – to take time out to hammer his recalcitrant narrative into a form that would satisfy his own requirements. He enjoyed his stint at Yaddo, working in a cabin in the woods, going for walks on the estate and accommodating himself, for the first and only time in his life, to a literary and artistic community. It was rather like being enrolled at a kind of superior boarding-school, he recalled.[33] As for *Coffey* – a note to himself at this stage spells out the need 'to make Sasha's ambition tragicomic instead of comic'. ('Sasha' had to give way to 'William Joseph', before the final name, James Francis – Ginger – was arrived at.) At the end of this particular draft, Brian Moore notes that Coffey has risen up 'into a control of that nightmare world which formerly he could not cope with'. But still he isn't satisfied with the novel, which goes into a completely new draft, beginning on 23 August.

At the time, the Moores were visiting Amagansett, at the eastern end of Long Island, as guests of the Ruddicks, with whom a reconciliation had been effected some time earlier. This stylish holiday resort so caught their fancy that they arranged to rent a house there in Meeting House Lane from May to September of the following year (1959). Then it was off to New York to see a few plays and show young Michael the Empire State Building and the Zoo. Back home in Montreal, Brian applied for a Guggenheim Fellowship, for creative writing in fiction, on the advice of Seymour Lawrence, with whom he'd spent a day in Boston in July. His sponsors included Graham Greene, Orville Prescott, Dorothy Parker and Irwin Shaw; and, to his jubilation, he learned that the award – $5,000 – had been granted, to come into effect for the year starting in May 1959.

At the end of April, Lansdowne Avenue was a flurry of packing, and a final social engagement – dinner with the Weintraubs – was entered into, before the Moores set off for Amagansett, where they promptly bought a couple of bicycles and rented a television set, and got their five-year-old happily occupied with a bucket and spade on the small town's amazing beach. The usual programme of intense work (still on *Ginger Coffey*) and engrossing sociability ensued, with an interruption occurring in the middle of June when Brian was rushed into hospital at Southampton to be operated on for a ruptured appendix. By 20 June, he is back on 'the Coffey rewrite', and the usual summer visitors – Sean and Cynthia Moore, Bill Weintraub, Seymour Lawrence, etc – are converging on the spot. Relations with Mordecai Richler were on a friendly footing once again, after Brian had recommended Mordecai's novel *The Apprenticeship of Duddy Kravitz* to Seymour Lawrence, who published it;[34] and the following summer the Richlers also rented a house in Amagansett, which – along with the presence of people like Wallace – Wally – Markfield, author of the novel *To An Early Grave* – turned the place into a kind of loosely knit but intimate literary colony, with much toing and froing, exhilarating activities such as shark-fishing off Montauk, and an abundance of vivid gossip. Diana Athill – who herself would come to stay in a year or two – told Brian in a letter how much she relished Jackie's enthralling details of life in Amagansett: 'She writes funnier letters than you do . . . *Not* meaning that I don't like getting yours. The Moore I get, the merrier.'[35]

Amagansett was, and is, one of those idyllic North American seaside towns, with broad, grass-edged sidewalks, decorative nineteenth-century clapboard houses spaced widely apart, carefully tended greenery everywhere, an immense sandy beach, an atmosphere at once select and sedate. Less pretentious than the nearby Hamptons, resort of the East Coast elite, Amagansett held a strong allure for those equipped to appreciate its offbeat charms.

There were certain conditions attached to the Guggenheim Award, the main one being that, if you were a Canadian citizen, you had to spend a year in the United States. In fact, whatever his intentions may have been around the time of the award, Brian Moore would not again inhabit his Westmount house, which was first of all rented to strangers, then rented to, and finally purchased by, his brother Sean, who lived in it with his wife and growing family until circumstances caused them to move elsewhere. Brian's days as a Montrealer were at an end. Montreal, however, remained in his mind the city in which he'd reversed the verdict of miserable Belfast (marked as 'Failed'), in which he'd finally grown up sufficiently to become a husband, father and householder, initiated some lasting friendships, and experienced his first taste of acclaim. One of the ways in which he expressed his gratitude for all this was to hold on to his Canadian citizenship. But now he was eager to uproot himself and his family, to try his luck in cosmopolitan New York while conforming to the Guggenheim requirements; and (he said), with typical writer's ruthlessness, he overrode every protest and dragged his wife and child along with him. Jackie Moore put up a lot of opposition: the child's life would be ruined, she insisted, if he had to leave his excellent Westmount school; the cost of living would scupper them; *she* would find it hard to function as a freelance writer so far away from her sources of employment. It made no odds. When they left Amagansett in September 1959 they were headed towards New York and the next phase of their life.

10

'AN ALIEN AMONG ALIENS DURING MY NEW YORK TIME'[1]

I said goodbye and made for the street. The bar door shut. A gust of warm air huffed down Seventh Avenue, ruffling the feathery coat of an Afghan hound which led a tall homosexual home; ballooning two cellophane-covered suits held aloft like a prize catch by a passing delivery boy; whipping the skirts of a little secretary tight about her hips; blowing my own forelock down into my eyes as I hurried down the subway steps.

An Answer From Limbo

ONE HUNDRED AND FIFTY, West 15th Street, NYC, was the Moores' new address; the apartment, on the edge of Greenwich Village, came complete with mice and cockroaches, and was in a neighbourhood in which crowds of Puerto Ricans came out to sit on their doorsteps, on chairs carried out of doors, in the warm September evenings, playing cards, strumming guitars, quarrelling, breast-feeding their babies and drinking endless gallons of beer. 'It's all quite Island in the Slum,' Jackie reported to Bill Weintraub.[2] Lots of amenities were just around the corner from them, she went on: 'But what a Big Corner.' Still, there were advantages. Michael got a place at a good public school near by (in which the short-story writer Grace Paley was a house-mother). Brian, whom the *Milwaukee Journal* immediately summoned to be interviewed about his life and work, praised West 15th Street as being in a great location for going places.

He was going places himself, with two 'literary' novels under his belt, and another in the pipeline. The 'final revision of the last chapter' of *Ginger Coffey* had been completed in August and the novel dispatched to Brian Moore's various publishers. However, he still wasn't satisfied with the ending, which was rewritten yet again in September and forwarded to Diana Athill at Deutsch. (He never believed that he'd got it right; and for this reason *Ginger Coffey* was never a favourite among his novels.) In the meantime, he'd started work on the story, first mentioned in his notebooks in August 1958 – 'Self and Mamma in S. France. The big blowhard rural son brings crippled old lady to S.F. with mousy niece companion. Boasts, boating etc with his wife and child' – which eventually evolved into *An Answer From Limbo*. The settings for his third and fourth novels, Montreal and New York, follow the pattern of his own migrations and dramatise situations which very nearly existed, which might well have existed, although, in fact, they didn't exist. Both Ginger Coffey and Brendan Tierney in *Limbo* (and especially the latter) share a number of characteristics and experiences with their creator, but soon branch out into a vivid fictional life exclusively to do with themselves. The immigrant status of both is important, indeed, though not entirely in the way it was for Brian Moore. And the novels signal a movement away from the social criticism of their predecessors, towards an exploration of character. It's not a hidebound society that does for Ginger, the Irish drifter in the pork-pie hat, but some fatal lack of drive and capability in himself. And, of course, luck. Washing his hands of Ireland, and its disparagement of initiative, Ginger has bundled his wife and daughter on to a boat and transported them to Canada, the land of promise. Alas, the jobs he's set up for himself as Canadian representative of a couple of Irish firms very quickly peter out, and, after a period of unemployment, he is forced, at nearly forty, to take a lowly post as proofreader under a slave-driver called MacGregor. This part of the novel reflects very closely the author's experiences at the *Montreal Gazette*: but then the lives of author and character diverge completely, as one, having gained a foothold, went up in the world, while the other goes down, as far as he can go, into realms of absurdity, frustration and desperation.

Coffey is, indeed, a type of Micawberish *émigré* Irishman, completely adrift, always waiting for things to take a turn for the better, buoying himself up with a tentative, good-humoured optimism, staving off disaster from one minute to the next. What happens? Despite MacGregor's promises, the night-time proofreading turns out not to be a prelude to a respectable reporter's job; to make ends meet, Coffey becomes a daytime delivery man for a diaper-distributing firm called Tiny Ones ('Now you're a regular member of the shit brigade,' a colleague tells him); his social standing plummets when a couple of his customers turn out to have known him in his palmier Dublin days; his wife leaves him, and his fourteen-year-old daughter throws a tantrum when he comes home early and interrupts a rowdy party she is having. At his lowest point, Coffey gets drunk on sherry and Coca-Cola in the company of some awful old winos – fellow proofreaders on the *Tribune* – and, on the way home, suddenly finds himself arrested and facing a charge of indecent exposure after having urinated in a hotel doorway (the Royal Family Hotel, to cap it all). However, Ginger's ill luck then goes into a kind of reverse, first with the unexpected leniency of the judge who tries his case, and then with his own arrival at a more level-headed assessment of his prospects – more level-headed, that is, than the self-delusions with which he'd been bolstering himself up. After all his grandiose notions, he comes to see the point of settling for what you can get.

After the hell of the first two novels, this one is situated in a kind of purgatory, with its build-up of near-comic contretemps, its zestful dolours and embarrassments and aggravations, and final emergence into an approximation, at least – and if only for the moment – of serenity. It's also the only Moore novel which is set completely in contemporary Canada (though there are others which contain Canadian interludes). The author has admitted to a certain trepidation over the prospect of evoking a milieu which – unlike Belfast – wasn't bred in the bone.[3] However, when it comes to tackling 1950s Montreal – rundown and wintry to accord with the protagonist's circumstances – not a single wrong note is sounded:

> Outside in the refrigerated air, snow as fine as salt drifted off the tops of sidewalk snowbanks, spiralling up and over to the intersection where a policeman raised his white mittpaw, halting traffic to let Coffey cross. Coffey wagged the policeman the old salute in passing. By J, they were like Russkis in their black fur hats. It amused him now to think that before he came here, he had expected Montreal would be a sort of Frenchy place.

French my foot: it was a cross between America and Russia. The cars, the supermarkets, the hoardings; they were just as you saw them in the Hollywood films. But the people and the snows and the cold . . . The noon crowd scurried along icy pavements from central heat to central heat. Six office girls, arms linked, high voices half lost in the wind, edged past him in a tottering chorus line.

Just over a year after it was published, Jack Ludwig, writing in *Canadian Literature*, referred to *Ginger Coffey* as 'probably the finest novel Canada has seen'.[4] It was a bit of an irony that, at this point, Brian Moore had ceased to be a Montrealer; but the novel stands as a testimony to his vicissitudes in that city, as well as encapsulating immigrant uncertainties and the dangers of over-reaching oneself.

In October, Brian heard from his agent Wing that John Huston had expressed an interest in making a film of *Judith Hearne*, with Katharine Hepburn in the title role; and then it turned out that producer Sidney Buchman had had the same idea, with Jack Clayton as director. In the meantime, Dan Petrie had presented a scene from the book at the playwrights' unit of the Actors' Studio. Brian missed this performance as he was in hospital at the time with another bout of bleeding ulcers; but according to Jackie, who went, it was completely dreadful. Some members of the audience, who included the playwright Bud Schulberg, Norman Mailer and Rona Jaffe, agreed with this verdict; and their comments were forwarded to Brian in a letter from Mrs Elia Kazan, who expressed the opinion that, on the evidence, he'd do better to stick to narrative writing. However, he remained convinced that *Judith Hearne* could work as a play; and so he said no to both proposed film deals, and then got into a flap about money, with bills in droves being forwarded from Lansdowne Avenue, and Jackie failing to contribute significantly to the family finances. (As she had predicted, Jackie's lack of contacts in the New York magazine world told against her, and she went from being an acclaimed and valued feature-writer for various Canadian papers to having her work rejected by such publications as the *Atlantic Monthly*. Naturally, she was not happy with the situation, and talked a good deal about going back to Montreal.)

He even – briefly – took on some reading for André Deutsch, reporting on a couple of novels and autobiographies – 'all n.g.'.

Brian Moore was sent home from hospital with instructions to stay off drink, eat carefully, rest a lot and avoid stress, a programme which elicited from him a sardonic laugh. The easiest bit was giving up alcohol – although, as he reported,[5] abstinence didn't seem to be causing his brain to function any more efficiently.[6] For some time he tired easily and often had to take a nap in the middle of the day, a cause of resentment and disbelief for someone still only in his late thirties.

New York, however, was still great, still incredibly stimulating, even *sans* booze. A typical day might unfold like this. By 9 a.m. he'd be in front of his typewriter, bashing out a paragraph, drinking a cup of coffee, rewriting the paragraph three times. Then interruptions occur. The phone rings, it's Josh Greenfeld inviting him to the Actors' Studio, to watch a class presided over by Lee Strasberg; by eleven, he's there sitting in the audience watching Viveca Lindfors act out a scene in her bra and knickers. Then it's lunch at the actors' café with Greenfeld and Herbert Gold – who is seething over having been referred to, in print, by Norman Mailer, as 'a fairy', when he is emphatically nothing of the sort. Indignation and sympathy are expressed, and phone numbers exchanged. Then Brian and Josh go off to Josh's apartment, from which location Jackie is telephoned and summoned to the Café Figaro for coffee and talk, which runs on until late in the afternoon. A walk through Greenwich Village follows, then dinner, after which Jackie goes off to a showing of *Les Enfants du Paradis*, while Brian gets back to his typewriter and composes a letter to Bill Weintraub. 'Tomorrow we Will Work. Or Will We Have Time?'[7]

The embargo on alcohol was relaxed a bit for New Year's Eve, when Brian 'drank real drinks sparingly'[8] at a party whose guests included Eli Wallach, Roger Straus (of Farrar Straus), Gwen Verdon, Carl Reiner and the stage actress Barbara Bel Geddes; he and Jackie left in a limousine with Barbara Bel G. and her husband 'Wink' Lewis, going on to the African Room and finally arriving home at eight in the morning. (If this pace was kept up, it's perhaps not surprising that he sometimes required a breather after lunch.)

At another party, held earlier in December for the playwright Peter Shaffer (whose *Five Finger Exercise* had just opened on Broadway), the Moores made friends with an English couple, Stanley and Judy Price. Stanley Price was working as a reporter for *Life* magazine at the time, and trying to write a novel; after graduating from Cambridge he'd gone into advertising, because he'd been advised that this was a way to earn a lot of money quickly, and he needed to finance his relocation to New York, on which he'd set his sights. (He was ten years younger than Brian Moore.) He and his new wife Judy were feeling a bit out of it at the Shaffer party, what with hordes of theatrical New Yorkers milling about, and Kenneth Tynan holding forth to an engrossed circle of friends, when they became aware of another couple standing almost directly opposite them, also on the periphery of the event: 'a small tubby man and a small tubby woman'.[9] Fortunately Brian and Jackie Moore never knew that this was the image they'd presented to the Prices on their first encounter, or the friendship might not have developed. They were all exiles in New York, all literary, and shared an irrepressibly dry sense of humour. If anything – Stanley Price recalled – Jackie was the wittier of the two Moores, possessing what he took to be a typically North American quickness of response, and talent for free-ranging association. She was also, he thought, more benign than Brian, whose wit had a cynical edge to it, a derisive undertone. However, he didn't underestimate Brian's kindness in encouraging and advising would-be novelists. (Others, including Bill Weintraub,[10] had cause to be grateful for the productively admonitory manner adopted by Brian towards dilatory writers – well, those whom he considered to be worth the effort.[11])

Stanley Price,[12] who hadn't heard of Brian Moore when they first got together at the Shaffer party, quickly became an admirer, and, indeed, came to consider the older novelist as something of a mentor, describing himself humorously as being in much the same relation to Brian Moore as Brian was to Graham Greene.[13] The two couples saw quite a lot of each other in New York throughout 1960, while Brian began work on an autobiography, or memoir, of his father (eventually scrapped), awaited the publication of *Ginger Coffey* (25 August in the US and a day later in England) and – in November – conceived the idea of a novel centred on a character called Mrs Tierney, and promptly got going on it. The as yet rudimentary plot-line harked back to the note to himself concerning his mother's visit to the South of France (p. 157, above), and also owed something to the story, 'Grieve for the Dear Departed', which the *Atlantic Monthly* had published the previous August. (This story, about a mother in Belfast preparing for her son's homecoming, had been salvaged from a much-worked and abandoned novel of the mid-1950s.)

In March 1960 Brian Moore was in Washington, where he had a couple of social engagements with the Irish short-story writer Sean O'Faolain and his wife Eileen. O'Faolain at the time was teaching creative writing at Princeton University; on 23 March he came to New York to see Richard Ellmann receive a National Book Award for his life of Joyce,[14] and afterwards dined at the Harvard Club with his American publisher Seymour Lawrence, and others including Alfred Kazin and Brian and Jackie Moore. There was a certain rapport between the two Irish writers, even though O'Faolain – born in 1900– seemed to Brian to have opted for precisely the literary preoccupations he himself was in flight from: making sense of the country and the state it was in, analysing the failures of Catholicism and republicanism. These were constricting, he thought, even if – as in the case of O'Faolain – an exuberant and cosmopolitan sensibility was brought to bear on every aspect of provincial Irishness. For writers of his own generation (Brian Moore believed), to stay at home was somehow to limit oneself, to settle for being in some sense second-rate. It was tantamount to entangling oneself in those famous Joycean 'nets': nationality, language, religion.[15] And, he couldn't completely dissociate even such pungent and virtuoso elders as O'Faolain and his contemporary Frank O'Connor, from what he perceived as 'professional Irishness', a hint of playing to the gallery. (Some years later, this judgement was extended to include younger, more reticent novelists like John McGahern who seemed, to Brian Moore, to have inherited the mantle of Irishness – all that old guff, as he saw it, about revered ex-IRA men, grim rural life, families down on their knees intoning decades of the rosary, and all the rest of the package he chose to have no truck with.)

According to his perceptive friend Stanley Price,[16] Brian Moore, for all his protestations to the contrary, was not entirely happy in New York, which nourished his large literary ambitions without enabling them to be completely fulfilled. The city made him conscious of being a foreigner, in a way that hadn't been true of Montreal. Wherever he looked, he saw powerful literary cliques, unofficial mutual advancement societies from which he was necessarily excluded, not being an up-and-coming Jewish writer along with Bellow, Roth and Malamud, or part of that Southern literary mafia which included people like William Styron and Walter Clemons. ('Very parochial it is over here, among this group of young Jewish writers,' he told Mordecai Richler.) And, even if he'd been willing to display a full-blown Irishness (which he wasn't) – no comparable New York-Irish confederation existed at the time; and his upbringing in the workaday North cut him off from the glamour of more romantic and supposedly 'authentic' parts of the country (i.e. the South and West). Well then – if circumstances (and his own temperament) had cast him as an outsider, unamenable to pigeon-holing, he'd make it a virtue, and create a *modus operandi* out of it. With his customary firmness of purpose, he went on to do exactly that, even if a certain ambivalence went on colouring his attitude to the socialising aspect of the literary life. In the end, he achieved an enviable balance between his gregarious instincts and his need for the kind of solitude that enabled him to get on with his work (a solitude *à deux*, it turned out to be). In the early days in New York, however, it still rankled a bit that he hadn't quite the reputation to which his drive and abilities entitled him.

All his transitions – from finding himself a misfit in Catholic Belfast, to living as an Irishman in Canada, then as a Canadian citizen in New York – saved him from falling into the 'classic Irish novelist' mould. At the same time, he took a certain glee in refusing, into the bargain, to be strait-jacketed with regard to plot or genre, so that eventually he became famous for confounding readers' expectations, as each new novel (by and large) turned its back on the theme or technique of its predecessor. Admirers of Brian Moore's early realism, for example, might find themselves bemused to the point of outrage by a work such as the quasi-Borgesian *The Great Victorian Collection*, or struck all of a heap on tackling a miracle-mongering thriller like *Cold Heaven*. If the practice didn't help to boost his income – well, by a certain stage he was free of financial worries, and it satisfied him to claim the freedom to go his own way, to jettison any obligation to please a particular audience by turning out more of the same. Consistent only in their ability to grip the reader, his nineteen[17] mainstream novels embody various forms, from historical re-creation to metaphysical skylarking. They all netted him admirers, and detractors, generating polarised verdicts.

Literary ambition is the theme of Brian Moore's enterprising fourth novel, *An Answer From Limbo* (1963), which – with great economy – draws on his New York experience to encapsulate the ruthlessness of the writer hell-bent on securing a niche for himself, overriding every obstacle on the road to celebrity. ('I must be ruthless. I have only one life . . .') Brendan Tierney is the exiled would-be novelist, editorial wage-slave on a lowbrow publication, who's stung into action by the success of an inferior fellow-aspirant in the novel-writing stakes.[18] ('How many works of the imagination have been goaded into life by envy of an untalented contemporary's success?') Max Bronstein is this person's name, and he's portrayed as being rather crass and seedy. What does Tierney do? To begin with, he imports his grey-haired old mother from Ireland to act as an unpaid nanny to his children, thereby enabling his wife to resume her old job as a magazine illustrator and himself to resign from his, in preparation for composing the masterpiece. By page 62 he's installed in a rented workroom, complete with writing equipment: old trestle table, typewriter, writing-board, pens, pencils and so on. On the shelf above the tiny, grimy window repose 'folders containing drafts and chapters of the novel which is now the substance of my hopes'. For someone saturated from birth in the vocabulary of Catholicism – like Brian Moore, like his *alter ego* Brendan Tierney – writing is 'a vocation', a revelation, an act of faith – or, as it may be, an inducer of fanaticism. It's also, less grandly, one in the eye for all those doubters of the writer's talent, the playground bullies who ducked him in the school fountain to cure him of his literary pretensions. Yah-boo. 'Preliminary Pages for a Work of Revenge' (see p. 63), the Moore short story that appeared in the *Dolmen Miscellany of Irish Writing* in 1962, gets another airing at the start of *Limbo*, with its shrillness slightly toned down and its effect less overwrought in the context of the larger work. But it still presents the instinct to retaliate as a motivating factor in the writer's resolve.

You can almost read *Limbo* as an exercise in self-mockery, with the author taking a good-humoured swipe at one after another of his own less creditable impulses. His own recent past, as we have seen, included actions akin to Tierney's: giving up the job, transferring the family's financial burden to his wife, concentrating all his energies on a single literary work. All this comes at a price – and the final reckoning for the novelist, he seems to be suggesting, is an emotional deadness: 'He can't feel. He can only record.' There he stands (or Brendan Tierney stands) at his mother's funeral, noting the mechanised descent of the coffin into the ground, the priest's impatience as some underling performs too slowly. He registers the clods of earth falling heavily on the coffin lid. But, if the novelist's ultimate realisation – 'I have lost and sacrificed myself' – borders on hyperbole, the bulk of the novel is cast in a more robust mode. It encompasses social comedy and the vigorous re-creation of an avant-garde milieu, and adds up to a sober account of cultural and generational friction. Mrs Eileen Tierney, transplanted from Belfast, comes bearing all the provincial and religious paraphernalia her son has disowned. From the minute she sets foot in the 'Japanese' bedroom her daughter-in-law has prepared for her, it's clear that things are not going to fall out satisfactorily. The crisis comes when, after an accident to Brendan's son Liam,[19] Mrs Tierney takes it on herself to baptise her 'pagan' grandchildren to save them from being consigned to limbo should they come to an untimely end. The ceremony is accomplished in a locked bedroom at Riverside Drive with a plastic beaker of water and a few ritual words. Fury erupts when this piece of play-acting is disclosed to the non-believing parents by their uncomprehending daughter. The interfering grandmother is banished to the home of an Irish-American relative – where, in due course, after a fall in the empty apartment, she succumbs to a stroke. In the meantime Jane – Tierney's wife – back at work, becomes entangled with a lurid embodiment of the erotic day-dreams which enlivened her housebound days, and encounters with this flashy and sordid, but irresistible, person leave her suffused with guilt. No matter: Brendan's novel is accepted by a publisher, and his major preoccupation, and crucial moral dilemma, is the question of whether or not he should compromise his artistic integrity by agreeing to go along with certain amendments to the narrative suggested by his editor.

An Answer From Limbo was written between November 1960 and the beginning of 1962, and published in the US and Canada in the autumn of that year. In despair over the book, Brian Moore had nearly scrapped it altogether late in 1961, but was persuaded by Jackie to carry on – only to cut down the part of Mrs Tierney herself. (*Mrs Tierney* was the working title; *An Answer From Limbo*[20] didn't come to Brian Moore until March 1962. He worried that the new title seemed a mite pretentious, but it made sense if one considered the various states of limbo suggested by the book: exile, old age, the novelist's pre-publication hiatus.) He went back to the beginning and rewrote the whole damned thing. The final version owes a part of its astringency to a certain contempt and bitterness directed against the protagonist (with whom the author may well have been fed up by this stage), a touch of dust-and-ashes about Tierney's literary breakthrough. After having investigated the social and temperamental causes of failure, in his earlier novels, Brian Moore has now turned his attention to the cost of success, a cost worked out in terms of its effect on others, and on the ethical soundness of the central character himself.

The New York social round continued throughout the spring and early summer of 1960, with sparkling parties (for example, one held in honour of Alexander Trocchi) and advantageous lunches (for example, with Charles Morton of the Atlantic Monthly Press). The Moores left for Amagansett on 28 May for their annual holiday, to be visited at intervals by the usual contingent: Seymour Lawrence, the Amussens, Bill Weintraub, Sean and Cynthia Moore. Brian went shark-fishing off Montauk, and wrote about this activity for the *Atlantic Monthly*. In July, he tried and failed his driving test. *Ginger Coffey* came out and was generally well received, with good reviews (among others) from Kingsley Amis in the *Observer* and Ronald Bryden in the *Spectator*. *The New Yorker*, however, 'Says I'm no good. Two weeks in advance of publication, mark you. Malicious? Paranoid he?'[21] It rained throughout August, and the charming, greenery-laden streets of Amagansett took on a saturated appearance.

Later in the year, *Ginger Coffey* is sold to the Canadian Broadcasting Corporation to be adapted for television (later again, in 1964, the book was filmed in Ottawa under the direction of Irvin Kershner, with Robert Shaw and Mary Ure in the leading roles). Brian accepts a commission from *Holiday* magazine to write an article on 'Dining in Montreal' and ropes in his friends Bill Weintraub and Alex Cherney for advice on interesting local restaurants. In return he passes on some items of gossip about members of the social circle such as Josh Greenfeld, who is marrying a Japanese girl, and John Vachon, due home from France at any moment with a twenty-five-year-old French bride in tow.[22] In December, Brian flies to Toronto for a CBC interview with Bob Fulford – the only interview to date that pleases him. ('I'm interested in Catholicism in a non-religious way,' he told Fulford. 'I'm interested in the traditions it sets up, and the conflicts.') He's back in New York in time to meet his sister Eibhlin – invited for Christmas – off the plane. Socialising extends well into the New Year: 'Drinks with Philip Roth, party at Vachons' his notebook records. Then, in February, comes the joyful announcement of two major new awards netted by *Coffey*: the Governor General of Canada Award for Fiction, and, hot on its heels, a Senior Arts Fellowship from the Canada Council.

A hiatus then occurred in the East Coast routine. These awards enabled the Moores to spend a year out of the country, and on 1 June 1961, they sailed for Ireland – first class – on the *Maasdam*. They were bound for Oughterard near Lough Corrib in Co. Galway, and a house belonging to their actress friend Barbara Bel Geddes and her husband 'Wink' Lewis. The house – stone – came complete with patio overlooking a lake, formal gardens, vegetable gardens, a Morris convertible in the garage and a man named Kelly to drive it. To every remark of Brian's this agreeable person would respond, 'Ah, you're very right, sir.' Brian immediately got to work on the revising of *Limbo*, entertained his brother Seamus and various sisters and their families when they came to visit, and made a trip to Belfast to research another *Holiday* article.[23]

In spite of good fortune and plentiful diversions, however, this summer was not a particularly happy time for Brian Moore; in fact

he succumbed to a severe bout of low spirits, which persisted until
the autumn. Was it Ireland, or, in particular, Belfast, which he
hadn't visited since shortly before his mother's death, that caused
him to feel so thoroughly out of sorts? (Belfast, he always claimed,
had a dispiriting effect on him; at the same time, he admitted to
feeling at home there, knowing the place inside out and understanding all its postures and peculiarities.) Perhaps Belfast had
something to do with it, but his inability to get the 'Mrs Tierney'
novel into a satisfactory state was certainly a contributing factor;
and worst of all, in the isolation of Oughterard, cracks were
starting to appear in the Moores' apparently sunny and compa-
nionable marriage. (Much later, Brian would insist that things were
never right between him and Jackie, an assessment that included
intimations of sexual incompatibility and the suggestion of a more
general conflict of personalities; however, friends who knew them
well during their twelve-year marriage received a different impression.) He also felt sick a lot of the time, due to continuing trouble
with ulcers. One thing that cheered him was the news, conveyed in
a letter from Willis Kingsley Wing, that the deal with John Huston
for the film rights of *Judith Hearne* had just been clinched. 'Mort
Leavy is drawing the contract,' Wing wrote.[24] However, correspondence about this was still going on in November (and in the
event, *Judith Hearne* became free again in August 1966).

At the start of September 1961, the family upped sticks again and
travelled to London where they spent ten days or so in a borrowed
flat (Diana Athill's, at Elsworthy Terrace). Then, through the good
offices of a friend named Gerry Slattery – a sort of society doctor,
according to Brian[25] – they found themselves ensconced in 'a pad of
such luxury and good taste that any other place we ever lay our
heads will be a sore comedown indeed'.[26] This impressive place of
residence was in Chelsea, at 31, Wellington Square, and belonged
to a descendant of the Marquis of Queensberry. The first thing you
saw when you entered the drawing-room was a painting by Francis
Bacon. There were conditions attached to their tenancy. They
weren't allowed to put up visitors, for example, and so Bill
Weintraub, when he came that Christmas, had to stay with the
ever-accommodating Richlers and their expanding family. Mordecai, as usual – Brian reported to Bill – 'has been kindness perso-
nified'.[27] It was at this period that Michael Moore, enrolled as a

pupil at the American School at Gloucester Gate, became very thick with one of the Richler boys. Brian and Jackie even considered 'dumping' their son on their friends for a couple of weeks while they enjoyed a child-free jaunt on the Continent, but decided that in the circumstances to ask such a favour would be unfair. They arranged to go during the school holidays, settled on Paris for the proposed holiday, and took their eight-year-old with them instead.

Just as Belfast was castigated for being a place inimical to the creative spirit, so Canada was approved by Brian Moore for having fostered his talent, and London applauded for publishing his first novel while the New World dithered and niggled. London had taken him on, moreover, as a writer, not as an Irish writer (the distinction was important). Yet the nine months he spent there didn't diminish his sense of being an outsider, detached in some crucial way from every clique or group that partially enlisted him. His friend Stanley Price – who with his wife Judy had returned to make a permanent home in London – considered it a bit ironic that Brian, who'd left New York to escape for a while from the prevailing literary freemasonry, should immediately be confronted by a similar state of affairs. It was just a bit more complex in London, and hard to pin down. 'Log-rolling cliques there certainly were,' wrote the academic and literary editor Karl Miller:

> but they were usually at odds with one another, and no single group could be thought to be in control of the reputation and reception of writers. All there was of that kind of thing was an amorphous upper-class presence given over to a resentment of upstarts and of the unfamiliar. At parties and long lunches journalists and publishers met, as they still do, to gossip about the book trade. Literary editors scanned the lists of over-producing publishers, as they still do, in search of stories and of a content for their journals and for the book pages of newspapers.[28]

And not only did Brian have the current London literati to contend with, but certain adherents of cliques in New York he thought he'd left behind kept popping up in front of him. Norman Mailer was about the place, for instance, and 'in a pub yesterday I look up and there, dour as ever, sitting opposite – just like in the Figaro Café bar on Blecker . . . is Edward Albee,' he told Bill Weintraub. 'Are these people following me around?'[29] He goes on: 'There could be a story in the fairly obscure writer who goes to London to escape the competition of big names and then finds that the Village has moved to Chelsea – Jackie's suggestion this.'

Brian was invited to review for the *Spectator* by its editor Brian Inglis,[30] and promptly contributed a piece[31] taking the British to task for their 'anti-Americanism' which, as he saw it, was fast becoming 'the anti-Semitism of British and French intellectuals'. This, when it appeared, caused the proprietor of the paper to rush into the office of the senior editor demanding to be told what he meant by commissioning 'fronts' from unknown writers. So much for the novelist's fame. Still, Brian began to be invited to those leisurely *Spectator* lunches in the boardroom at the paper's Gower Street headquarters, complete with wine, and cheese boards, and literary gossip, and an atmosphere he described as that of 'a cottage industry' – agreeably ramshackle, in other words, in comparison with the streamlining of the late twentieth century.

So – he sat amiably at tables in Gower Street and elsewhere, a glass in his hand in defiance of his ulcers, casting a cold and amused eye over solidifying or dwindling reputations, random instances of advancement or comeuppance. In London, he attracted overt hostility from certain competing novelists such as the formidable (and as yet underrated) Olivia Manning,[32] who couldn't set eyes on him without proclaiming herself at a total loss to understand why *he* should be so successful . . . Great reviews, endless fellowships: it wasn't fair. Brian would see Olivia Manning quite often at Gerry Slattery's, and her displays of undisguised envy bewildered him, though he laughed it off. Then, at Mordecai Richler's, he'd find himself among a bunch of brawny Canadian expatriates whose practice was to leave their wives sitting demurely in a corner exchanging items of domestic gossip while they gathered in the kitchen to lark about while swilling beer and chewing specially imported slabs of beef. Such gatherings reinforced Brian Moore's sense of not being one of the boys.

He was also especially critical of the English class system, which, in his view, perpetuated rebarbative schisms in society, as well as relegating him, personally, to an incorrect stratum. He had only to mention that he'd been brought up as an Irish Catholic to have a working-class orientation foisted on him. In any intellectual discussion of proletarian literature he was the one expected to have a personal insight into it. It was useless to protest that his childhood had, in fact, been as middle-class as anyone's; everything, down to his vestigial Belfast accent, was against an acceptance of this – to him – incontestable fact.

One advantage of London was the scope it afforded for Brian to indulge his leanings towards swanky dressing. 'Bought coat at Aquascutum,' his notebook records; and, a bit later, 'Suit Hawkes £40 10 0.' He probably wore the latter when he and Jackie went to Cambridge as guests of the Prices, to see Stanley Price's brother graduate as a doctor. It was a great day. They had lunch with a metaphysician, were taken on a sightseeing tour of King's College, conducted by Ronald Bryden,[33] attended evensong in the chapel, had drinks in a Fellow's rooms, and dinner at the Arts Theatre. It was all quintessentially English and intriguing. After the graduation ceremony was over, Brian, engaging in a bit of tomfoolery, put on Dominic Price's fur-edged gown and was photographed by Stanley in these borrowed robes, looking exactly like an owl.[34]

His high spirits may have been due, in part, to the fact that on the previous day he had finished the final version of *Limbo*; now only the final revision remained. Hard work and intense socialising were still the order of the day, but he wasn't alone in this: in one week, he received presentation copies of books by three of his friends (Diana Athill, Bill Weintraub and Stanley Price). In February, he was in Brighton for the opening night of a play put on by another friend, the theatre director Ted Kotcheff (this was Doris Lessing's *Play with a Tiger*).[35] 'The fact that it was so brilliantly directed was hardly noticed,' Lessing observed drily, referring to the reviews[36].

In London, there were clubs such as Ronnie Scott's and Raymond's Revue Bar to be visited nightly. London was at last casting off its image of post-war staidness as the effervescent 1960s got into their stride. 'I can even envisage the day when it would be a wrench to leave these shores,' Brian admitted in a letter to Bill Weintraub,[37] succumbing for a moment to a vernal enthusiasm. However, the day was not far distant. Jackie Moore, despite the resistance she'd put up to the prospect of settling in New York, was now eager to get back there. 'She was very much a North American woman,' Brian said years later, looking back to this period; and not amenable to transplantation. Not that he was ever seriously drawn to the idea of mapping out a life for the three of them in England; New York, he'd already decided, was 'the place where we shall lay our heads for ever'.

First, though, came the postponed trip to Italy, at the end of March ('Venice, Florence, Roma, Napoli, Capri . . . we loved that country, the pictures, the food, the sun, the drinks – everything'[38]), after which – for a complete change of scene – Brian dashed up to Bolton in Lancashire, to see his sister Eilis in her convent there. From another sister, Peggy, in Dublin, he learnt that 'Quidnunc' in the *Irish Times* had announced the imminent implementation of John Huston's plan to film *Judith Hearne* at the Ardmore Studios, with Katharine Hepburn and Stephen Boyd (an inappropriate duo) in the leading parts. Negotiations in connection with this glamorous project had been going on for nearly a year: but in fact, like many another attempt to get that novel on to the screen, it proved to be a non-starter. Brian, in the meantime – on the advice of his lawyer Morton Leavy – had turned down a proposed London stage production of *Lupercal*, and was feeling agitated about the consequent loss of an $800 advance. (This, Leavy advised, was for the good of his career, the proposed director being a man of no reputation.) And, following the euphoria of having had both his publishers declare *Limbo* to be the best thing he'd done so far, he was getting into a panic over the question of what to embark on next. Being seriously overweight was another worry: he and Jackie kept trying to follow one fashionable diet after another, to minimal effect.

At the end of May, the Moores returned to New York, where they'd arranged to spend a week off 5th Avenue staying with the reinstated Ruddicks, before going on to Amagansett and their rented holiday home. The summer then passed as usual, with guests arriving in droves. Diana Athill came – in between staying with Norman Mailer and then John Updike, and going on to visit Philip Roth in Nantucket. Mordecai and Florence Richler came, and Seymour Lawrence. Subjects of gossip during beach parties and lunchtime gatherings included speculation as to whom President Kennedy was currently sleeping with, and the fact that Philip Roth had turned into 'last year's sensation' as an author. That July, the Moores secured a four-and-a-half-room apartment in New York, at 239, East 79th Street, but it wouldn't become available until 1 October, which meant they had to stay in a hotel for a week before this date, while they shopped for furniture and so on. Brian opened an account at the Chase Manhattan. He also acquired an office to work in (following in the footsteps of Brendan Tierney) – 'a small sleazy room with a view of tenement washing', was how he described it. In fact, as far as work was concerned, he was still casting about for the subject of his next novel, and in the meantime he accepted a commission from Time-Life to write a book about Canada. Novel number four was about to hit the bookshops: *Newsweek* sent a photographer over to the Croyden Hotel in preparation for *Limbo* publication day (10 October); and then came a television interview in Boston, followed by a bookstore tour of New York. In November, a Canadian trip was organised by Brian's publishers McClelland & Stewart, which included a talk to be delivered at the universities of Toronto and British Columbia. 'Voices of the Novel' (or as an alternative 'The Voices of Fiction') was the title. Also on the tour programme were numerous interviews, radio and television appearances, and cocktail parties. The half-apprehensive, half-gleeful author steeled himself to undergo what he termed 'a whirl of immense proportions'.

Brian Moore kept a commonplace book for most of his professional life, in which he'd inscribe passages from his reading which struck a particular chord, or endorsed some perception of his own, which he hardly knew he'd been harbouring. One entry reads as follows:

> Breton [André Breton, the French philosopher] felt that coincidence was everywhere like a hidden pattern, and one ought to look out for it. He liked to say that 'one had to put oneself in a state of grace with chance'.

A thundering coincidence in his own life concerned Brian and his friend of the Cambridge excursion, Stanley Price. The 'engaging and witty' Price (Brian Moore's description) was a fairly close and valued friend for a time during the late 1950s and early 1960s, and not at all thereafter. This friendship was a casualty (there were others) of the distressful period following the separation of Brian and Jackie Moore, and their new alignments.

To give an account of this particular coincidence, it's necessary to backtrack a number of years, to 1953. Stanley Price had recently graduated from Cambridge University, and, being desperately keen to relocate himself in New York, took, in the meantime, the most lucrative employment he could find, in the furtherance of this ambition. It was in an Advertising Agency in St Martin's Lane. One day a new employee was brought to Price to be shown the ropes: a personable young Canadian named John Lewis, an experienced copy-writer recently arrived in London, a few years older than Stanley Price, with whom he was destined to share an office. The two young copywriters immediately took to one another, and in fact, ended up sharing a flat for a time. Lewis 'was a nice man, very funny, very droll';[39] the thing that had brought him to London, it transpired, was the defection of his wife, a part-time model and publisher's PR girl, very beautiful, who had left him, and – some time later – taken up with a magazine editor in Toronto. (This was Lewis's version of the story. It was not quite so dramatic from the point of view of his wife, for whom the marriage amounted to nothing more than a youthful indiscretion, best forgotten by both participants.) John Lewis was very cut up indeed at the time – though in due course he recovered sufficiently to marry again, in England, his second wife, and the mother of his children, being the best friend, from her college days, of Stanley Price's future wife Judy.

That was John Lewis. Fast-forward to 1965, and Stanley Price is in Hunterdon County having a conversation with the nature writer Franklin Russell, the previous husband of Brian Moore's second wife Jean. Though he was a New Zealander, Russell had arrived at his present habitation via Canada, where he'd worked as a freelance contributor to magazines, and then as an editor. For some reason it came up that his wife – Jean – had been a model in Toronto. The by-now-agog Price couldn't resist putting a query: had Jean by any chance been married before? Indeed she had. And what was the name of her previous husband? John Lewis. 'God knows,' Stanley Price recalled,[40] 'how I made the connection – but there it was. Out of all the women in Canada, that was Jean. Brian's Jean.'

11

BRIAN'S JEAN

I went up to Jody Terrel's for a drink and that was how I met Terence. That was something, I can't explain it, but we met again the next day, and then every day I took the train to town to be with him, sometimes even staying overnight in his apartment on the Lower East Side. Which was foolish and dangerous, of course, but how can I explain it, I was living in a state of elation, waking up in excitement every morning, finding myself smiling in the street when I thought of Terence and me, hating to go to sleep, feeling there never was, never would be a time like this, that New York was the greatest city, that, oh, that I had no nerves any more. For the first time in my life, I was happy.

I Am Mary Dunne

THE CANADA TRIP TO promote *An Answer From Limbo* took place as planned. On 24 November 1962 Brian Moore was in Toronto attending 'a large booze party'[1] thrown by Jack McClelland, his 'playboy publisher' (as Brian styled him). The association went back a number of years. As Brian told the story, Jack McClelland and a colleague had come to visit him one day at Lansdowne Avenue, bearing gifts for Jackie and Michael. This was after *Judith Hearne* had been published in England, but hadn't yet come out in the States. McClelland's idea – which he carried out – was to put Canadian writing on the map by marshalling a stable of significant authors[2] and bringing them out under his own imprint, rather than acting as a distributor for English and American publishers, which was how the system had tended to work in the past. (*Judith Hearne* was published by Collins in Canada, using plates supplied by

Deutsch.) Handsome and charismatic, according to Brian, and fond of a drink, Jack McClelland supplied the impetus to get Canadian publishing going. And this particular social occasion at his home in Toronto, in November 1962, was a glittering affair, in accordance with his usual style, full of pressmen and publishers and literary celebrities, not all of them Canadian. It was also the occasion when Brian threw away an opportunity to ingratiate himself with the editor of Penguin Books in Canada. It happened that this influential figure bore down on him, with a friend, while he was talking to a young woman he'd just met, and – ignoring her completely – started, 'This is Brian Moore . . . I'd like you to meet . . .' ('All that sort of stuff,' Brian recalled, with wry amusement, and spoken in a high-falutin voice.) Whereupon Brian announced, very firmly, 'This is Mrs Russell . . . would you excuse us . . .' and steered her off to the kitchen for a drink.

Inexpedient it may have been as far as his career was concerned, but this action had the most profound effect imaginable on Brian Moore's personal life. Not that it was apparent at the time, or for some time afterwards, that anything out of the ordinary had taken place. The meeting between him and Jean Russell seemed felicitous, certainly, but not momentous. It is always agreeable to meet a kindred spirit – and, as an additional cause of jubilation (or so it seemed), both Mrs Russell's husband and Jackie Moore were quickly drawn into what looked set to become a devoted foursome. First, though, came the exchange of telephone numbers at the Toronto press party, and promises to keep in touch: the Russells were about to move to New York where Jean, whose talents included a considerable flair for interior decoration, was going to fix up an apartment for them.

Jean Russell, née Denney, who was some years younger than Brian, came from Glace Bay, Cape Breton Island, Nova Scotia, and was educated at a private boarding-school in Ontario. Like Jacqueline Scully – whom she didn't resemble in any other respect – Jean was the child of divorced parents. Her father had studied for the ministry before his readings in philosophy had awakened a certain scepticism in him, eventually leading him to abandon religion altogether. He became an officer in the Canadian Army at the start of the Second

World War. Both her parents came from Newfoundland, married in Massachusetts, and settled in Nova Scotia, where Jean and her older brother were born. Her mother – like Brian's mother – had been an operating-theatre nurse, who counted efficiency, imperturbability and an energetic approach to living among her characteristics, in contrast to her more volatile husband. Both were amusing and sociable, though, and Jean described her childhood as exceptionally happy, before her parents' separation and eventual divorce. One consequence of the divorce was that Jean lost touch with her father, only re-establishing contact with him shortly before his death – from a heart attack – in the spring of 1967. (It was a cause of regret to Brian that they never met.)

After leaving school, Jean had a number of jobs which included modelling, acting for television and working in textbook publishing before she moved on to the publicity department of *Maclean's* magazine, where she met her second husband Frank Russell. She and Russell had got to know Jack McClelland: hence her presence at the fateful party on 24 November. In fact, Jean very nearly gave this social occasion a miss, only deciding to attend at the very last minute. Well, everyone's life contains such apparently insignificant choices and their unpredictable outcomes.

After Toronto, Brian went on to Vancouver to read his paper – now called 'The Voices of Fiction' – at the University of British Columbia. The jet trip back to New York, on a clear day at 30,000 feet, 'was one of the greatest air trips of my life . . . Rockies, prairie, plains, wilderness, Toronto – you have a great land here, son', he assured Bill Weintraub,[3] in buoyant mode. It was, indeed, helpful for him to obtain a bird's-eye view of the country, in all its vastness and variety, since he was just about to start work on his Time-Life book.[4] Once back at East 79th Street, he got down to it in earnest: reading, reading and more reading. With *Limbo* off his hands, and no new work of fiction yet in preparation, he was able to devote his considerable energies to this commercial undertaking, spending Christmas that year in Halifax and Montreal, and never ceasing to immerse himself in relevant material.

The project was completed quickly and efficiently and the book came out the following year. It is mainly a picture book, but the text, as one would expect, is clear-sighted and informative on everything from the country's industrial development to its conflicting cultural inheritances. At the same time, Brian was elated to find his books on the syllabuses of several universities, and it seemed an indication of his growing literary stature that a young female thesis-writer at New York University should come to talk to him about his work. (She was the first of many.) Also around this time, certain significant entries start to appear in his notebook: 'Call Jean Russell No 21484'; 'Russells – dinner'; 'to country w/ Russells'.

It wasn't until October 1963 that Brian Moore got down to the novel he called his *Bildungsroman*, the deferred, and comically framed, account of his academic unsuccess and ARP experiences in wartime Belfast. Once it was under way, he described it to Bill Weintraub as being 'of anything I've written, the least likely to succeed with the great American public'[5] – who, the implication is, would find the wartime exigencies of provincial Northern Ireland of limited interest. Nevertheless, he had decided he wanted to express something about 'the odd, faintly comic set of attitudes with which we in Ulster met the advent of Hitler',[6] and he worked on the book with his customary diligence and application until he got it right. On Friday 11 December 1964 a note in his diary records the completion of *The Emperor of Ice Cream* – but the following day he is back at work on 'the final rewriting' which continues into the New Year. The novel, published in the US on 15 September 1965, makes a strong finale to the Belfast trilogy with its pungent dissection of the city's social and moral climate during the middle part of the twentieth century. It is, indeed, a more up-beat work than its predecessors, what with the drama of war action which enlivens the drab Belfast milieu, and the optimistic portrayal of young Gavin Burke, whose way of life is clearly not at risk from indigenous enervating forces, however unsatisfactory it may seem to himself at seventeen. Even the notorious Ulster weather, which did its worst all through *Judith Hearne* and *Lupercal* – 'The rain began to patter again on the windows'; 'Her hair was wet with rain' – has finally brightened up: 'It was a Sunday afternoon and . . . a warm one, with no sign of rain.' (Still the characteristic Ulster garment remains a raincoat, whether it's the hideous red creation worn by Judith Hearne, Mr Devine's unfashionable mackintosh, the big rubber-looking waterproof, all tabs and toggles and flaps, sported by a lout, or the unexceptionable coat carried up the Cave Hill on a sunny afternoon by Gavin Burke, with lechery in mind.)

The droll, buoyant tone of the novel gives way at last to a flagrant piece of self-indulgence (which is almost its only flaw). Gavin, having acquitted himself superbly in a crisis, comes face-to-face with his shaken old father in the blitzed family home, and – in a complete reversal of family relations – assumes the dominant (and protective) role. This scene reads like a bit of over-compensation for the fact that 'my father died thinking I was a wimp' (as Brian Moore claimed more than once). In fact, he didn't, as we have seen (see p. 81 above); but indubitably Dr Moore's death occurred before his second son had a chance to show what he was capable of achieving, and this was something of a cause of chagrin to Brian for the rest of his life. Burke Senior in the novel is not, indeed, an out-and-out portrayal of Dr Moore ('an exceptionally nice and honest man', his son is still reiterating in a television interview not long before his death);[7] Brian Moore is exercising the novelist's pre-rogative to tamper with remembered realities in the interests of dramatic effect. But the fictional character acts as a conduit for certain ineradicable aggravations on the part of his creator.

Life, in the meantime, continued at its customary headlong pace. Early in 1963, Jackie and Michael Moore go off to the Laurentian Mountains for a skiing holiday; *An Answer From Limbo* is published in England to mostly enthusiastic reviews; Brian is in Montreal in May, and then goes to Amagansett to await the arrival of his wife and son early in June. On 12 June, he is editing the script of *Ginger Coffey*; three weeks later, he's off to Montreal again on an assignment for *Maclean's*; then it's back to New York before returning to Amagansett and putting in an offer to buy their rented house (this is withdrawn when it turns out that plans are under way to build a parking lot just a hundred feet from their front door). By the middle of September he's alone in Amagansett again – aside from the dog – with gusts of rain assaulting the house and branches dripping and swaying outside the windows. All the summer visitors have fled – 'Bill Cole and friends, Stanley Schachter and friends, Costellos, Ruddicks, Moores, Moe Stein and others . . .'[8] Soon he is on the move himself, to Hollywood and San Francisco, to consult with Irvin Kershner over the *Coffey* script. Back in New York, at 239, East 79th Street, he and Jackie give a dinner party for Bill Weintraub's ex-wife Bernice and her new husband (a Mr Shanet); Brian accepts $500 to be 'a consultant' on a half-hour television programme on Canadian–American relations; and he notes the funeral of President Kennedy on 25 November. In December comes a fan letter from Sir John Heggate in Londonderry, Northern Ireland, which relays a comment on Brian's first two books from the novelist Elizabeth Bowen – 'What, ah what a good writer! What he writes burns into one';[9] this must have pleased him. Robert Shaw and Mary Ure are signed up to do the *Coffey* film. Brian flies to Montreal at the end of January 1964, and again at the end of February, to go over the script once more and watch part of the shooting. Jackie is also in Montreal around this time in connection with the sale of the Lansdowne Avenue house to Sean and Cynthia Moore. A tremendous amount of toing and froing is taking place.

Things are changing. By now (early 1964) relations between the Moores and their new friends the Russells have progressed to such a stage that the two couples are planning the joint purchase of a property not too far from New York, something in Bucks County or Hunterdon County, for example, which might be converted into separate holiday homes to suit both pairs. An intensive programme of house-hunting is got under way (interrupted by Brian's having to leave for Ottawa in April, for another rewrite of the *Coffey* film script); and, early in May, a suitable farmhouse is located, an offer is made, and the purchase completed, all within a couple of months.[10] The property, in Hunterdon County – 88 acres – includes a number of barns and outhouses, and the idea is that the Moores will occupy the house, while the Russells – using Jean's remarkable talent in this direction, and Frank's abilities as a handyman – will transform the outbuildings into a set of splendid living quarters. It's an exciting departure, this new blueprint for a kind of joint property-owning, and everyone is thrilled by it.

The writing of *Emperor* continues alongside these abundant activities, with Brian taking time out whenever he can to get on with his spirited *Bildungsroman* (for example, he re-starts it alone in New York, at the beginning of June). His editor at the Atlantic Monthly Press, Seymour Lawrence, was 'axed' around this time by the company's millionairess owner (due to some dispute over the publication of J.P. Donleavy's *A Singular Man*), and promptly became Vice-Chairman of Knopf, to which Brian considered transferring his allegiance. In the event, however, after meeting, at a party, a very congenial editor named Aaron Asher, and taking up his offer of publication, he went first of all to the Viking Press, with his novels of 1965 and 1968, and then stayed with Aaron Asher through his moves to Holt, Rinehart, and Farrar, Straus and Giroux, after which, he decided, he'd had enough. All this chopping and changing, Brian knew, was not good for his career.[11]

In the autumn months of 1964, forces were massing which would bring about a radical transformation of Brian Moore's life. He had been dissatisfied with his personal circumstances for some time, though carrying on in his usual amiable and high-spirited manner. (It is possible that some of his dissatis-faction was manifested in his continuing problems with ulcers, and his constant attempts to change his appearance by resorting to one unsuccessful diet after another.) His thoughts about his marriage, and about what he wanted from life,[12] were increasingly focused on one of the participants in the new house-sharing venture; and, in fact, it wasn't too long before an upheaval occurred whose constituents call to mind an observa-tion of Alice Munro's narrator in the story, 'An Ounce of Cure' (1967): 'I felt [she remembers, thinking of an evening during her adolescence when things got farcically out of hand] that I had had a glimpse of the shameless, marvellous, shattering absurdity with which the plots of life, though not of fiction, are improvised.'

Some of the Moores' friends, confronted with the new develop-ment, blamed themselves for failing to notice that anything was amiss between Brian and Jackie (but what could they have done if they had?). The Deutsch director Diana Athill, who'd become a great friend of the Moores, and especially of Jackie, was with them at Amagansett during the summer of 1964. Their other house guest at the time was Jean Russell, whose husband Franklin Russell was off in Newfoundland on a nature-trail in connection with his latest book. The English publisher remembered an occasion at Amagan-sett when they were all making their way down to the beach, Jackie and young Michael striding ahead, and she, Brian and Jean following after; and the thought crossed her mind before she could stop it: 'Oh, darling Jackie – perhaps she really is going a bit too far in not bothering about how she looks.'[13] Jackie had put on a lot of weight, she wore an unflattering old pair of ragged denim shorts, and her unkempt short hair, stiff from sea-bathing, stuck out from her head like the bristles of a well-used scrubbing-brush. 'When you couldn't see her vivid face and the brightness of her hazel eyes, you noticed that she was looking a mess.'[14] And there was Jean – irresistibly beautiful, effortlessly elegant – whose presence may well have triggered this passing thought.[15] Jean, according to Diana Athill, had a natural charm and attractiveness on top of her outstanding looks; she was nice, 'really so nice that one forgave her for being so lovely!'.[16] But Diana Athill's primary concern was for her devastated friend Jackie, when the news reached her in London, a couple of months later, that the unthinkable had happened and Brian and Jean had run off together.

'You won't believe what's happened,' Jackie Moore had written to Diana Athill – who retained an impression that her friend had discovered her husband's infidelity 'through some cliché of marital disaster such as finding a note in a pocket when sending a jacket to the cleaner's',[17] thereby precipitating a crisis, and driving the adulterous pair to take flight. But it hadn't happened quite like that. Jackie was alerted by a friend who took it on herself to mention that she thought 'something was going on' between Brian and Jean. She wasn't wrong. Being thrown together in connection with the purchase of the farm had opened the way for the two to fall irreversibly in love. For Brian, it was Margaret Swanson and the allure of romantic passion all over again – but this time recipro-cated; while as far as Jean was concerned, Brian – right from the moment when he walked towards her at Jack McClelland's party in Toronto – was 'simply the most attractive man I had ever met'.[18] They were both honourable people, however, and very much aware of obligations and responsibilities; and for as long as possible, they resisted the force that looked set to overwhelm the pair of them, and everyone around them. Whatever happened, though, it was clear that things would not, and could not, be the same again. *If* they had turned their backs on one another, it was likely that repining and guilt over displaying an insufficiency of courage at a crucial moment would have poisoned their lives: this, at any rate, was plain to Brian, who saw before him, on the one hand, his best chance of happiness (rightly, as it turned out), and on the other, discontent and an endless sense of loss. Jean hesitated for much longer. The major sticking-point for both of them was ten-year-old Michael, and the hurt about to be inflicted on his happy family life. So the peculiar situation, the proposed house-sharing with all the surface amiability and attention to practicalities, and the powerful undercurrent poised to disrupt it, dragged on for some time.

It couldn't continue, of course. Something had to give: what gave was the pretence of normality, as things came splurging out into the open. This was a relief, in one sense, but also traumatic: the Rubicon was well and truly crossed. The date was 13 October 1964 (three days after the New York première of *The Luck of Ginger Coffey*). Brian and Jean left for New York, and booked into a suite at the Chelsea Hotel, until things could be sorted out. Then came the searing business of recriminations, settlements, breaking the news to people who needed to be told what had happened, and so on – all made bearable only by the fact that the two of them were together, and never experienced an instant's doubt that they had done the right thing. What they had entered into was a lifetime's commitment to one another, and it endured.

However – just for the moment, they had stirred up a hornet's nest of anger, misery, shock, opinionated gossip, the indignation of friends on Jackie's behalf, blame apportioned over-hastily, agitations of all kinds; and it was going to take some time for all this to die down into an acceptance of the *fait accompli*. Jackie, back at the farm, understandably distraught, was phoning everyone she knew with her version of the story;[19] Michael was predictably upset by his father's desertion; everything was awry. In the middle of all this, Brian was trying to finish his novel (he did finish it, as we've seen, on 11 December, and then began the 'final rewrite'), as well as looking for somewhere to live. At the end of November, he and Jean moved into a flat at Gramercy Park, New York (three pleasant rooms, $133 a month) and began shopping around for furniture. In the hurry to get away, some irretrievable belongings, including antiques donated by Jean's parents, had been left at the Hunterdon County farm, where the two abandoned spouses remained in possession, before having it officially made over to them. Brian and Jean spent Christmas that year in Vermont (driven there by Jean), while Jackie and Michael Moore went home to Montreal, where Jackie enlisted the sympathy and support of such old friends as Alex Cherney. Brian was inclined to take a wry and sarcastic tone about those who – as he saw it at that moment – were *for* Jackie and *against* him. He wrote to Bill Weintraub[20] about 'the stern wrath of Godly A. Cherney' – Bill himself having managed the seemingly impossible feat of remaining on the old affectionate terms with both parties.

At the start of December, Brian had heard through his agent Wing that the great Alfred Hitchcock had expressed an interest in working with him – Hitchcock having read *The Feast of Lupercal* and admired it, since it corresponded with things he recalled from his own Catholic schooling in London. Brian had already refused an offer from Sam Goldwyn Jr. to write a screenplay for *Limbo*; and – with proliferating financial obligations – he needed to boost his income in every possible way. On 14 February 1965, he and Jean were in Hollywood dining with the Hitchcocks; intensive discussions about various possibilities took place the following day. The main thing Hitchcock had in mind was a thriller based on the Burgess-and-Maclean defection in 1951,[21] with events unfolding from the point-of-view of Mrs Maclean, for which Brian would provide a script. However – 'I listened to it all – and God knows the money would have come in handy – and I turned it down.' He did this because he wasn't persuaded that it was a good idea (in fact he referred to Hitchcock's outline as 'a piece of nonsense'), and because he didn't want to be back in a situation in which he'd be committed to a stretch of trivial but time-consuming work, instead of getting on with his proper task of writing novels. It would be easier, he thought, to turn out the occasional well-paid travel piece, when money worries became pressing. But as it happened, Brian and Jean had only been back in New York for a day or so when news came through that Hitchcock was now prepared to double his original offer. 'And [Brian's lawyer advised] I really think you should accept it this time.' It wasn't only the money that made him – albeit with misgivings – utter a hesitant yes to the new proposal; New York, where it seemed to the beset pair that everyone 'was on Jackie's side', was getting them down. The West Coast, if only for six months or so, offered a new start away from censure and innuendo. They were back in Hollywood by the beginning of March, arranging to rent a house owned by an actor named Herschel Bernardi, whose wife was an admirer of Brian's novels. So, while Bernardi was in New York performing in a musical, Brian and Jean lived magnificently in an ultra-modern house on the edge of a canyon, complete with all sorts of electronic devices, many spare bedrooms, and tremendous views across the San Fernando Valley. The address was 12200, Iredell, Studio City. As for 'L'Univers Hitchcockien' (as François Truffaut dubbed it), Brian was soon in the thick of it, going every day to 'huddle' with the master in his sumptuous suite of offices, working to expand a two-line idea of Hitchcock's into a full-blown plot. 'Our yarn', Hitchcock called it. In the afternoons, Brian and Jean would visit the screening room where a projectionist stood ready to screen any movies they wanted to see.

Brian's task was to prepare an outline, which – if accepted – would form the basis for a screenplay, also to be written by him. All this went ahead as planned. There were few distractions. Hollywood, it soon transpired, was not the place of glamour and endless sociability that might have been expected. The Amagansett shore had more to offer as far as the latter was concerned. Consorting only with a hermit – as he described Hitchcock – Brian and Jean lived a bit like hermits themselves. (Though they did enjoy a weekend at the Hitchcock estate at Santa Cruz, flown there by private plane.) Jean, at the time, was acting as Brian's chauffeur, and not looking for work on her own behalf. For the moment, their relationship with 'one fat Englishman'[22] was the central fact of their lives. Hitchcock was an enigma and a source of fascination to Brian, though eventually he came to believe that 'the master's' mind was essentially trivial, aside from the one area in which he excelled. It was hard to make head or tail of him: in person, he conveyed an impression of a Hampstead butcher or a Chelsea undertaker, yet there he was commissioning the likes of Braque to paint a mural at the Santa Cruz home, and amassing a collection of paintings at his house in Bel-Air that might have been the envy of any provincial museum. This was a man, *gourmet* or *gourmand*, who had his ham shipped directly from Ireland, his sole from Dover, his lamb from

San Francisco and his caviar from Iran, but who, at the same time, seemed to own only the suit he stood up in, and whose driving force was the need to maintain the power and resources he enjoyed as a filmmaker whose power and resources depended on the success of each subsequent film. He was also caught in something of a double bind – desperate to be taken seriously, but unable to provide the authentic Hitchcock touch whenever he tried to be serious. Hence his enlistment of high-grade authors – although, according to Brian, his literary judgement was such that he made no distinction between Ernest Raymond (say) and George Bernard Shaw. His favourite among his own films was *Shadow of a Doubt* (written by Thornton Wilder), and his constant objective was to get some 'character' into his characters. But how, Brian wondered,[23] do you achieve 'character', 'when you are opposite a great visual farceur'? That was one of the problems he was facing 'here in Lotusland'. Another was the disorientation overtaking him and Jean as they sat down to lunch every day alongside such Hollywood icons as Jimmy Stewart and Cary Grant: 'We used to go out in the evenings to see such people on the screen,'[24] and, Brian added, it was disconcerting to have the 'evening fantasies' turn before their eyes into nothing more than people around the office.

'Moore's Folly' was the rueful epithet bestowed by Brian on the Hunterdon County farm where Jackie, Michael and Franklin Russell remained in residence. (The barn was sold off.) Writing to Bill Weintraub,[25] Brian asks for news of Michael, who hadn't replied to any of his letters and, once when Brian had telephoned, had hung up on him. Bill had visited the 'legendary farm' that Easter (1965), and was able to reassure his friend that things in that quarter were as well as could be expected. Brian was hoping to have Michael out to stay with him and Jean during the summer; in fact, he came in August, after the trip had been postponed several times at Jackie's instigation, and Brian loftily informed that it would not take place at all – 'It was decided,' he told Bill, 'that Michael would not like to come to Disneyland and California.'[26] However, for some reason Jackie then changed her mind and accepted, on Michael's behalf, an airline ticket mailed by Brian at the end of July. Michael came, but before long his mother was ringing up to summon him home; and after this had happened on several occasions, Brian made the decision that, for the child's sake, it was better if he didn't see his father at all. A long gap then ensued, before father and son met by arrangement in Boston (see p. 224 below) and close relations were resumed. Michael had naturally been adversely affected by the upheaval in his life, but it did not, to Brian's everlasting relief and gratitude, inflict any irreversible damage either on Michael himself or on the bond between the two of them (a bond that was later extended to include Jean). At the same time, Michael's devotion to his mother remained unshaken.

In March 1965 Brian had confided in a letter to Bill Weintraub[27] that Jackie 'seems to be making it very big with F. Russell and I am offering up a novena to their future entanglement'. The novena, or some other intangible expedient, paid dividends. Frank Russell's book, *The Secret Islands*, published in 1965, bore the dedication, 'To Jacqueline and Michael'. (In a similar gesture, *The Emperor of Ice Cream* was – like all Brian's subsequent novels – dedicated 'to Jean'.) This was the first public acknowledgement that a new relationship had been salvaged from the wreckage of the other two. The pair who were left behind discovered they had things in common, aside from their predicament. The 'shameless, marvellous, shattering absurdity' of the plots of life was about to be exemplified. Jackie Moore and Frank Russell began an affair, and by the beginning of 1967 Jackie was pregnant. Her son Alexander was born in September. (He was born with a congenital defect which required a series of operations to be put right.) Some time after this, Brian's ex-wife and Jean's ex-husband got married.

It was undoubtedly these personal events that caused Jackie to relent in the matter of the divorce sought by Brian as far back as the autumn of 1964. The very fraught relations between the two, following on from the agonising split, had ensured that heels were dug in and attitudes hardened. Brian never denied that he had behaved badly towards his first wife, though he came to believe it was in marrying her, not leaving her, that the crucial transgression lay. None of it was her fault, he said in later years. 'It was my fault. If you marry someone without being in love with them – you're to blame.' At the time, though, it seems to have come as something of a surprise that Jackie didn't make things easier for him. *She* claimed the slowness of lawyers was responsible for any hold-ups in the resettlement of his affairs; however, in a letter to Bill Weintraub dated 17 March 1967, Brian gave vent to a rare outburst on the topic. It would suit him fine, he said, not to have to contribute $12,000 a year to Jackie's income, to be able to marry Jean and see Michael whenever he chose. And 'Jackie, not lawyers, has prevented all this'. For the moment, he'd prefer it if she remained in ignorance of his address (where he and Jean had been for the last six months). This was on the advice of *his* lawyers, because of some episode during the previous year, when she'd 'put the Cossacks' on him over an imagined financial wrong. Moreover, he'd been forced to curb his annoyance and be polite to her for two and a half years, since she held the trump cards (especially in relation to their son). Was it any wonder, he wanted to know, that he'd finally succumbed to the urge to state all this without equivocation? He went on to state it again, with pardonable exaggeration, in his novel *Fergus*:

He walked through the house and out on to the terrace facing the sea. Rage weakened him, making him dizzy, his vision blurring as he stared down at the shore. Rage at his wife, at her vengeance, her lies, at her refusal to let him see his daughter, at her lawyers, the detective agencies she had hired, her impossible demands, which had driven him out to this Pacific coast.

What occasioned this outburst was Bill's suggestion, in a letter, that he was being put in the position of having to decide between the two of them. This was not the case. 'Let me dispose of the Jackie loyalties question' once and for all, Brian wrote, in a tone of exasperation. 'When I said – make up your own mind – I merely meant about the facts of the case . . . Of course I haven't asked anyone to choose . . .'[28] Nevertheless, many people believed that this was precisely what they had been asked to do. Brian, by moving to California and by rebuffing the overtures of certain former friends, managed to give an impression that he'd taken umbrage at their continuing association with his ex-wife. One typical instance of his unwarranted withdrawal concerned his English friends the Prices. Stanley Price, in the course of a business trip to the States, had gone to stay with Brian and Jean at Malibu and had a splendid time. On the way home via New York he felt he couldn't pass up the chance to visit Jackie, for whom his feelings of friendship had in no sense diminished. Back in London, he wrote to Brian and got no reply. He next sent to Malibu a copy of a novel he'd written and still got no response (and this from the friend who'd advised and encouraged him through hours and hours of literary discussion). A further letter also went unanswered. Stanley Price then wrote care of Brian's agent, still to no avail. At that point he gave up. The only way to make sense of the thing was to form the conclusion that Brian had succumbed to irreversible pique on account of Stanley's visit to Jackie.

However – it is equally possible that Brian's silence was less an act of deliberate rejection than a consequence of his preoccupation with new realities and concerns. (It may of course have had to do with his habit of 'taking a scunner at' someone or other, for no apparent reason.) Certainly, in the circumstances, it would have seemed appropriate to put the past behind him, as far as possible. He hadn't kept in touch with anyone else among Jackie's friends, he told Bill Weintraub, 'or anyone who once was mutually a friend of the Moores, with the exception of Mordecai who, I feel, understands the situation'.[29]

The reference here is to Mordecai Richler's divorce and remarriage, which had taken place in circumstances curiously similar to those experienced by Brian. In the summer of 1958, Mordecai and his wife Cathy had rented a villa in the South of France together with their great friends Stanley and Florence Mann. By the end of July, however, Mordecai was writing to Bill Weintraub to tell him that 'Cathy and I have separated, and will be getting a divorce one of these autumn days.'[30] The letter ended with best wishes 'to Bernice, Brian, Jackie'. A further letter, dated 29 August, contained the throwaway remark, 'Florence and Stanley are getting a divorce, I think.' Within a year – and in response to a letter from Bill announcing that his and Bernice's marriage was irretrievably on the rocks – Mordecai had disclosed that he and Florence Mann planned to marry, once her divorce was settled. This information was 'highly confidential': no one else was to be put in the picture, aside from the Moores. Ironically, in the same letter, Mordecai Richler expressed his conviction that 'Brian and Jackie are about the only couple I know who seem to have a happy marriage. A solid one. I've never seen them go at each other – score mean points jokingly as I've seen . . . others go at it again and again.'[31]

In her memoir *Stet* (2000), Diana Athill gives an account of her broken friendship with Brian Moore. Shocked and dismayed by the hurt inflicted on Jackie – though trying not to apportion blame; such things happened, she knew, and it was foolhardy for outsiders to attempt an assessment of rights and wrongs in these matters – she'd written to Brian to suggest that, for the moment, they keep their correspondence strictly on a business level. No doubt she'd soon adjust to the new state of affairs, and feel towards him as warmly as ever; in the meantime, gossip and pleasantries were off-limits. His reply to this communication, as she recalled it, came at her like a thunderbolt, upsetting her so much that she threw it away (first showing it to André Deutsch). It began by announcing shortly that 'there would be no business letters because there would be no further business'. Brian had been dissatisfied for some time by the treatment meted out to him by the firm of Deutsch – in particular, their dereliction in the matter of publicity – and so he was taking his books elsewhere. The letter – according to Diana Athill – then launched into a diatribe against Jackie, and against her for having 'sided with Jackie'. She was shocked by its tone; André Deutsch was shocked by its tone; and Mordecai Richler confirmed that other friends of the Moores had been surprised by his unrelenting attitude, or what struck them as an unrelenting attitude. Indeed the perception was strong in certain quarters that Brian had destroyed his marriage and then compounded the offence by going about running down his wife, thereby revealing a whole new and deplorable side to his character. But for all its neatness and simplicity, this judgement was actually pretty wide of the mark.

Certainly Diana Athill had reason to be upset and angry on behalf of her friend Jackie Moore – '*She* had not wanted anything from the marriage that it didn't give her'[32] – and no doubt she wrote to Brian in the terms she describes, in the first flow of her indignation. This would have been in the autumn of 1964. But relations with Deutsch were not severed until some time later. Deutsch published *The Emperor of Ice Cream* in 1966; it wasn't until 1968 and *I Am Mary Dunne* that Brian moved to the firm of Jonathan Cape, which had made him a better offer. 'I have shed André Deutsch like an old skin,' he told Bill Weintraub, 'and am now about to swing . . . with Tom Maschler the hooded Capeman'.[33] (In that year, too, he received a chatty letter[34] from Diana Athill, thanking him for sending an advance copy of *Mary Dunne*.) And, writing to Bill Weintraub from Hollywood, he says he has 'promised Diana'[35] an account of his Hitchcock experiences, which is hardly the tone of someone observing a frosty and vindictive stance. He learned about Jackie's pregnancy from Jackie herself, when he'd telephoned her about something else; and he was told as soon as the baby was born. Of course the whole area of the separation and remarriages was rife with harshness and recrimination: how could it not have been? But it was also less clear-cut than the verdicts of some concerned, or intrigued, observers might suggest.

By May 1965 Brian had completed the final draft of his outline for the film which became *Torn Curtain*, and – after getting the go-ahead from Hitchcock – promptly began work on a screenplay. The screenplay was finished and delivered in the middle of August, Julie Andrews and Paul Newman were signed up to play the leading roles, and Hitchcock declared himself satisfied. A silence then ensued, with no further word from the master himself, or from Universal Pictures. Brian and Jean had decided to stay on in California for the time being, and early in September they moved to a new address, 8884, Lookout Mountain Avenue, Hollywood, where Brian got down to a new novel, provisionally entitled *A Woman of No Identity*. (It was hard at first to find the right style for this: he wanted it to be colloquial and immediate, not anecdotal.) *The Emperor of Ice Cream* was published in America netting enthusiastic reviews, including a 'rave' in *The New York Times*. After a trip to San Francisco, Brian visited a doctor complaining of pains in his chest: 'coronary insufficiency' was diagnosed. He immediately gave up cigarettes and went on a diet, under Jean's adept supervision. (He would never again be described as overweight: the short chubby figure of the 1950s had gone the way of Judith Hearne's hopes and Brian's first marriage. A new, more streamlined form had taken its place. Photographs from the period show Brian looking as close to handsomeness as he would ever manage. Even his handwriting underwent a sea-change, becoming more distinctive and elegant to correspond with his upgraded image. When his sister Una commented on his new calligraphic style, he told her, 'It's not difficult. You buy a 7-shilling Osmiroid pen and a Penguin – or other – handbook on italic writing. Within a few weeks you can learn to write, as I am doing now, at a normal writing speed. And it's fun to learn.'[36] Later he acquired a Mont Blanc fountain pen.)

In his novel *Fergus* (1971) Brian Moore describes the state of mind of a screenwriter anxiously awaiting confirmation of the acceptability of his script; and no doubt, with permissible novelist's exaggeration, this nail-biting scenario draws on his own experience following his submission of the *Torn Curtain* screenplay. The silence dragged on for so long that he began to assume – rightly, as it turned out – that some other writer had been enlisted to tidy up what 'the master' perceived as infelicities in his script. This fear was confirmed in November 1965, when a letter arrived proclaiming that Keith Waterhouse and Willis Hall were the authors of 'the final version of the screenplay', and that their names should therefore appear alongside that of Brian Moore among the screen credits. A week later came a copy of the 'revised' screenplay, which Brian read with increasing outrage, as he found only minimal alterations to his own original typescript. At a loss to see why he should share screen credit with the two sluggish newcomers, he immediately contacted his agent, his lawyer, and the Writers' Guild of America, and for the next few months was embroiled in legal battles to assert his claim to sole screen credit, which he eventually won. In his autobiography, *Streets Ahead* (1995), Keith Waterhouse makes the bare-faced assertion that *Torn Curtain* – not Alfred Hitchcock's most successful film – 'would have ranked even lower in the *oeuvre* had we not been called in to improve the script and polish the dialogue'. Waterhouse acknowledges Hitchcock's efforts to get screen credit for him and his co-writer, but says – disingenuously – that they, on the other hand, were doing their best to keep their names from being associated with the tinpot production. Brian Moore himself, indeed, considered *Torn Curtain* to be a negligible part of the Hitchcock output; but naturally he was satisfied to have won his case, guaranteeing a proper share of the royalties generated by the film. He had tackled his Hollywood project in much the same spirit he'd brought to the early thrillers. He believed – truly – that he'd done a professional job, nothing more. One thing, however, he liked to take credit for: the prolonged episode of murder in *Torn Curtain*. From his doctor father he had learnt years earlier that it was actually quite difficult to kill someone; and this piece of information, passed on to Hitchcock, gained an embodiment in the film:

> I had told Hitch one day that my father was a doctor, and that I knew death was often a long and painful business. People didn't always die as quickly as they did in movies. As soon as I said that, Hitch got really excited. He just went mad thinking of all the ways we could prolong a murder scene. He would sit and sketch on paper the various frames of action, occasionally looking up at me and asking, 'How be's if we do this?' And when everything was sketched out, he would dismiss me with the words, 'All right now, you go and dialogue it up.'[37]

At the memorial gathering held for Brian Moore in London in October 1999, the Moores' friend Alice Trillin spoke affectingly about the relationship between Brian and Jean, as she'd observed it over many years. It was, she said, impossible to think of one without the other; their marriage amounted to 'the most equal partnership between a man and a woman that I've ever known'. Brian, she went on, never ceased to think of Jean as 'beautiful, wise and funny': the ideal wife, friend, companion, literary critic and arbiter of taste and judgement. From the moment of taking a deep breath, burning their bridges behind them and eloping to New York in a strung-up state, to the day of Brian's death over thirty years later, the two were hardly separated for more than a night, and then only for some unavoidable reason, such as illness.

Their extraordinary closeness was evident from the beginning, to themselves and to others who got to know them, and needed no bureaucratic props; but just to make it official, as it were, they married as soon as it became possible to do so – on the day that Brian's divorce eventually came through, 14 October 1967. It had been a long wait. (That the divorce became a reality was due to the exertions of Brian's solicitor, Morton Leavy. A couple of years later, writing to his sister Una asking if she'd be kind enough to devote some time to looking after Leavy's student daughter Annette, who was going to Ireland for a holiday, Brian mentioned that he had consulted Jean about the best way to persuade Una to take on this task. '. . . and she said, "Tell her he's the man made it possible for you to divorce Jackie and marry me." So I'm telling you . . .'[38]) The marriage took place at the City Hall in New York, in the presence of only two witnesses, Sean and Cynthia Moore. The brothers and their wives then went for a ride on the Staten Island Ferry – 'a great way to see the New York skyline'[39] – had lunch at a favourite French restaurant, visited an intriguing medieval museum, the Cloisters, overlooking the Hudson River, before going on to the Plaza ('very grand') for afternoon tea. At seven, they met for a glass of champagne at Sean and Cynthia's hotel; next came an evening at a theatre on Broadway, with the exultant quartet finally winding up having supper at a South American restaurant called the Fonda del Sol. 'A great wedding!' Brian exclaimed. The newly-weds then had a couple of days in Toronto, where Bill Weintraub – himself also about to get married for the second time – dashed down to see them, overbrimming with enthusiasm and felicitations. Then it was back to Los Angeles and the Pacific Coast Highway, before the two Moores 'emplaned' for Sacramento, California, on behalf of the London *Sunday Times*, who'd commissioned Brian to write an article on the prospective presidential candidate, Governor Ronald Reagan. 'If elected,' Brian joked to Bill Weintraub,[40] Reagan 'will be the first leader of the Western world who once did a two-week gig as MC of the floor show at the Last Frontier Hotel in Las Vegas.'

12

QUIET DAYS IN MALIBU[1]

'Living very quiet life with Jean and cat.'
Letter to William Weintraub, 1971

JUST OVER A YEAR before their New York wedding, Brian and Jean had moved to a new address, this time in Malibu, along the Pacific Coast Highway. The house they moved into, rented to begin with, was to be their principal home for the rest of their lives. Referred to by Brian as 'a shack on the Pacific', and 'a slum by the sea', this, over the years, evolved into a comfortable and stylish backdrop to his industrious and enviable life. When the place came up for sale early in 1969 they immediately put in a bid for it, and, after prolonged negotiations and setbacks in connection with exclusive access to the cliff steps leading to the beach down below, became its owners in the June of that year. The price was $75,000, which necessitated a bank loan. It's an extensive, one-storey, sequestered dwelling, full of a halcyon warmth and tranquillity – handsome redwood garage door, gleaming white terraces of exterior paintwork, elegantly appointed double-ovened kitchen, furniture resplendent with new white slip-covers, richly upholstered velvet sofas, sandblasted brick floors of incomparable 'cleanth', lamp and chair appurtenances from various contemporary design stores, including a swivel Eames chair for his study, bookshelf fittings and so on: this was how Brian described some of his newly acquired riches to Bill Weintraub,[2] in an outbreak of unabashed home-owner's enthusiasm. Troops of plumbers, painters, carpenters, handymen and upholsterers took over the house (under Jean's direction) and transformed it into a place of beauty, in its exotic, richly coloured garden, high above the Pacific, with swarms of pelicans flying past the kitchen windows and hot Santa

Ana winds swirling round the homestead at night. It wasn't all roses, of course – another letter describes flood water, 'intermixed with good red mud',[3] pouring down the driveway during the wettest Californian winter for seventy-nine years; and brush fires were another hazard.[4] But it was sufficiently idyllic to cause jubilation in the one-time Belfast boy with his memories of damp Lagan fogs, endless grotty terraces with mean back yards, and a combative, church-going populace.

Indeed, the Malibu beach house is about as far removed as one can get from Belfast drabness and crabbedness – and there were many sybaritic days on the terrace above the Pacific with the typewriter poised on a marble table and the temperature seventy-six degrees in the shade. However, the new situation wasn't without anomalies of its own. Malibu, in the popular mind, is redolent of the utmost wealth and glamour, and the glittering sociability one associates with the Hollywood film industry. But as they'd found with Hollywood itself, the Moores were able to live as quietly as they chose in this supposedly frenetic locality. There was no literary community to incorporate them (though their friends Joan Didion and her husband John Gregory Dunne, whom they had known in New York, came to live nearby for a time during the 1970s). In fact Malibu itself is hard to pin down. 'It is not a resort,' Joan Didion says in her essay, 'Quiet Days in Malibu'. The place has 'no hotel, no passable restaurant, nothing to attract the traveller's dollar'. It consists of twenty-seven miles of coastline, with a parallel highway, along which 'Greyhound buses and refrigerated produce trucks and sixteen-wheel gasoline tankers'[5] accelerate. Coming from Los Angeles, you pass through a bleak industrial landscape, gigantic in scale, makeshift dwellings in dirty pastel colours, everything seedy and rundown and grim. Further out, things change for the better; but it's only when you turn off into the driveway leading to the Moore house – or any of the other million-dollar houses lining the Pacific – that the atmosphere becomes luxuriant and alluring.

The house itself had a new wing added in 1987, which enlarged it considerably; it acquired such furnishings as a nineteenth-century dresser, stained blue, from the Laurentian Mountains, a large quilting table and a pair of nineteenth-century samplers from Nova Scotia. Brian was happy to live in the environment created by Jean –

elegant and idiosyncratic – but retained such an aversion to Victoriana and its associations with pomp and oppressiveness that he could rarely be persuaded to set foot in an antique shop: Jean had to do her treasure-hunting on her own, or in the company of like-minded friends. Brian relished the effect, indeed, but opted out of participating in the chase – though he always had a say in the final purchase. (His novel of 1975, the quasi-Borgesian *The Great Victorian Collection*, concerns, among other things, the experience of someone sinking under the weight of a vast, unreal accumulation of Victorian artefacts, as the dream that brought them into being rapidly becomes a nightmare. You can read the novel, too, as a fable about oppressive – paternal – values rising up 'to haunt the present'[6] as a favourite Moore metaphor gets another airing.) Troops of outdoor workers, at Malibu, kept the garden in order, while a Mexican maid attended to indoor cleanliness. A clever and beautiful Siamese cat, called Teddy, was part of the entourage. The result was a kind of domestic perfection undreamt of in Brian's Montreal days.

At the end of 1965, *The Emperor of Ice Cream* had appeared in the 'best-of-the-year' lists of *The New York Times* and *Tribune*. A couple of months later it came out in the UK and attracted – among other instances of enthusiasm – praise from the critic and Oxford don Christopher Ricks, whose long review article in the *New Statesman* was printed under the heading, 'The Simple Excellence of Brian Moore'.[7] 'The sort of head we all admire,' Brian joked.[8] Philip French, who, with his wife Kersti, became a friend of the Moores, wrote a review of the book for Alan Ross's *London Magazine* (it appeared in the February issue of 1966) which dealt with the whole of the Moore *oeuvre* to date, and produced an extremely inspiriting effect on its subject: 'It is really a joy, out here in the Hollywood Hills, to know that one is not writing into a void.'[9] Brian was struck by one comment of Philip French's in particular: 'Indeed there is in *The Emperor of Ice Cream* a sense of reconciliation, a personal and artistic resolution of tension which Moore has been working towards for ten years.' Brian found this 'uncannily exact', thinking, no doubt, not only of the struggle to perfect an individual style of writing, but also of tensions and inadequacies in his personal life which only now had achieved a triumphant resolution. At last, things were going exceptionally well – and all the praise and attention, far from being a distraction, provided an incentive for Brian to get on with his work-in-progress. Much of this year, 1966, was taken up with a film script for Irvin Kershner, *The Slave*, which came to nothing; and with completing and revising *A Woman of No Identity*, eventually to be published under the title *I Am Mary Dunne*.

Brian Moore has often been praised for his ability to enter into the consciousness of his female characters from Judith Hearne on (though in fact, since every character is either male or female, it would be a poor novelist who made a hash of impersonating one or the other). It's true that, perhaps to a greater degree than many of his male contemporaries, he brings his fictional women centre-stage, with no loss of authenticity or complexity. *Mary Dunne*, for example, is a very subtle portrayal of a young, urbane Canadian woman living in New York – a woman in the grip of a fluctuating sense of identity, partly caused by premenstrual tension, and partly by the kaleidoscopic circumstances of her life: three marriages, various occupations and preoccupations, a susceptibility to name-less fears and irrational apprehensions. If *Emperor* was Brian Moore's *The Awkward Age*, *Mary Dunne* is his *Portrait of a Lady*. It begins with a moment of amnesia in a hairdresser's, with Mary unable to remember her current name. (Something similar had happened to Brian himself: at one point, when he needed a new passport, he wrote in a panic to Bill Weintraub[10] asking for the name of the church in Montreal in which he had got married, and which he couldn't for the life of him recall. It would be too pat to attribute a psychological cause to this instance of forgetfulness.) But it's only a temporary lapse. Mary ultimately assumes control of her life – or recognises that this resource has always been available to her, as the events of her past are ordered, in her remembering consciousness, into a secure pattern. This novel exemplifies the author's sureness and lightness of touch, including, as it does, some moments of social comedy, and a few striking set-pieces, such as the episode of the two female friends engaging in a squabble in a restaurant, or the arrival for dinner of a bore from the past.

It should be made clear that Mary Dunne is not Jean Denney, any more than Brian himself was Ginger Coffey or Brendan Tierney; however, the book would not have been written without Jean and her Nova Scotia background, and she herself undoubtedly provided a starting-off point, after which the novelist's inventiveness was able to take over completely. 'Actually, I'm quite pleased with my inventions,' Brian assured Bill Weintraub,[11] 'Mary – Jimmy – Hat etc, because they *are* inventions . . .' Just as he'd asked his brother Seamus to check *Lupercal* for inadvertent reminiscence masquerading as fiction, so Bill was conscripted to cast an eye over the Montreal and Toronto sections of *Mary Dunne*, in case anything potentially libellous might have slipped in. 'There may be those who'll play guessing games and try to put names to characters.'[12] In fact, the few particulars drawn from life tend to be pieces of transposed autobiography, as when Mary remembers her brother carrying her on his shoulders as he scaled a cliff (Brian's escapade at Portstewart with his brother Sean), or a very minor character recalls sitting down to take tea with Rasputin (harking back to Aunt Maggie Moore).

I Am Mary Dunne – final draft – was completed in Rome in September 1967, and Jean immediately began reading the book, finishing it on Palatine Hill. 'I have finished my new novel . . . [it] is shockingly *dirty* and not something Seamus will be able to let his children read,' Brian joked to his sister Una.[13] 'It is set in New York.' Throughout that summer, Brian and Jean were in Europe, having arrived via Montreal and Nova Scotia (Bill Weintraub was roped in to help with arrangements for their cherished cat, which was shipped as excess baggage to Montreal and then forwarded as air freight to Halifax, where Jean's mother collected it, driving seventy miles there and back). They reached London in the middle of July, then had a couple of weeks in Ireland, visiting Belfast and Dublin. Their base in London was a flat just off the Kings Road, at that time the heartland of the carefree and colourful. Brian enjoyed strolling through Chelsea flanked by beautiful Jean on his right, in a white Irish hat, and on his left 'my sister the nun', whose habit seemed especially attuned to the era of fancy dress.

Eilis Moore was among the Irish relatives coming in droves (or so it seemed) to inspect Brian's new inamorata, who stood up well to the ordeal. The rest of their time in England was taken up with such diversions as a trip to Brighton, lunch with Brian's agent Michael Horniman, drinks with Peter Crookston of the *Sunday Times* at the

Royal Court bar. At the end of August, the couple left for Paris; then it was on to Lausanne, Geneva, Munich, Innsbruck, Venice, Siena, and finally Rome. (In the course of these travels they learnt that Jackie Moore had given birth to a boy.) On 2 October they flew from Rome to New York, where they were married twelve days later. Their European trip established a pattern which would be repeated, with variations, during the summer months over many years.

Another *Judith Hearne* script had been completed by Brian for United Artists, but – as ever – some blockage immediately occurred, and the project hurtled into limbo yet again. Indeed, the main purpose of the recent Irish trip had been to conduct Irvin Kershner, who accompanied the Moores, round some possible locations for the film: Camden Street, the lower part of the Stranmillis Road opposite Friars Bush Cemetery, Smithfield Market, Royal Avenue including the Central Lending Library, and Lavery's Pub. Una Maguire and her husband were roped in to help with the sightseeing agenda.

By the start of 1968 – and after a post-Christmas break for himself and Jean at the Plaza Hotel in San Francisco – Brian was making tentative notes in connection with a new novel. This, he confided to Jean, would, if it went ahead, constitute something of a new departure, being totally unlike *Mary Dunne* or anything else he had written. He was getting into the swing of it by March, when he took some time off to visit New York with Jean, having arranged to meet up there with Sean and Cynthia, and Bill Weintraub and his new wife Magda. All went to plan. Brian had been invited to give a couple of lectures at the Universities of Arkansas and Texas, and arrived at the former in blizzard conditions, very untypical for the area; the next day, for the first time ever, the university was closed because of snow. The Moores then flew on to Love Field (the Dallas airport), at which point they were met by their host, a professor at the university, who drove them forty miles into Texas cow country, a Protestant, white, fundamentalist locality, full of shabby small towns and old-fashioned farmhouses, a locality that hardly seemed to have changed in sixty years. They saw the bank robbed by Bonnie and Clyde, exactly as it was in the film, and marvelled at the degree to which this town (Ponder), and another called Pilot Point, had resisted the innovations of the twentieth century.

*　　*　　*

I Am Mary Dunne was published in the US on 19 June 1968, and in the UK on 17 October. Its reception in both places was enthusiastic. The *Saturday Review Syndicate* called it 'a virtuoso feat', and the *Atlantic Monthly* judged it 'His best work to date'. The Moores were in New York in June, then went to Montreal, followed by Nova Scotia – where they stayed with Jean's mother on the shores of the Bay of Fundy – before flying to London (27 July) and then on to Dublin, where Brian had arranged to write a piece on the Horse Show for *Holiday* magazine. Back in London, there were dinners with Tom Maschler of Cape, the literary agent Ed Victor, Brian's old friends the Slatterys, Philip French and his wife, lunches with Peter Crookston and Francis Wyndham in a restaurant in Chancery Lane, with the film director Jack Clayton . . . the usual social round. After their summer abroad, Brian and Jean returned home via New York, where they saw their friend the illustrator Tomi Ungerer, and had lunch at Columbia University with Hallvard Dahlie, who was working on the first critical study of Brian Moore.[14] At home in Malibu, Brian got down to work again on the book called *Musée Imaginaire*; and by the middle of November, he'd settled on what was to be its final – simple – title, *Fergus*.

Both *Mary Dunne* and *Fergus* encompass vivid recitals of each protagonist's life history – or at least, its more significant portions. With *Fergus*, however, a new note is sounded, a note of supernatural capering. Comic realism meets comic immaterialism, with resounding effect. Fergus Fadden, thirty-nine years old, Belfast author of a couple of novels, is living in California with a girl nearly young enough to be his daughter, and, in order to pay for his divorce, has produced a screenplay of one of his novels, at the instigation of a Hollywood producer. The screenplay has been delivered and no word has been heard from the producer, which is a cause of anxiety, one of many anxieties by which Fergus is beset. Nothing out of the ordinary so far. But the upshot of these anxieties of Fergus's is the materialisation, in and around his Californian home, of figures out of the past, some dead, some rejuvenated. His sister Maeve, a mother-of-four in Dundalk, is incarnated in front of him as a sixteen-year-old schoolgirl in her Cross-and-Passion uniform, full of sibling backchat. Old girlfriends pass before his eyes in the fashions of another era.

The tableau begins, as we have seen (p. 32 above), with the

wraith of Dr Fadden (Dr Moore to the life) suddenly taking shape in the incongruous setting of the laid-back Pacific Coast. After Fergus's father comes Fergus's mother, admonitory, placatory, as the occasion demands; and then the whole *galère* of one-time antagonists, friends and relations, rising up to excuse or accuse, every one having his (or her) say, while 'real life' – Fergus's life as a Hollywood screenwriter, with his girlfriend Dani, 'young Miss California in a miniskirt', and Dani's drunken mother being tactless on the terrace – continues on a parallel plane. It's Fergus himself – whether he's taken leave of his senses, is the victim of hauntings or hallucinations – who holds the novel's fragments and figments in a breathtaking equilibrium. *Fergus* is a *tour de force*, a balancing act, and an entertaining exercise in deflected autobiography. It's also a self-reflexive piece of fiction, with the author's imaginings gaining form and substance on the page. Its central device, perhaps, owes something to the Waugh of *Gilbert Pinfold*,[15] and other compar-isons suggest themselves – most notably Joyce, with a Joycean relish and exuberance being brought to the novel's scenes of outrage and desperation. Like Leopold Bloom, for example, in the 'Nighttown' section of *Ulysses*, Fergus finds himself the butt of charges both reasonable and ridiculous: yes, he did behave badly towards this one or that one; no, he isn't 'a very anti-Christ of iniquity, a moral cesspool'. But for all that, *Fergus* is wholly original, and singularly diverting.

It's the heady mix of the remembered and the invented that gives it its edge. It was an audacious choice of the novelist to insert his own house – the swing chairs on the terrace, the bank leading down to the sand covered in small rubbery banana-shaped creepers known as ice plant – into his narrative, along with his parents, teachers, aunt, childhood and adolescent friends (there is even a bit-part for Niall Dempsey – Ownie Dempster in the book), girlfriends like Isobel Hammond, business colleagues and so on. Zuma Beach, California, has a scene from Portstewart Strand, *c*. 1932, super-imposed on top of it:

> In the lee of the tree trunk, a white linen tablecloth already spread with food from opened wicker baskets, unbreakable picnic teacups and saucers laid out in a row, ready for tea, and, fussing, pulling a piston in and out of a primus stove, Dr

Fadden, kneeling, an old-fashionedly elegant holiday-maker in white Panama hat, the brim pulled rakishly down all around, brass-buttoned navy blazer, cream woollen flannels, white buck golf shoes with red-brick rubber soles, a cream tennis shirt with a striped silk foulard. And in a temper. 'Damn stove! Damn petrol's flooded the wick!'

'*Memento ergo sum*,' thought Mary Dunne: I am the sum of my memories. The novelist has remembered everything, down to the matchbox – Swift's Blue Bird – locally made in Belfast long ago. Such details contribute authenticity, indeed; while the wry, out-landish[16] approach makes the whole thing compelling. Even the final scene, in which a kind of down-to-earth explanation is proffered in the form of an impending heart attack, doesn't damage the novel's invigorating artifice. All the dead, and undead, dears take off for heaven, or wherever, in an old Morris Minor car. It's time to go – not for Fergus, however, who raises an arm, releasing them, and releasing himself from his waking dream. The heart attack has not proved fatal.

Work on *Fergus* continued throughout 1969; that and chores connected with the Malibu house purchase occupied the early part of the year. In March, Brian was back in Arkansas reading from his work-in-progress (dialogues with his 'young self', which were cut from the final version). The book was finished in January 1970, read by Jean and dispatched to Aaron Asher at Holt, Rinehart,[17] who pronounced it 'an original and otherwise splendid novel'.[18] Rereading it, Brian himself concluded that, of all the books he'd set out to write, this one approximated more closely to the aims he'd had for it than anything else since *Lupercal*.

Reviewers, by and large, did not agree with this assessment. The first ominous note was struck by Professor Julian Moynahan of Rutgers University who, writing in the Sunday Review Section of *The New York Times* (27 September 1970), judged *Fergus* 'a failure'. Other reviewers, curiously, considered it might have worked better as a play. When the novel was published in England (on 25 March 1971), it fared a bit better, though the reviews were 'mixed'; the *Sunday Telegraph* praised it for bringing 'absolute conviction to this terrible and comic haunting', while its daily counterpart called Brian Moore 'a versatile and compelling' novelist. Susan Hill, writing in the *New Statesman*, commended the author for taking 'a calculated risk' which 'almost comes off'. She found a good deal in the novel 'which is wise, perceptive, and also funny'.[19]

'A smash hit it wasn't,' Brian wrote ruefully to Bill Weintraub,[20] *à propos Fergus*, his hopes for the novel not having been realised. *Mary Dunne* had struck a keener chord with the American reading public. And yet: attention should be paid to the author's view of this work. It's a simple matter to underestimate *Fergus*, whose ease of manner masks a tremendous artistry and resonance. Those critics who complained about the novel's inclusion of 'stock scenes'[21] and commonplace characters are wide of the mark. Few novels show such insight into Belfast mores of the inter-war, and post-war, years, or present their findings with such aplomb and individuality.

Dispirited by the cool reception of *Fergus*, Brian Moore abandoned work on a novel he'd begun in the spring of 1970, another engagement with the *outré*, this time centred on a 'secular miracle', the materialisation of a collection of objects (not people) in a Californian parking lot. Instead, he took on what you might describe as the least surreal project imaginable, a quasi-fictional re-run of Canada's 'October crisis' of 1970. The Senior British Trade Commissioner in Montreal, James Richard (Jasper) Cross, was kidnapped on the 5th of the month by the Front de Libération du Québec (FLQ) and held for sixty days in a dilapidated area of French-speaking Montreal; then Pierre Laporte, Deputy Premier of Québec, Minister of Labour and Immigration, was snatched in his turn by a different Liberation group, and executed. While all this was taking place, Brian received a telephone call from his publisher Jack McClelland in Toronto, suggesting that he should write a non-fiction account of these exorbitant occurrences. Within a couple of days, Brian and Jean had left for Montreal, where they rented an apartment. Cross was still in captivity at this time. Brian began by interviewing newspaper and television commentators, finding out as much as he could about the background to the crisis. At this stage, he wasn't sure if a book would result from his investigations, or, if it did, what sort of book it would be.

He was drawn to the unfolding story for a number of reasons. There were obvious parallels between French-Canadian separatists and Northern Irish nationalists – second-class citizens, both of them, both accustomed to fomenting rebellion in their shoddy enclaves. And now, it seemed, the time had come for both these groups to get up off their knees, to take matters into their own hands and set their own agendas. Brian understood disaffection: it had tainted the air around him during his earliest years. And – as a one-time newspaperman in the city – he understood a good deal about the specific grievances of French Montrealers. Then, the thriller element in the story appealed to him, the strong, readymade plot, with all its political nuances and implications. To get anywhere near the full picture required a lot of research: 'Hard work this factstuff,' Brian confided to Bill Weintraub. But the excitements generated at that moment carried him along. He decided to do the book, but to write it as a novel, albeit a documentary novel. Having talked to contemporaries and associates of the politically motivated kidnappers, 'I found them to be young, ex-Catholic, nationalists, totalitarians,' he said,[22] 'dedicated to violent uprising. It was a mixture I had known back in Ireland. I felt I could write about it.' And he told his agent: 'I want to use the "theatrical" and the staged elements to show that the whole thing had about it something of a staged event, with both kidnappers and Trudeau working as television performers and with the capture of the national media the real point of the game.'[23]

He began work on the book on 13 January 1971, the day after he and Jean returned to Malibu after a seven-week stint in Montreal. (At the end of February they were back in Montreal for another month's work there; before that, they'd had a couple of days in the pretty town of Richmond, Virginia, where Brian was taking part in the Richmond Festival.) The first draft was finished in the middle of April, and two days later Brian had an idea for a title: *The Revolution Script.* He'd decided to approach the subject from the point of view of the FLQ activists, the six young people who planned and carried out the Cross kidnapping, and ended by obtaining negotiated asylum in Cuba after their victim's release. Treating the story as fiction allowed him to get inside the minds of the major players, and to bring in certain minor characters of his own invention.

It also enabled him to take a sympathetic attitude, by and large, to the Cross kidnappers; indeed, what struck certain commentators,[24] many years later, was the difference in presentation between these FLQ terrorists and the IRA terrorists of Brian Moore's later, Northern Irish thriller, *Lies of Silence* (1990). However, there were sound reasons for the change of view, if change it was. Throughout the late 1960s and even the early '70s, the Civil Rights aspect of revolutionary activity in Northern Ireland (and in French Canada) was paramount; no one of a liberal persuasion could deny the genuine grievances that cried out for redress. (Fergus Fadden, accused among many other things of indifference to political events taking place in his own home territory, protests that he sent a letter of support and a cheque to Bernadette Devlin: 'I wrote that I admired what she had done.'[25]) Twenty years later it was a different matter, the Provisional IRA having alienated liberal opinion everywhere by its campaign of destructiveness, with atrocity piled on atrocity. Subjecting the people of Northern Ireland to onslaughts of bombing, intimidation and terror did not seem a reasonable way of effecting reforms in the social sphere.

Brian Moore's later repudiation of the IRA's 'revolutionary' tactics was a reasoned, if distant, response to the circumstances prevailing at the time (i.e. the late 1980s). He never questioned the justice of resentments which simmered away through the years of Unionist misgovernment and finally erupted, only the channel the eruption was directed into, which ended by shifting universal sympathies away from the erstwhile underdog. (The final transformation of the century, of ex-IRA activists into peacemakers, had yet to come about.) When he wrote his 'Bloody Ulster' article, which the *Atlantic Monthly* published in September 1970, he was still bemused by the sudden 'newsworthiness' of his backward native province, by the terrible upsurge in sectarian violence (when things – *pace* the Civil Rights movement – had seemed to be slowly improving), and by the sight – relayed across the world – of British soldiers carrying guns on Northern Ireland's streets. At that moment, he judged direct rule from Westminster to be the only hope for the North: 'We cannot be left any longer in the dead hands of our Unionist masters, those masters who, in fifty years, have made us incurably, terminally sick with foolish religious prejudice and thus completely incapable of managing our own affairs,' he wrote,[26] resorting – untypically – to hyperbole, in response to scenes he'd witnessed, instances of ineradicable bigotry, 'the same old garbage . . . same old stupid mess'. He worried about his relatives who were there in the thick of it: 'You are . . . often in my thoughts these days,' he told his sister Una. 'It must be ghastly and it would seem it can only get worse . . . I have a vision of Belfast now looking worse than it did in the worst days of the Blitz.'[27]

It made him angry, because there'd been a moment at the end of the Second World War when he believed the international crisis had put things in perspective, causing Ulster to grow up, and grow out of its silly childish squabbles, Protestant versus Catholic (this belief is dramatised at the end of *The Emperor of Ice Cream*, when the ultra-nationalist father is brought to adjust his way of thinking). But no – bloody Ulster remained addicted to its infantilisms. Brian, indeed, applauded the Civil Rights movement in its drive to eradicate injustices, but couldn't contain his exasperation when the old tribal assertiveness proved so horribly irrepressible. It was back to his old instinctive belief that the only way to deal with Northern Ireland was to spend as much of one's life as possible away from it. And yet: when he stood with Jean in their Californian living-room watching bits of Belfast burning on the television screen, he understood that total deracination was not an option as far as he was concerned. Belfast was his birthplace, and he couldn't quite detach himself from its incorrigible goings-on.

The 'fact-finding tour of the Ulster barricades'[28] had taken place in August 1969, when all hell had just broken loose; Brian and Jean were staying at the time with Brian's sister Una and her doctor husband Diarmuid Maguire, at their home in Lurgan, Co. Armagh. Dr Maguire had driven them along the motorway, the M1, into Belfast where they joined a queue of cars 'sightseeing' the Troubles.[29] They had come North from Kerry and Dublin, and were going on to London, Paris, Amsterdam etc: the usual European tour. Their London address, on the borders of Hampstead, was a house loaned to them by Tom Rosenthal, then a director of the art publishers Thames & Hudson, and an admirer of Brian's work. While there, they gave a dinner party whose guests included old friends such as the Richlers, Frenches, Crookstons and Diana Athill. After returning home via New York and Montreal, they had Bill Weintraub to stay with them in December, and threw a party in his honour the week before Christmas. Early in the New Year, Bill came again with his wife Magda; and Brian turned down the offer of a job as Visiting Writer at Bowling Green, Ohio. Brian and Jean then had a short break in San Francisco, indulging their taste for staying in plush hotels.

Once he'd finished *The Revolution Script* and sent off the manuscript to his various publishers, Brian got back to *The Great Victorian Collection*, only to put it to one side again as a new idea took hold of him. (The new idea, centred on a community of monks on an almost inaccessible island off the coast of Ireland, evolved into the novella *Catholics*, which was published in 1972.) Meanwhile, after a short delay caused by the tardiness of Jack McClelland, *The Revolution Script* came out in Canada and the US at the end of 1971, and in the UK a couple of months later. The book did not do as well as expected in Canada, but in England it received full and conspicuous coverage,[30] with reviewers being about sixty–forty per cent in favour. Some, however, expressed misgivings about the lumping together of fact and fiction, a view with which Brian himself was inclined to agree. Eventually, he would dismiss the book as 'journalism', a blind alley as far as he was concerned, something he should never have been persuaded to undertake. It seemed a bit ironic, though, that he should be blamed for being too 'fantastical' in *Fergus*, and too 'documentary' in his next work. Such judgements, however, confirmed his own belief that, as an artist, he should simply follow his nose and write whatever he felt impelled to write, irrespective of potential sales, or predictable kudos. As he remarked to Bill Weintraub, *à propos* an early draft of *The Great Victorian Collection*, 'It proceeds with a spooklike life of its own, to my wonder and fingers-crossed pleasure.' That pleasurable take-over of the writing consciousness, though it didn't last at the time, was the spirit in which fiction was best composed. (In the same letter,[31] he mentions having turned down a 'lucrative offer' to write a biography of Charles Laughton, 'who it seems was raving queer and pander living in Hollywood in marriage of convenience with Dike Elsa Lanchester . . .'. The offer didn't tempt him at all.)

Part of the original attraction of the Cross kidnapping story was its cinematic possibilities, though in the event it became another of the many film scripts of his novels slaved over by Brian to no avail. It never was produced as a film, despite its suitability; along with all, or nearly all, the rest, it generated enormous interest, only to fall at the first or second hurdle. The producer Sidney Glazier had a point, one feels, when he invited the Moores to dinner at the Connaught Hotel in London, and, after an expensive meal and rather a lot of wine, advised Brian that he should give up writing film scripts and stick with good novels. Brian chose to interpret this remark as a ploy to establish whether he was serious about film writing, or considered it beneath him; but in fact, it seems a rather shrewd piece of counsel on Glazier's part. Brian's screenplays had a way of evading a practical outcome.

However, *The Revolution Script*'s immediate successor, *Catholics*, was successfully filmed in 1973 – though not by the proposed director, John Huston,[32] despite fraught and protracted negotiations. Sidney Glazier was the producer, the script was the work of Brian Moore, and Jack Gold directed the film for television, with Trevor Howard in the leading role, and Cyril Cusack playing Father Manus. Shooting took place in Ireland through the spring and summer of 1973, and the film was scheduled for the autumn. It won a Peabody Award in 1974, and some years later it was released for screening in the cinema. *Catholics* had begun life as a story, which grew to such an awkward length that Brian despaired of having it published at all. The idea was mooted that it might form the centrepiece, and much the longest contribution, to a collection of Moore stories; but in the end it came out separately, as a 'novella'. (It was around this time, at a dinner party, that Brian, hearing some pompous writer claim he had trouble keeping his novels to under 700 pages, chimed in: 'That's funny, I have trouble getting mine up to 200.')

It was clear from the start that *Catholics* was going to be a success, at least a *succès d'estime*. Tom Maschler of Cape called it 'a gem – absolutely wonderful'; and the *Bookseller* reported: 'The novel reviewers were all singing in sweet harmony over Brian Moore's *Catholics* . . . Indeed it is surprising that such a song of praise should not have wafted this novella on to the Booker shortlist.'[33] It missed the Booker, but it won the W.H. Smith Award – £1,000 – for the best novel of 1972, announced in August

1973, and presented in November. Brian was unable to get to London for the presentation, so Tom Maschler stood in for him. 'The missus and I celebrated quietly in our cottage with a fattening dinner and a bottle of rare California vintage vino,' he told Bill Weintraub.[34]

Brian Moore humorously divided novelists into two categories, 'putters-in' and 'takers-out', assigning himself firmly to the second category. *Catholics* represents the most extreme application of the principle of literary economy; it is pared down as far as it will go. This makes it probably the most austere and elegant of Brian Moore's works. It is set some years into the future (the 1990s), and on a remote island off the West Coast of Ireland where a community of monks is adhering to age-old traditions – the Latin Mass, private Confessions, etc – in the face of edicts from Rome and Amsterdam enjoining modernisation on them. A brash young American Catholic priest, James Kinsella, is sent to Muck Island on a mission to bring the mothballed monks into line with the rest of the contemporary Church. Catholicism has always been about conformity, indeed, but there are certain ironies prevailing in the situation depicted here. The Church in the world at large has almost been reformed out of existence as the spiritual element in Catholicism, its *raison d'être*, has given way to an overdose of ecumenism and updating. In *Catholics*, spirituality is equated with traditionalism; the most eloquent speech in the book is given to the old monk Father (sic) Manus, who sticks up for customs sanctified by immemorial usage, 'the mystery and the miracle of the Mass', as opposed to all the 'singing and guitars and turning to touch your neighbour, playacting and nonsense [designed] to make the people come into church the way they used to go to the parish hall for a bingo game'.

However, Muck Island and the nearby mainland, where traditional Mass is celebrated in the open, at what was once, during the Penal Days, a 'Mass Rock', have become places of pilgrimage for Catholics nostalgic for the old ways, and consequently are attracting considerable media interest, which is turning the whole caboodle into a show (a holy show). The Mass Rock is turning out to be no better an emblem of continuity than the Rock Mass.

So – Catholicism as a force is either an anachronism in the modern world, or a newfangled adulteration of inveterate doctrines; and to complicate matters, in this short novel, the Abbot of Muck Abbey, Tomas O'Malley, has himself suffered a crisis of faith – understandably enough, after being exposed to the hellish tawdriness of Lourdes – and now runs his religious community more as a secular enterprise than anything else. He hasn't arrived at this position without a good deal of angst. (Some critics have suggested a connection between O'Malley's moral crisis and that of Judith Hearne, but the difference is that the eponymous heroine was not a very intelligent or spiritual woman, and it was a failure of previously held certainties that assailed her, not a loss of faith as such.) Brian Moore, in *Catholics*, casts an ironic but not unsympathetic eye over varieties of belief and unbelief. After *Fergus*, it seems, he no longer felt the urge to spell out his bracing repudiation of the exorbitant Belfast Catholicism of his earliest years. Henceforth, Catholicism in his novels would appear in a wider context, allowing a more subtle appraisal of its uses and abuses. At one point in *Catholics*, for instance, someone justifies the Church's continuing existence in the modern world by designating it 'the quintessential structure through which social revolution can be brought to certain areas of the globe'; this aspect of its function was something to which Brian Moore would return in few of his later novels. Though he was and remained an agnostic, Catholicism and its effects continued to engage his imagination. As a force (he claimed) it was interchangeable with other forms of belief or commitment, guiding principles such as political idealism (*The Revolution Script*), sex (*The Doctor's Wife*) or the literary impulse (*The Mangan Inheritance*). He also claimed, because of his familiarity with the tenets of Catholicism, to find it a convenient metaphor for faith of whatever variety.

Catholics is beautifully written, as everyone agreed; it is neatly and cleverly composed and raises interesting (well, fairly interesting) questions about the continuing role of the Church. And yet – one misses the comic gusto of *Fergus*, the interaction between male and female characters (there are no women at all in *Catholics*, which may be an oblique dig at the religious mentality), the involving and ingenious plot. The Muck Island novella is indeed a 'purer' work of the imagination than its FLQ predecessor; but *The Revolution Script*, for all that, didn't really merit the final critical consensus which pronounced it 'readable, but a mistake'.[35]

It is, in fact, a compact thriller, a perfectly creditable and engrossing reconstruction of a striking sequence of events.

Early in 1971, Brian heard via 'the New Jersey Oberkommandatura' (as he jokingly put it) that his son Michael was set to embark on a medical career – following the family calling – and that he, Brian, was expected to foot the bill for this (it wouldn't, he was assured, amount to much more than Michael's current Solebury School fees). So it was necessary to keep the money coming in. Plans were still afoot to make a film of *Judith Hearne*, and the newest scriptwriter on the project was Shelagh Delaney, author of the celebrated play *A Taste of Honey* (1958). Delaney had been shipped over to New York on the *Queen Elizabeth II*, flown to Chicago (where the author Studs Turkel gave her a conducted tour of the city) and ferried on to Hollywood, arriving in due course to lunch on the Moores' 'sundrenched patio'.[36] 'Imagine me – wiv Katharine Hepburn!' she kept exclaiming, in broadest Lancashire. (Hepburn, still a contender for the leading role, was another of the Moores' luncheon guests, along with director Anthony Harvey.) And, 'Imagine *me* wiv Katharine Hepburn!' Brian quipped, describing the actress's appearance in a darned coolie jacket, cotton drill trousers and torn sneakers.[37] A week or so later, the Moores were dinner guests of Katharine Hepburn at her home in the hills above Sunset Strip, where considerable gossip took place concerning old Hollywood stars such as Mary Pickford, Jimmy Cagney, Spencer Tracy *et al*. Summer had come, with a vengeance, and back in Malibu surfers rode the waves outside the picture window from dawn till dusk. 'And so it goes,' Brian said, quoting Kurt Vonnegut.

13

ALARMS AND EXCURSIONS

She took a bus to the airport hotel . . . She woke at six a.m. San Francisco time, showered, dressed, and by eight o'clock was in a rental car driving south. Shortly before ten she turned off the freeway on to a road that led out to the Monterey Peninsula. She bypassed the resort town of Carmel to drive further south, down a coastal road built by convicts, into that lonely region known as the Carmel Highlands. Here, grey-green hills eased down to empty beaches, past arroyos over which seagulls wheeled and screamed.

Cold Heaven

WRITING TO BILL WEINTRAUB from Paris in September 1970, Brian Moore mentions a significant sighting in the street (near Rue Monsieur Le Prince). A lithe boyish figure, sockless in loafers and wearing a tan suit, and childishly rapping the windows of a medical textbook shop with a rolled-up newspaper, had passed by as Jean and he strolled along. Samuel Beckett. This, Brian said, was his second Nobel prizewinner – the first, W.B. Yeats, having been 'glimpsed eccentrically in pink shirt & with flowing white hair loping along a Belfast street'[1] over thirty years earlier. As it happened, a third – future – Nobel Laureate was about to come into his orbit. This was Seamus Heaney, who, in January 1971, with his wife Marie and children, drove down the Pacific Coast Highway during his stint at Berkeley to visit a revered senior – i.e. Brian Moore. Heaney had been including Brian's novels on his literature courses for some time, and was keen to say hello to his celebrated compatriot. Brian, in his turn, was impressed by Heaney's progress: 'Belfast to Berkeley in one year. V. good poet and getting old at 31!'[2]

The visit was a great success, and some years later it resulted in the Heaney poem, 'Remembering Malibu' – 'a memento of that terrific windy afternoon', Heaney wrote to Brian Moore, adding, 'I suppose in the end it is an admission that I can't shift myself out of the dirt I grew up in'.[3] 'Remembering Malibu' was published in the collection *Station Island* (1984).

Remembering Malibu
for Brian Moore

The Pacific at your door was wilder and colder
than my notion of the Pacific

and that was perfect, for I would have rotted
beside that lukewarm ocean I imagined.

Yet no way was its cold ascetic
as our monk-fished, snowed-into Atlantic;

no beehive hut for you
on the abstract sands of Malibu –

it was early Mondrian and his dunes
misting towards the ideal forms

though the wind and sea neighed loud
as wind and sea noise amplified.

I was there in the flesh
where I'd imagined I might be

and underwent the bluster of the day:
but why would it not come home to me?

Atlantic storms have flensed the cells
on the Great Skellig, the steps cut in the rock

I never climbed
between the graveyard and the boatslip

> are welded solid to my instep.
> But to rear and kick and cast that shoe –
>
> beside that other western sea
> far from the Skelligs, and far, far
>
> from the suck of puddled, wintry ground,
> our footsteps filled with blowing sand.

If he'd come at a different time of the year, perhaps, Heaney might have encountered a more stereotypical Pacific; however, as the poem implies, things are often less simple than the standard image suggests. The beehive hut, the storms and the Skelligs make an oblique allusion to *Catholics*, and the poem also refers to Brian Moore's more-or-less frictionless transplantation, in comparison with the poet's stronger local attachment. More or less, because, like Louis MacNeice's father, Brian 'Kept something in him solitary and wild'.[4] (The last line of 'Remembering Malibu' echoes MacNeice's '. . . no sign/Remains of face or feet when visitors have gone home'.) The places in which he felt most at home were by the side of oceans – the West of Ireland, Amagansett, Malibu, and, later, the Atlantic coast of Nova Scotia.

It was around this time that Brian began to be accepted as an Irish writer by other Irish writers; it was, he said, the generation which included Heaney and Brian Friel that first held out to him the prospect of assimilation (well, partial assimilation); as ever, he shied away from complete identification with any literary group, however nebulous or diverse. And he was often very funny about the kind of Irish writer he *wasn't*: the sort that had the auld da in the corner laying down the law, the obsequious parishioners kowtowing to the priest, and flamboyant gestures of patriotism. The idea of Northern Ireland as a centre of literary excellence took him by surprise, indeed – as well it might, given the doldrums of the years in which he'd passed his childhood there – but he saw it as a welcome and incredibly inspiriting departure. Ulster might have reverted to a lethal juvenility in its political strategies – you bomb ours, and we'll bomb yours – but the poetic efflorescence that overtook the province in the late 1960s testified to its achievement of maturity in another sphere. Its roster of poets, all of them to become famous to a greater or lesser degree, was as 'grown-up', complex, subtle, inspired and unprovincial as anyone could wish.

Even before he met Seamus Heaney, Brian had been in correspondence with the Co. Tyrone poet John Montague,[5] whose connection with small literary magazines such as *Threshold* had led him to solicit contributions from his fellow expatriate. (Montague lived in Paris at the time, and he and Brian had arranged to meet there on several occasions before they actually succeeded in doing so.) A piece on the erupting Troubles was suggested early in 1970, to go into a book on this theme, and Brian worked on it for a couple of months (in the event, it was amalgamated with the 'Bloody Ulster' article that was published by the *Atlantic Monthly*). Another Ulster poet was Derek Mahon, whom Brian had met in the bar of the Shelbourne Hotel in Dublin in the summer of 1969; Mahon was to become a valued, if distant, friend. This was true also of the playwright Brian Friel: Friel, at Brian's suggestion, prepared a *Judith Hearne* screenplay for Anthony Harvey after the one knocked off by Shelagh Delaney had proved unacceptable (it was, apparently, 'the result of 2 weeks' work and very poor', Brian wrote).[6] Friel's, which was in the hands of the proposed producer/director early the following summer (1972), was in a different category, Katharine Hepburn was free at the time and ready to start work, and a good crew was lined up. But financial problems with backers intervened to scupper the project: '*sicut erat in principio et nunc et semper*', Brian observed with resolute ruefulness.[7] (In the same month he was having fits over the dust-jacket Cape had commissioned for *Catholics*: with its helicopter, cute monks etc – he said – the thing looked like 'some book of religious votive exercise, or some leaflet which might be handed out by the Catholic Truth Society'.[8] He got his plain jacket in the end, but this delayed publication by a couple of months.)

In the late 1960s, Brian Moore's work attracted the attention of a broad-minded Irish Jesuit ordinand, Michael Paul Gallagher, who interviewed the novelist for *Hibernia* magazine (10 October 1969). A friendship[9] then developed between the two, with the priest – ordained in 1972 – assuming something of the role of theological adviser in connection with future novels of Brian's (starting with *Catholics*). Possibly each of them, the lapsed Catholic and the priest, felt himself to be exceedingly liberal in cultivating a *rapport* with the other, irrespective of ideological scruples. At any rate, an enthusiasm for philosophical and metaphysical matters drew them together, even if Brian's approach to the latter remained disinterested. They met up in Dublin in August 1972; Brian and Jean had just come from Donegal, where they stayed with the Friels and heard how, a week previously, Katharine Hepburn had swept into this 'rocky fastness' and amazed the locals by tearing about over the rocks on a bicycle, and ordering breakfast at 7.30 a.m. Before getting to Dublin and the Shelbourne – via Kildare – the Moores had managed 'a flying visit' to Belfast, which, Brian reported, 'was like spending an evening and afternoon in the ward of an insane asylum'.[10] To his sister he added, 'Belfast was grim and the Antrim Road is not exactly Fun City these days. However, I was fascinated to see it.'[11]

Ireland was, as usual, followed by London: 'Lunch Peter Crookston; Dinner Maschler; Party Martines', Brian's notebook records, sounding for the moment a bit like 'Jennifer's Diary'. (Lauro Martines and his wife Julia O'Faolain – novelist and short-story writer, and Sean O'Faolain's daughter – were friends from Los Angeles, who also spent part of the year in London.)

By the end of 1972 Brian was back at work on the novel he'd abandoned twice already: *The Great Victorian Collection*. When his brother Sean came to stay at Malibu in late November, he read the manuscript as far as it went, and declared himself to be gripped by the events depicted: though of course the success or otherwise of the novel would depend on how its metaphysical manoeuvrings were resolved. It was indeed 'a tough nut', Brian said; but one he was keen to get his teeth into. He was enjoying life – wouldn't have had any other, even if it entailed going out to lunch with Aaron Asher and being regaled with endless talk about Philip Roth and his million-dollar advances – an occasion that prompted Jean to make a joke about Brian being treated like the wife, and Roth like the mistress.[12] On Christmas day, the Moores were invited to the Dunnes', where guests dined on a ham cooked by Jean, turkey cooked by Joan Didion Dunne, and dessert supplied by the actress Katherine Ross.

So the social round continued. A few weeks later – barely

recovered from an attack of flu – they were back at the Dunnes' for a birthday party, and Brian was sitting mentally comparing himself to Count Dracula at the dinner table around ten at night, when the door burst open and in trooped a lively bunch of revellers, who included a young rock producer named Earl McGrath (a new friend of the Moores), the 'British pop painter' David Hockney, and Bianca Jagger wearing a strange hat and circus clothes. All this was a joy to the novelist, who felt he'd been vouchsafed a glimpse – albeit updated – of the world of Waugh.

In February, Brian and Jean attended an academic conference at the Banff Springs Hotel in Alberta, Canada, where Brian experienced an upsurge of Ulster common sense in the face of what had struck him as pretentious, heavy bullshit and academic jabber over the heads of the audience, the like of which 'I never did hear'.[13] Impelled by outrage, up rose 'professional hack' Moore to confess his bewilderment at all the stupendous nonsense he'd been forced to listen to, and to assert that, for his part, his 'main metaphysical concern daily was waiting for the mailman'.[14] Thunderous applause greeted this declaration, and a voice from the back of the audience was heard to shout, 'Thank God for Brian Moore!'

However, the organisers of the conference gave him the cold shoulder following this performance – a fact that dismayed him not a jot. *Someone* had to stick up for plain speaking. Academic jargon was anathema to him – and if denouncing it entailed denying his genuine 'metaphysical concerns', then so be it. After this triumph of sorts, it was on to beautiful British Columbia and the Bayshore Inn ('a dullish . . . hotel'), sightseeing excursions north of Vancouver and visits by boat to Vancouver Island. Before returning home, the Moores went to Calgary to see their friend Hallvard Dahlie (author of the first critical study of Brian's work). Back in Los Angeles, they attended a dinner in honour of Mordecai Richler.

It wasn't long before Brian was invited to contribute his own expertise to a segment of academic life. The University of California at Los Angeles approached him in connection with a ten-week course on the short story, which they thought he might run, beginning at the end of September (1973). This would involve nothing more arduous than conducting seminars, with ten or twelve selected students, one afternoon a week, reading their work and 'handing out gentle criticism',[15] and being paid around $550 per session. Money for jam. He was happy to accept. The course went ahead as scheduled, and was such a success that, the following year, Brian was offered an appointment as Regent's Professor for the Fall and Winter Quarters (September to March). These professorships were reserved for 'distinguished persons not formally associated with colleges and universities, who are able to spend a brief time with us . . .':[16] W.H. Auden had been an earlier recipient. Brian, gratified by all this, enjoyed the contact with students, and discovered that teaching – well, teaching at this advanced level – came easily to him. Before he started, he confessed, he'd had 'no notion of how I will hold my class or what to do with it',[17] but very soon it was going 'swimmingly'[18] – so swimmingly, in fact, that when the Regent's Professorship expired, he was asked to stay on, and continued holding his weekly seminar at UCLA right up until 1990. Out of forty or fifty applicants each year, he would choose around ten, and do his best to guide them through the pitfalls and technicalities of creative writing. Among his early students was a six-foot black boy in a woollen mob cap whose previous occupations had included selling vacuum cleaners and being an odd-job man in a whorehouse ('King of the Dirt Suckers' was the title of his story). And one would-be recruit, regretfully turned down, was a 'stunning' ex-airline stewardess who 'submitted a leather-and-bondage story to Prof Moore': it just wasn't up to scratch.[19]

Joking aside ('Prof Moore' and so on), Brian Moore's entry into academic life was a source of considerable satisfaction: at last he could consider himself on a level with such bygone luminaries as his uncle Eoin MacNeill, and know that his university appointment would have impressed his father, if only he'd been alive to applaud it. Indeed, Dr Moore would have appreciated the honour far more than Brian himself, whose late-twentieth-century, cosmopolitan knowingness had him constantly on the alert for ironies and anomalies, in his own life and elsewhere, of which there were plenty. At a very basic level, he was jubilantly aware of having overturned the verdict of bad old Belfast, all those years ago (whose disparagement of his abilities had struck deep). At the same time, he had no illusions about universities and their accoutrements, and would have had to resort to self-mockery if he'd found himself taking his academic upgrading seriously. As it was, the position at UCLA, on the periphery of the English Department, suited him fine; as with other aspects of his life, he found himself simultaneously attached and detached, somewhat to his amusement.

The position suited him, but he'd hardly set foot in the place before his critical faculties were aroused; everything seemed strangely casual, haphazardly organised. The English Department he judged to be 'very bad', and his academic colleagues on the whole confirmed his view of the species as irretrievably tedious. He found no brilliant lecturers or thinkers there, no Frank Kermode or Christopher Ricks. He claimed to have made only one good friend during his entire time at UCLA – Eugen Weber, from the History Department. Others, he felt, slightly resented his status as privileged outsider ('Not one of us') – though he didn't have tenure and posed no threat to them. 'They were just dull guys.' It was no hardship, however, to mingle even with unappealing colleagues at compulsory social events such as the Departmental Chairman's Reception or the Chancellor's Garden Party. The novelist's beady eye was ever on the *qui vive*.

One UCLA undergraduate (1979–82), whose opinion of the university more or less coincided with Brian's, was the writer Scott Bradfield, who later became a creative-writing tutor himself, and a friend of the Moores.[20] Arriving at the start of the autumn term in 1980, walking up and down a corridor and trying to recall the name of his English supervisor, to whom he had to deliver an essay, Bradfield was greatly excited to spot pinned up on a board a notice proclaiming, 'Brian Moore: Short Story Class'. He couldn't believe it – Brian Moore was one of his favourite novelists, and had been ever since he'd read *Judith Hearne* in the departure lounge of London's Heathrow Airport; by this time he'd got through about half of the Moore opus. So he started accosting people, demanding to be told if this was *the* Brian Moore, the author of *Judith Hearne* and other splendid novels; but even from Faculty members all he got was, 'Oh, I don't know – I guess so' – nobody had heard of him! This he considered typical: 'English professors don't read anything!'[21] In the middle of his loudly expressed enthusiasm, the ebullient Scott Bradfield noticed a door open across the corridor, and remain ajar; this was Brian's room, and there he was in person, sitting in it, and possibly overhearing the exclamations of an admirer. Bradfield went across and introduced himself, and in this way the two got to know one another. The following year Scott Bradfield took the course himself, and was impressed by Brian's conscientiousness, patience, and sensible, straightforward approach to teaching. He followed a pattern: each session was begun with a twenty-minute presentation, on creating character, how to make an impact in your opening paragraph, or whatever; after this came a discussion of students' work. 'He didn't throw a lot of theory at you.'[22] Alas, not all the students were there to pay homage to a master storyteller and thank their lucky stars that he happened to be available: some merely considered the creative writing option 'trendy'. And there was a further hazard for Brian: because of the individual attention he was able to bestow on the small number of students, a few developed the idea that they were in a special relationship with him, and for years after he'd resigned from the job he was pursued by letters beginning (playfully), 'Do you have nightmares about former students taking over your mailbox?' or (plainly), 'Do you remember me? I was your student when . . .', letters causing the recipient's spirits to wilt.

In the spring of 1974, Brian was in Toronto at York University taking part in an 'Irish Studies' conference organised by another of his fellow Northern Irishmen, the academic and theatre critic D.E.S. Maxwell (who also became a friend). The theme of the conference was 'The Writer in Society' and Brian was co-opted to sit on a panel discussing this topic with fellow panellists, playwrights Brian Friel and Denis Johnston – whose memoir of his wartime experiences, *Nine Rivers from Jordan*, Brian admired – and a Canadian crime writer named Hugh Garner.

He kept in touch with D.E.S. Maxwell, and at the end of the following year he was back in Toronto, giving a talk to students. At the celebratory dinner afterwards, in a nearby restaurant, Professor Maxwell mentioned that he'd held a seminar that afternoon on *The Feast of Lupercal*, whereupon Brian became very anxious to be assured that the students had picked up the symbolism of the blinkered horse in the closing sequence. Unlike many writers, he was never averse to discussing his work, explaining his intentions or pointing imperceptive readers in the right direction.

Brian, as Regent's Professor, was required to deliver a public lecture, and one was duly prepared by him under the title, 'The Writer as Exile'. However, on the scheduled date – 20 November 1974 – he was in hospital suffering from bleeding ulcers, inflammation of the pancreas and anaemia. It was an intensified outbreak of his old complaint. He was ministered to in a Hyatt House Hospital and released, after a week or so, with the usual caveats: no coffee, no alcohol, Gelusel every hour and no social activities whatsoever. After being checked by his doctor – and blood count permitting – he might, *might* be able to resume his teaching by the end of the month ('*Deo gratias*, as it is the present source of steady income').[23] All this, he said, made him feel decidedly *old*.

His ex-wife Jackie had a more serious complaint. In August 1973 Brian had telephoned Frank Russell at the Hunterdon farm and learnt that Jackie was ill; then in the post came 'a very nice and sensible letter'[24] from Jackie herself; awaiting the result of tests, she said, she should know by 20 September whether the news was good or bad. It was bad. Cancer was diagnosed,[25] and through the dismal round of treatments that followed, chemotherapy, surgery and so on, Jackie – by all accounts – behaved with great fortitude, and tried to live as normally as possible during her periods of remission. But it was a harrowing time for everyone concerned, especially for Frank Russell, who looked after her at home, and for Michael, who had to witness his mother's deterioration.

Brian's attitude to his first wife had undergone a number of adjustments by this time. First guilt, then anger at her crippling financial demands had turned her into a sort of bugbear in his life, but as time passed and his own fortunes improved, his earlier hostility was modified into a grim jocularity which came out in allusions to 'the New Jersey Oberkommandatura' and so forth. After he'd heard about her illness, and especially in view of her 'nice and sensible letter', sympathy for Jackie in her appalling plight was in the ascendant, as far as he was concerned; but it wasn't too long before she got slightly on the wrong side of him again. In his weakened state, still with a pancreatic infection, he had to endure a 'doom-friendly' phone call from his ex-wife, in which she told him all about *her* diseased pancreas and seemed to imply that his was in a comparable condition: not the most tactful of suppositions. (His illness elicited a much more satisfactory phone call from his son Michael, who possibly felt himself in danger of losing both his parents.) Thinking about Jackie, he concluded that – because of everything that had happened – all his old affection for her had evaporated; though naturally he felt sorry for her, as he would for anyone facing imminent death. That was what he believed at that particular moment; but it was, perhaps, an undue simplification, given everything that *had* passed between them.[26]

Jackie died in January 1976.[27] This freed Brian to resume, as far as possible, a fatherly role in the life of his son: since Michael was now a handsome, well-adjusted and confident young man (in fact, he possessed all the qualities Brian would have wished for himself, at the same age), it was more on terms of friendship than anything else that their new understanding was established. Brian, of course, had missed his son's turbulent teenage years (not that Michael had been a particularly turbulent teenager), the time when friction is apt to occur between parents and children.[28]

They had met, for the first time in a number of years, on Boston Common: this 'long-sought meeting' (on Brian's part) took place in the summer of 1974. Michael was a student at Boston University, and had a job lined up at Massachusetts General Hospital as a laboratory assistant working on tissues. But he was already thinking of switching from medicine to nursing, having come to the conclusion that doctors 'were a bunch of crooks' (as Brian had it). Eventually, Michael Moore was able to combine his nursing qualifications with his other interest, computers, to become a software designer for a variety of medical software companies. But first, by a long way, came the rapprochement with his father – encouraged by his mother Jackie, whose attitude had altered as a consequence of her condition. Brian (with Jean) flew to Boston from Toronto, where he'd been working on an article for *Travel & Leisure*. He and Michael had lunch at a small fish restaurant chosen by Brian, where, by a coincidence, the manageress turned out to be an ex-girlfriend of Michael's, whom he'd been trying to dodge for a couple of weeks: this circumstance generated a certain amount of merriment, and helped to overcome any awkwardness that might have existed between father and son. Then, in April 1976, three months after Jackie's death, Brian once again made the journey to Boston to visit his son; he'd been on a trip to Michigan for a conference at Wayne State University, and afterwards went on to Detroit and Toronto (where he dined on separate occasions with his old friends Kildare Dobbs and Jack McClelland). The friendly relations already reestablished were consolidated at this point.

A couple of months earlier, Brian had learnt that *The Great Victorian Collection* had won the James Tait Black Memorial Prize, in the UK, for the best novel published in 1975; and it was also about to net the Governor General's Award in Canada. It hadn't got to this stage without a struggle. This was the novel Brian had turned his back on several times, only to return to it as a new way forward occurred to him. 'Working on "new" GVC,' his notebook records at the start of 1973; exactly a year later, the same announcement appears. Between these dates, the book was finished and went to the typist, Miss Phyllis Terry, then it was revised and rewritten and went to the typist again. Eventually it made its way to Brian's agent Perry Knowlton, who – to the author's astonishment – not only liked it, but saw commercial possibilities in it. And Aaron Asher agreed, once the manuscript was forwarded to him. However, Tom Maschler put a damper on this initial enthusiasm by telling Brian that, in his view, although the 'fantasy' element of the book was satisfactory, it fell a bit flat when it came to characterisation. These comments set Brian off on yet another dogged rewrite – mostly carried out in London during the summer of 1974, which necessitated retyping by a London typist, who performed this task so badly that the manuscript had to go whizzing back to Los Angeles and Miss Phyllis Terry yet again. And so it went on.

The Great Victorian Collection is Brian Moore's 'Borgesian' novel, though another influence is Franz Kafka, the Kafka of *Metamorphosis*, for example: 'an impossible premise treated realistically'[29] was how Brian defined his central objective. The impossible premise is his 'secular miracle', the materialisation of a group of priceless artefacts in the parking lot of a motel in Carmel, California. (Carmel seems to have been associated in his mind with supernatural goings-on.) These objects have been dreamed up, literally, by a twenty-nine-year-old Canadian professor of history,

Dr Anthony Maloney (a near namesake of an earlier, less engaging character, boorish young Tony Maloney in *The Feast of Lupercal*); Maloney will find, like Frankenstein's creator before him, that he's brought into being more than he bargained for.

This is an extraordinary work, with all its *outré* elements – fantastical, allegorical – subsumed under a cast-iron realism (in accordance with the author's design). The realism keeps you reading, while the narrative inventiveness makes you marvel. When the *Irish University Review*[30] brought out a special 'Brian Moore' issue in 1988, one of the contributions that pleased the subject most was an essay by the Irish critic and academic Seamus Deane,[31] which begins by citing Umberto Eco's 'Travels in Hyperreality' (1986). What Eco has in mind, the instance 'where the American imagination demands the real thing and, to attain it, must fabricate the absolute fake', is exemplified in the Moore novel, which is, among other things, about questions of fakery and authenticity – and also, of course, about the inventions of the creative writer, the plots he dreams up. 'Moore's fable, so ingeniously wrought,' Seamus Deane goes on:

> is supple enough to intertwine several themes – the relation of the work of the imagination to reality, the history of sexual liberation and of anxiety, the relationship between America and Europe, the exploitation of culture in the industrial capitalist system, the issue of representation and representability, the authority of the secular world and the vengeful rebellions of the marginalised 'spiritual' energies. What has happened is either a miracle – the real thing – or a 'secular miracle' . . . not quite the real thing, but not a fake either.

One might add to these themes the oppressive residue from Victorian forebears; this strand, and all those identified by Seamus Deane, do indeed get into the novel, but in such an unportentous form that it's easy to overlook them altogether. On the other hand – as Philip French noted in his *TLS* review[32] – by stressing the novel's implications, rather than its content, you can make it sound 'a sombre thing indeed'. Which is misleading, he says, for it is in fact a work 'of great exuberance and inventiveness'.

*   *   *

Brian Moore had set himself a formidable literary task and pulled it off, though not without immense application. Before the final – Maschler-inspired – rewrite of *The Great Victorian Collection*, another setback had occurred, this time a practical one. Aaron Asher had fallen out with the president of Holt, Rinehart and resigned his position there, and Brian decided to resign along with him. Having accepted no advance, as yet, he was free to do as he pleased with his manuscript, and he preferred to stick with his editor rather than his current publisher (about whom he'd had reservations all along). But this left him publisherless for the moment, and meant that the book could not come out, as planned, in the autumn or winter of 1974. In the event, it appeared in June 1975, under the imprint of Farrar, Straus & Giroux (Ballantine reissued it a year later), while UK publication took place the following October.

By the time it came out in England, he was well into the final draft of his next novel, then called *Mrs Redden* but eventually to appear under the title *The Doctor's Wife*. This, a return to the naturalistic mode, was to figure among the most popular and commercially successful of Brian Moore's works, getting him, for the first time, on to the Booker shortlist (though its critical reception was, as ever, 'mixed'). 'On this book, unlike others, I have finally tasted the smell of riches which most successful authors must sense,' he told Bill Weintraub.[33] And to Aaron Asher he confided: 'When I began writing novels I rode a bicycle. I am now driving a new Mercedes 450 SI sports car (8-cylinder engine).' (It was, of course, out of the question to live in California without being able to drive; and after many lessons from Jean, Brian had passed the test in 1973. He became a proficient driver.)

Tom Maschler, when he read the typescript, wanted to know if the book was written consciously to get its author on to the bestseller lists: it's full of sex, he said. Of course it is, Brian countered; sex is its theme, sex as a credo, a substitute – one of his characteristic substitutes – for religion. Even in the face of complaints from reviewers – his two previous novels had set up expectations that this one didn't fulfil, the characters weren't interesting – he maintained that *The Doctor's Wife* was a good novel, because the sexual longings and risk-taking at its centre are undercut by the bleakness, the return to reality, of its resolution.

But this – twentieth-century – reality doesn't require a death to round off its exaltation/doldrums cycle. Mrs Redden is no Anna Karenina, though Tolstoy's heroine might figure among her literary predecessors, along with another. Within the Moore opus, there are several contenders for the 'Bovary' mantle; but this one, right down to its title,[34] surely comes closest to the Flaubertian prototype. It is, quite simply, a story of ecstatic adultery. And as with all such stories, there's a less ecstatic outcome. Sheila Redden is the Belfast doctor's wife who succumbs to passion in the South of France – Villefranche to be exact – with an American student ten years her junior. It was supposed to be 'a second honeymoon' for Mrs Redden, but her husband Kevin, in the thick of various emergencies in Belfast, postpones joining her in France until it's too late to come at all: this puts responsibility for what happens partly on his shoulders, though the implication is that the marriage was going to fall apart in any case. (One critic, Edna Longley, who disliked the book, notes drily – a fact important for anyone who lived through the Troubles – that Kevin gets scant authorial credit 'for his ministrations to bomb victims'.[35] In truth, the Northern Irish imbroglio and concomitant horrors function merely as a backdrop here, part of the provincial dreariness and lunacy Sheila Redden is escaping.)

In the narrative view, Mrs Redden has come to her senses, while in the view of certain other characters in the book, including her brother Owen, another doctor, she has taken leave of them. ' "This decision of yours could be a sign of mental illness." ' Sheila herself, harking back to her Catholic upbringing, is sure of one thing only: this is grace, she has achieved a state of grace, whereas her whole previous life was lived in a state of sin. You can read this and other narrative flourishes as a way of elevating a fairly commonplace story, or as an elaboration of the heroine's complex personality: and both responses were current at the time of publication. No one, however, was in any doubt about the sheer professionalism of the undertaking, even if, for one or two commentators, professionalism was not enough.

The Doctor's Wife did not win the Booker Prize; the story was told that Mary Wilson, one of the judges that year, had disliked its sexual explicitness and therefore ruled it out. The prize went to

David Storey for his *Saville*. This was a disappointment – but the book had already done well enough to make it a minor one. And many people had enjoyed reading it, and wrote to tell Brian so, including his son Michael: 'A bit strange at first (naughty bits by one's father) but after that barrier, I found a really good book.'[36] Inevitably – as with *Mary Dunne* – among those in possession of even the most meagre biographical information about the author, there arose considerable speculation as to whether or not the story had a foundation in reality. If the title phrase was construed as a clue, rather than a gesture in the direction of the nineteenth-century predecessor, there was indeed no shortage of candidates for the part. But this is no *roman-à-clef* (or if it is, to any degree, it's irrelevant by the time the transforming power of fiction has been to work). It is, basically, a celebration of the sexual drive and its potential for cutting the dead wood out of one's life.

During the London sojourns, throughout the 1970s, there were many splendid occasions: 'big Slattery party with Peter O'Toole et al.',[37] at which the most interesting episode turned out to be a conversation with Anthony West (son of Rebecca West and H.G. Wells); tea with Tom Maschler and Doris Lessing; dinner with the hard-drinking Kingsley Amis whose talents as a mimic went down well (this was a gift he had in common with Brian). There were lunches with Richard Ellmann, Lindsay Anderson, Julia O'Faolain and Lauro Martines – before Brian took 'a scunner' at the latter; dinners with V.S. Pritchett (whose view of Belfast, which he called 'detestable',[38] may well have coincided with Brian's – unless it drove Brian to defend his birthplace), Tom Rosenthal, Mordecai Richler. Life – at least the literary life – was being lived to the full. A few of the Moores' trips abroad took place under the auspices of the magazine *Travel & Leisure*, which dispatched them to the West Coast of Ireland for a piece on Irish country house hotels, to the French Riviera, and (once back home) to Santa Barbara. In Ireland, as well as enjoying the luxury-hotel round, they stayed in a house rented from the journalist Penny Perrick in Roundstone, Connemara – a three-storey, five-bedroom manse; and (a couple of years later) in 'a simple Irish farmhouse' in Goleen, Co. Cork, borrowed from their old friend Tomi Ungerer, the recent purchaser, to the bafflement of many, of 230 acres of rough Irish soil complete with twelfth-century ruined castle: a quixotic purchase which the Moores applauded.

Whenever they found themselves in Ireland, or anywhere within reach, they'd scurry across for a 'nervous visit' to Brian's home town. They were there in October 1975, for example, for an Irish Television documentary featuring 'Brian Moore in Belfast', and registered the streets filled with soldiers, guns trained on passers-by, the close body-searches at every checkpoint. When Brian appeared briefly on a local news programme, he received a letter from his sister Grainne in Ballymena, in which she commented on his resemblance to Aunt Maggie Moore and Grandfather Moore. 'She has a wonderful way of making you feel at home.'[39] Belfast was sinister and disorientating – a far cry from stately Clifton Street, horse-and-cart traders and shawled old women trudging past the Central Lending Library. The things they saw were filed away in Brian's mind for future reference. To keep his spirits up, he writes to Bill Weintraub mentioning an advertisement for the film *Deep Throat*, which he has relished, and which Bill will relish: 'After Jaws there is only Deep Throat.'

For a time in the mid-1970s, the Moores were in danger of losing their house: Los Angeles County had plans to turn the whole area into a County Beach, and this entailed the compulsory purchase of properties along that stretch of coast. Several of their neighbours, including the Dunnes, moved away as a consequence, and this left Brian and Jean more isolated than ever. But they stuck it out, feeling a bit like squatters, and eventually gained a reprieve from the State; encouraged, they promptly 'set about doing all the things that have needed doing these last two years'.[40] Painters, carpenters, electricians and plumbers took over the house and restored it to scintillating order. Part of the money to pay for this refurbishment came from the sale of Brian's papers to the University of Calgary in Alberta. Negotiations in connection with this sale had been going on since 1974 – the original idea having come from Hallvard Dahlie. The Calgary librarian, Kenneth Glazier, had visited Malibu to discuss the proposed acquisition. By May 1975, Brian was able to report to Bill Weintraub,[41] 'Eight cartons of Moore memorabilia etc. stand packed and waiting the Bekins man tomorrow *en route* to Calgary and oblivion'; and the following November a small ceremony took place in the Library at Calgary to inaugurate the Brian Moore Collection.

Brian, at the time, was basking in 'the respectful status' finally being accorded to him in Britain, as he told his old friend[42] (à propos The Great Victorian Collection). He also mentions an interview in the Guardian 'which describes me as a "wide" man, with "a face that looks lived in"'. Another instance of his growing literary stature was the publication of Jeanne Flood's book on him in the Bucknell University Press 'Irish Writers' Series in 1974. Brian wrote a polite letter to the author of this study, though in private he deemed it pretty wide of the mark, especially in the area of psychoanalytic assumption (see p. 72 above). 'When it comes out over there,' he told his sister drily, 'you will see that I have a very "complicated relationship" with Daddy. According to Miss Flood.'[43]

The death from cancer of his old friend John Vachon in April 1975 was a blow to Brian Moore, as was the death of his first wife – though, as we've seen, the emotions aroused by the latter were not straightforward. ('I felt very sad about her,' he wrote to his sister Una.) Add to these his own health scares, and it's easy to see why death was on his mind when he wrote, or revised, his best-known short story, 'The Sight' – commissioned for a collection of Irish Ghost Stories, edited by Joseph Hone and published by Hamish Hamilton in 1977. This concerns a New York lawyer whose doctor has summoned him back for a further medical test, following an earlier examination, and whose Irish housekeeper is possessed of second sight . . . It's a succinct and skilful exercise in the uncanny.

The year 1976 was something of an 'annus Moore mirabilis',[44] as Brian put it, what with the James Tait Black Memorial Prize, the Governor General's Award, the Booker nomination, and the UK screening of Catholics on ITV. The year ended on a happy note, too, with Michael Moore and his girlfriend Karen (later to be his wife) coming to Malibu for Christmas. At the same time, plans were afoot for a dramatisation (by Bill Morrison) of The Emperor of Ice Cream to open in Dublin at the Abbey Theatre. But Brian, cautious by nature, and never one to take good fortune for granted, was unable to glory in all this without adding a caveat for himself: 'Surely the fates have some terrible retribution in store for me.'[45] In fact, when it came, it wasn't as terrible as it might have been, though it was pretty appalling at the time. It happened in Dublin, in July 1977, on the opening night of the re-run of Bill Morrison's play based on Brian's novel. Things had gone well, the performance was over, and the author was on his way up the aisle to join the cast back-stage for a celebration, when he suddenly collapsed and had to be rushed into Jervis Street Hospital. ('My God,' said a member of the cast when he heard the news, 'surely we weren't as bad as all that!') It was the old trouble – duodenal ulcers – but a devastating attack. Brian was in Intensive Care for three weeks, and in hospital for five. During this fraught period Jean stayed on at the Shelbourne Hotel but spent most of her time at Brian's bedside. He was subjected to surgery immediately after being admitted to hospital, but it transpired later that the operation was botched, and it was going to take a further operation – whenever he was up to it – to put things right. 'The luck of Lazarus' ('twice he's come back from the dead') was a phrase coined by Hermione Lee[46] to describe Brian Moore's two dramatic brushes with death – the swimming accident, and then the Dublin débâcle.

While he lay in his hospital bed, Brian was visited by several relatives and friends, including the Jesuit priest Michael Paul Gallagher. Sean O'Faolain sent his greetings – 'from one old hospital lag to another'.[47] Rumours about Brian's health abounded. 'I was shocked to hear how ill you were in Dublin,' Seamus Deane wrote to him.[48] Diana Athill was told categorically that it was 'a very massive heart attack'[49] that had laid him low, before a true version of events was relayed to her by John Gregory Dunne. ('It must have been an unimaginably dreadful experience for both of you . . .') Released from hospital on 31 August, Brian spent a week at the Shelbourne recuperating, before he and Jean set out for London. From London they flew to Montreal, returning home at the end of September. There followed a succession of doctor's appointments, blood tests, etc, before the second operation in April 1978 (at UCLA Hospital), and a further period of convalescence.

The previous October, restored to a kind of health, Brian had begun work (again)[50] on the novel which was to follow *The Doctor's Wife*, and which had required some research in Cork and Galway (for local colour) and in Dublin (to check certain biographical facts). Possible titles for this novel went as follows: *Brothers and Sisters Have I None, His Father's Son, My Father's Son, Family Album, The Closing Ritual*. But it was published (in 1979) as *The Mangan Inheritance*, and it extended the author's range by dovetailing Irish gothic into North American realism. Jamie Mangan, minor poet, born in Montreal, living in New York, is the central character who inherits a lot of money from his actress wife, having already inherited his face from an ancestor who may or may not have been the original *poète maudit*, James Clarence Mangan. Mangan, dissolute Dubliner, drunkard, opium addict, passed his life 'Amid wreck and sorrow,/And want, and sickness, and houseless nights . . .'[51] while managing to turn out an impressively pain-racked body of work, including the well-known 'Dark Rosaleen' ('Woe and pain, pain and woe,/Are my lot night and noon . . .'). He died in 1849 aged forty-six. The Moore novel is based on the speculation that Mangan, just possibly, might have married a Cork farmer's widow and produced a son. If this was so, the face, the poetic ambition and the bad end – all three going together – were supposed to recur in each successive generation.

The Mangan Inheritance is, among other things, a satire on the impulse to track down one's ancestors, on romantic Ireland and on poetic pretensions. To underline a few of its points it has to go over the top (hence the gothic overlay); but its hero's relative colourlessness balances the highly coloured ingredients of the plot. It's centred on a number of ironies, the first of these being the fact that Jamie Mangan's famous wife had just decided to divorce him, before going off with her lover to get herself killed in a freeway accident; it's her money that finances his trip to Ireland to investigate his family history, from the starting-point of Drishane, Co. Cork. It isn't long before Jamie uncovers some Irish relatives, other Mangans, tight-lipped, mad, sluttish, dwarfish and abominable in succession, and discovers that his blood-line incorporates horrors, incest and mutilation among them. These horrors caused at least one reviewer, a bit unkindly, to cite *Cold Comfort Farm*,[52] before concluding that the book wasn't up to the usual standard of 'a prodigiously talented novelist'. Others, including Christopher Ricks, disagreed.[53] This novel, Brian Moore's twelfth, succeeded no less than its predecessors in generating conflicting responses.

Tom Rosenthal, praising the book, believed it might come to be regarded as Brian Moore's 'richest and most adventurous and most powerful novel',[54] and indeed, in its narrative control, its playfulness and intensity, and its deflation of a myth or two in the Irish armoury (the poetry, the wild blood), it stands alone. The Irish inheritance, if you like, in this reading boils down to a deluded sexual pervert inhabiting a roofless ruin.

The ruin, in fact, can be located precisely to the Co. Cork territory acquired by the Moores' friend Tomi Ungerer, just as the background of Jamie Mangan, the fictional character, includes an upbringing in Lansdowne Avenue in Montreal, with a father who's a managing editor with the Montreal *Gazette*. This accords with Brian's usual practice: items imported from real life, creatively juggled, contribute authority to all the Moore fictions.

At the start of 1979, Brian was engaged in research in connection with what he called his 'nuns novel', but by April this had been put aside while he reconsidered a different story, the 'Mary Ellen story'. This evolved into *The Temptation of Eileen Hughes*, after the nationality of the characters concerned had been changed from Canadian to Northern Irish. In fact, work on both these projects, the nuns and Mary Ellen, continued in tandem, along with teaching at UCLA, an end-of-term party at the Moore house for fifteen students and their partners, Rolling Stones concerts, a dinner for André Deutsch (six guests), visits from Moore siblings including Marie-Therese from New Zealand, and the usual trips abroad. (The year ended with the Moores in Hawaii as guests of the Dunnes.) After the Dublin health upheaval, the vigorous social round, with accompanying periods of intensive work, was resumed as soon as possible.

14

A SIXTY-YEAR-OLD SMILING PUBLIC MAN

Belief is an obsession of mine. I think everybody wants to believe in something – politics, religion, something that makes life worthwhile for them . . . So faith is my obsession. And politics in a general way. Not documentary. But politics as . . . Well, look at the great Russian writers. They were often dealing with highly political situations, but they didn't turn them into newspaper stories. They managed to find something universal and truthful in them. That's what I try to do in my political books. I try to look for that sense of truth in the character, never to make somebody do something that I don't believe in, simply to make the plot work.

Interview with Joe O'Connor, 1995

THE DAY BEFORE *The Mangan Inheritance* was published in the UK – 8 November 1979 – Brian Moore made a new start on the 'Eileen' story; but two weeks after that, his notebook records bluntly, 'Stuck on book'. A couple of breaks then occurred; in January Michael Moore came for a visit, term began at UCLA, and Brian signed up for a course of lessons to enhance his swimming capabilities (for health reasons; he'd also joined the Malibu Riding and Tennis Club). In March, the Moores had a couple of days in San Francisco, and when they got home Jean read a draft of the novel, which was going under the title, 'The Girl Who Was God'. She pronounced it humourless, the central character shadowy, unlike Brian's other work. However, she was much happier with a revised version which she read some weeks later. Then it was off to Seattle for the world première of the stage version of *Catholics*,[1] followed by a brief visit to London, meetings with friends such as Derek Mahon, a dash up to Manchester to see Eilis in her convent, and back home via Halifax, Montreal and Toronto.

The Temptation of Eileen Hughes, the novel that had caused such bother in the writing, required further adjusting after Aaron Asher had read the manuscript and suggested a few amendments. It's an odd story (and oddly unconvincing) about an Irish Catholic businessman in the grip of a chaste obsession with one of his employees. Eileen Hughes is the twenty-year-old sales assistant who lives with her mother in a Northern Irish market town (Lismore – Lisburn), and has attracted the attention of her rich employers the McAuleys, who kindly take her with them on a trip to London. Eileen thinks she's a protégée of Mona's, but in fact it's Bernard McAuley – ex-seminarist married to a worldly wife – who has lost his head in the face of the shopgirl's allure. His wife Mona goes along with his *idée fixe*, to preserve her marriage and the security it brings – just as Bernard goes along with Mona's practice of picking up strange men in pubs and taking them back to her hotel room. Eileen herself is presented as rather dim-witted and friendless – in fact, they make an unsavoury trio, the spoiled priest, promiscuous wife and guileless (not to say gormless) employee.

The Temptation of Eileen Hughes presents a further exploration of the various secular outlets for quasi-religious fervour which forms an important strand in Brian Moore's work: Eileen is, explicitly, a god-substitute as far as Bernard is concerned. We know this because the author tells us so, but cannot understand why it should be. The story is eloquently told, and after a certain point it grips the reader; but the narrative isn't free of irritations, aside from the central implausibility: for example, these Northern Irish people keep saying 'someplace' in the American manner, instead of *somewhere*. This betokens a most unusual carelessness. And this is the book in which the whole of the violence, sectarianism and disaffection in the North of Ireland is crammed into a single embittered observation on the part of a minor character, and virtually left at that: 'Nothing but British Army patrols and searches and bombs and shootings and burn-outs.'

However – *Eileen Hughes* was generally well received when it came out in 1981, and some years later it was adapted successfully for television, with Ethna Roddy, Jim Norton and Angharad Rees in the leading roles, and Tristam Powell as director.[2] By the time the book was published, Brian was well into his next novel, which started life as *The Call*, became *The Troubled Midnight*, then *The Marian Legend*, and finally *Cold Heaven*. (It was a new incarnation of the 'nuns' story which dated back to 1979.)

During the 1980s, Brian Moore's reputation was consolidated. In May 1981 he was in Worcester, Massachusetts, to receive an honorary degree from the Assumption College there; a month later, Thames Television sent a production team to Malibu for a South Bank film with Melvyn Bragg; in 1982, Brian was invited (by Canadian film producers John Kemeny and Denis Heroux) to prepare a script for a television dramatisation of Simone de Beauvoir's *The Blood of Others*, to be directed by Claude Chabrol. Brian agreed to this, even though he didn't like the book ('such an awful novel'), and his script was approved after it had gone through several drafts. The project entailed meetings with Chabrol, and with de Beauvoir herself, from whom he concealed his true opinion of her fiction. The Neil Gunn International Fellowship came to him in 1983, courtesy of the Scottish Arts Council: £3,000 for a three-week tour of Scotland, plus fares and expenses for himself and Jean. This was a delightful interlude – all he had to do in return for the VIP treatment and enjoyable sightseeing was to prepare the official Neil Gunn lecture to be delivered in Edinburgh. A couple of years later, the National Film Board of Canada produced an hour-long documentary on Brian Moore, beginning with an interview out-of-doors in Malibu, and including shots in Belfast. In 1986, his novel *Black Robe* walked away with the Heinemann Award of the Royal Society of Literature, and more was to come: the *Sunday Express* Prize, the Canadian Authors' Association Prize, and (jointly with John Montague) the Hughes Prize in Dublin, all for *The Colour of Blood*. Back in Malibu, social engagements continued to proliferate (in the intervals of the quiet life), including dinners in the company of celebrities ranging from Christopher Isherwood to Mick Jagger.

All this was splendid; however, the tribute Brian Moore found most gratifying, perhaps, was the award of an honorary degree of Doctor of Literature from Queen's University, Belfast – 'the city whose scrupulous meanness he [had] bitterly exposed'.[3] A wheel had come full circle, as the one-time unsuccessful university aspirant achieved a triumph unimagined in his St Malachy's days. Because of his indisputable eminence, Belfast had had to back down, just as he'd vowed it would in his 'Preliminary Pages for a Work of Revenge'. Revenge, however, was no longer an element in his standpoint; the mood was mellower now, as he followed Yeats in his guise of 'sixty-year-old smiling public man'.[4] Professor John Cronin, in his citation for Brian Moore, described him as 'the most internationally celebrated of contemporary Irish novelists', and went on to praise his 'commitment to the Horatian principle of combining instruction with delight'. For, he added, with justice, 'Brian Moore is, above all, that most traditionally Irish of creatures, a great storyteller.' It was an appropriate commendation, the implied linkage being not only with the boy in Clifton Street who made up stories to amuse his siblings, but harking back to the great Donegal *seanchaidhe*, storytellers, entertainers, wordspinners whose recitations were among the glories of the Gaelic oral tradition.

Brian Moore's storytelling expertise is greatly in evidence in his novel of 1983, *Cold Heaven*. Given the plot, in connection with which the word 'preposterous' springs to mind, a lesser author would never have achieved the necessary suspension of disbelief on the part of the reader. You have to suspend disbelief to enter into the mood of the novel which is actually *about* disbelief – and the ultimate triumph of free will – though it's cast in the form of a thriller, albeit with a central metaphysical motif. It opens with an incident taken directly from life: the accident with the speedboat during the writing of *Judith Hearne*, and its near-fatal consequences. The scene is shifted to the Baie des Anges, in the South of France, where a Dr Alex Davenport, on holiday with his wife Marie, is struck on the head while swimming and apparently dies. Marie, who'd been planning to leave him in any case (another Moore motif), is overtaken by guilt and misery. But an extra complication enters into her state of grief. 'Is it because of what I didn't do?' she wonders. 'Did they kill him because of that?'

The effect of Marie's musings, at this point, is to make the reader imagine some shady conspiracy or intrigue at the back of an ordinary holiday disaster, and one goes on envisaging something of the sort even when Alex's body disappears from the hospital morgue, apparently under its own steam. In the Davenports' hotel room, later that day, there are signs to indicate that the corpse has been back to collect its belongings. Marie tracks it to the airport at Nice, to their New York apartment, and finally to a motel in Carmel, California, where at last she comes face-to-face with the husband she had left for dead.

Misdiagnosis? Nothing so rational is at the root of this particular piece of fiction. Here indeed is a dead man who won't lie down, a very testy Lazarus who prefers to say nothing at all about his singular experience: poor Alex, with reason, is terrified of acquiring fame as a medical freak. Besides, he isn't altogether out of the tomb yet; his state of animation depends very much on his wife's state of mind. While Marie is rebellious, Alex becomes comatose; when she is tractable, he revives. She sees the three of them, herself, Alex, and her lover Daniel – another doctor – as puppets jerked out of true by some peeved celestial being: these odd and frightening events, she understands, are due to her failure to act on instructions issued to her by an apparition, an apparition of the Virgin Mary.

This heavenly vision, Our Lady of Monterey, had materialised in front of Marie, during a previous visit to the spot, and ordered her to see to it that the site in question, a rock along the coast of the Monterey Peninsula, should become a place of pilgrimage. She had shirked the task – hence the accident to Alex, as a reminder to her of a duty undone. Marie – not even a Catholic, despite a convent schooling – increasingly feels herself to be the object of some extra-terrestrial persecution. Bits of the natural world are roped in to reinforce the divine notification: a cloud of butterflies leads Marie, the reluctant visionary, to the uncanny spot; and later, a small earthquake causes a crucifix-shaped split in the sacred rock. 'Rocks', as the Irish poet Joseph Mary Plunkett[5] once reminded us, 'are His written words' – and earthquakes, no doubt, a means of emphasising a point.

W.B. Yeats's 'The Cold Heaven', however, is the poem which supplies a title, as well as containing a clue to the novelist's purpose: Yeats's phrase, 'the injustice of the skies', directs us to the book's main theme. There is, though, another, gaudier poem, 'The Hound of Heaven' by Francis Thompson, which would have done just as well as an explicating agent. *Cold Heaven* is the story of a divine pursuit: ' "the sinner pursued by God, so to speak" ', someone says towards the end of the book.

Or is it? As one critic[6] remarked, Marie Davenport is like the governess in *The Turn of the Screw*: 'brave if there are ghosts, crazy if there aren't'. But the drift of the narrative encourages us to rule out madness on Marie's part; as in the conventional thriller,[7] these things are really happening, suspense builds up, and the denouement is managed with verve and conviction. It's only the aftertaste that sticks in the gullet, with the theophanic device, the Virgin on the rock with her ridiculous demands, seeming as lurid as Lourdes, as fatuous as Fatima. Of course Brian Moore is saying that one can choose to do without religion, in particular the Catholic religion, but this entails – if only in the realm of the imagination, only as a system of belief – taking it seriously in the first place. It's as if the Belfast pragmatist is subordinated, if only for the moment, to the California visionary: and for this reason, the central conceit seems considerably less satisfactory than the complementary 'secular miracle' (also located in Carmel) of *The Great Victorian Collection*.

By the time *Cold Heaven* came out in 1983, Brian Moore had parted, amicably, from Aaron Asher, whose moves he felt he could no longer keep up with; and on the recommendation of his agent Perry Knowlton, had acquired a new editor, Billy Abrahams. Brian and Jean were having lunch one day on the terrace at Malibu, when 'Billy came bouncing in – and I immediately took to him. Very witty, very bright . . . a couple of years older than me . . . being roughly the same age, having been around much the same circuit . . . this meant we had a lot to talk about.' Going with Abrahams entailed moving back to Holt, Rinehart, with this one book, before switching to E.P. Dutton with *Black Robe* in 1985. (Dutton sent Jerry Bauer to photograph Brian for publicity purposes.) Under the terms of his employment with both these firms, Billy Abrahams was entitled to issue works by his particular group of authors under his own imprint: 'A William Abrahams Book'. His small select list of authors included Lillian Hellman, Muriel Spark and Joyce Carol Oates: 'All those ladies – and you!' he used to joke to Brian. He and Brian became great friends – 'phone pals', Brian put it, since, in his isolation at Malibu, he'd often ring Billy in San Francisco to get all the news and gossip. (Billy Abrahams was a homosexual whose partner was Peter Stansky of Stanford University.)

At one point during their association, Billy advised Brian that the publishing firm of Dutton was about to be taken over by a large conglomerate, and that it would be in Brian's interests to move elsewhere. Brian acted on this advice and went with Nan Talese at Doubleday for a time, before returning to Billy Abrahams when the Doubleday venture proved unsatisfactory.[8] 'And we've had a happy marriage ever since,' he joked. His last novel, *The Magician's Wife* of 1997, came out under the William Abrahams imprint (Billy died the following June). Brian was always at pains to stay on good terms with those he worked with, through all the vicissitudes of the publishing enterprise. If a person was a colleague, he said himself, or involved with him in some commercial capacity, he'd make endless allowances for any shortcomings they might reveal, rather than acting on the 'scunner' principle that operated in other areas of his life. (Of course, he added, if the latter did come into play, then the severance would be total.) This is no doubt the reason why so many colleagues, or co-workers, did become close friends.

The 1970s was Brian Moore's most productive decade (five novels, or six, if you count *The Revolution Script*). Four titles were published during the 1980s, and a further four in the last decade of his life. *Cold Heaven* was followed by *Black Robe*, Brian Moore's unearthing of unimaginably shadowy terrain: seven-teenth-century Canada, north-west of Quebec, with its savages and savageries, its fur-traders and missionaries and powerful sense of menace. It's the story of a journey into the heart of darkness (the Conradian echo contributes to the novel's resonance), undertaken by a Jesuit, Father Paul Laforgue, with a young French boy for company and a troupe of unpredictable Indian guides. Laforgue is another of Brian Moore's morally afflicted priests, the would-be worshipper beset by doubts, embodiment of the struggle between a humanistic appreciation of the complexity of moral issues, and a monolithic devoutness. 'Black Robe' is cut from the same cloth as the Abbot of *Catholics*, or Father Michel in *No Other Life*.

The Jesuits in North America, by the nineteenth-century Amer-ican historian Francis Parkman, made a starting-point for this fictional exploration of clashing cultural beliefs and traditions.

(An 'Author's Note' at the start of the novel acknowledges Graham Greene's discussion of this work, in his *Collected Essays*, which directed Brian Moore's attention to it in the first place.) From Parkman, Brian Moore went on to the *Relations* themselves, the series of letters from the Jesuit missionaries to their superiors back in France, which had been the historian's primary source. (The UCLA Library was always a great help to Brian in his researches.) Having immersed himself in the literature of the period, he then allowed his imagination to come into play, and the result is an adventure tale, an account of a journey towards enlightenment and a striking exercise in historical re-creation, right down to the scatological speech of the Huron, Iroquois and Algonquin Indians, with their fucking this and asshole that. (For some reason, these obscenities in the mouths of Indians sound oddly endearing – ' "Shit!" she said. "Eight nights?" "We will drive hard. With any fucking luck we might do it in seven" ' – and so on.)

Brian Moore often deplored the fact that traditional narrative forms (the quest, the epic journey), along with so-called 'genre' fiction (the historical novel, the thriller), tended to be left in the hands of inferior authors; part of his objective, in the latter part of his writing life, was to reclaim such forms for mainstream literature. 'I've become fascinated with tension, narrative, pace,' he told one interviewer.[9]

The writing of *Black Robe* had begun in the summer of 1983, shortly before the publication of *Cold Heaven*, and while revision of the five-hour television drama, *The Blood of Others*, was still going on. (The title[10] didn't come until the following year, when it was suggested by Jean.) Grants from the Canadian Arts Council enabled the Moores to visit places in Canada where records were kept of 'Iroquois, Algonquin and Huron history and customs, and sites of early Iroquois and Huron settlements, in particular, the village of Midland, Ontario, where the Ontario government has accurately reconstructed longhouses, a village, and the original Jesuit mission established there'.[11] Parts of the novel were written at a house on the wild southern shore of Nova Scotia, not far from the town of Liverpool (and close to the site where the Moores were to build their second home, within the next ten years or so). Most years, they'd managed to visit Jean's mother during the summer at her Annapolis Valley home; and after her death in 1982 they came round to the idea of establishing a base of their own in Jean's native province, though it was some years before conditions were right to enable this project to come to fruition. (Jean was drawn to the South Shore because of her memories of happy childhood holidays spent on an island off the coast, with a lighthouse keeper and his family.) In the meantime, an isolated, pastel-coloured, timber-framed house was available for them to rent, during the summer months. It had to be the summer, since their years in Malibu had made them disinclined to put up with the worst extremes of the absolute Canadian winter.

Their friend Denis Heroux read the manuscript of *Black Robe* in a single sitting, and immediately telephoned to say he'd like to make a film of it (this was in August 1984). In fact the deal was agreed by the following March, shortly before the US publication date; though the film – directed by Bruce Beresford, and with the Quebec actor Lothaire Bluteau in the leading role – only went into production in 1990, and received its first showing in June 1991. It was something of a disappointment that *Black Robe* failed to make the Booker shortlist, despite excellent reviews, and despite Tom Maschler's high hopes for it: he told Brian that, of all his novels, this was the one he'd considered most likely to walk away with the prize;[12] and critics such as Hermione Lee deplored its exclusion from the shortlist. Brian, who was in Ireland at the time, in Dublin and then in Belfast, claimed to have forgotten all about the Booker until he opened the *Irish Times* and discovered that he wasn't a contender. But by now – as ever – he was more interested in his next novel, which was still at a rudimentary stage: it concerned a cardinal in an Eastern European country, caught between the security police on the one hand, and a right-wing faction of the Catholic Church on the other, and drew on Brian Moore's recollections of Poland in the immediate post-war era, along with Graham Greene's account of a visit to Poland in the mid-1950s as a guest of the Pax Movement.[13] As it happened, three Moore protagonists over a period of eight years (1985–93) were Catholic priests.

Some new friendships took root during the 1980s, and others were strengthened. The fashion journalist Georgina Howell, for example, whom the Moores had known since the late 1960s, became a great friend of Jean's, and whenever the Moores were in London, the two would indulge in merry shopping sprees together. 'Lunch at Georgina's', Brian's diary records in June 1985, alongside dinner with the Maschlers, drinks with John Gross, and an evening in the company of Julian Barnes, Pat Kavanagh and Hermione Lee. The last, academic, biographer and critic, had first met Brian when she interviewed him for the Channel Four programme *Book Four* in 1984: this interview inaugurated a friendship that lasted until his death. She and her husband John Barnard went to stay with the Moores several times, both in Malibu and in Nova Scotia. There was one particular dinner party in Malibu which stuck in her mind, because of the odd conjunction of a couple of earls among the company around the table on the tropical terrace: the Moores' friend Earl McGrath, and an English guest he'd brought along, whom he introduced as 'Brookie'. It then transpired that 'Brookie' was the Earl of Warwick – and so you had the two of them, Earl McGrath and the Earl of Warwick. It was an intriguing juxtaposition.

Peter Crookston of the *Sunday Times*, a friend of the Moores from the 1960s on (introduced by Mordecai Richler), remembered the novelist's endearing habit of clasping his hands between his knees, bending right over and positively whooping with laughter, whenever some comic anecdote was relayed to him. As far as wit was concerned, too, he was pretty quick off the mark himself. For example: a friend of Peter Crookston's had a lodger who used to make a great deal of noise with his girlfriend banging about overhead in the throes of unrestrained coitus. Fed up with the continuous disturbance, the friend instructed his wife to ask the lodger to be a bit less boisterous late at night; she, however, through an understandable embarrassment, could bring herself to utter only an inexplicit reprimand, 'I wonder if you'd mind wearing slippers.' This didn't really address the problem; but much was forgiven the lodger due to the beauty of his girlfriend, a doe-eyed sylph whom everyone compared to Bambi. Hearing this story, quick as a flash, Brian came out with the sharp rejoinder, 'Oh aye – Bambi and Thumper.'

The novelist Julian Barnes and his wife Pat Kavanagh (who later became Brian's English agent, with his book *The Statement*) also proved to be kindred spirits; on at least one occasion, the Moores borrowed their North London home while they were on holiday.

Barry Humphries and his wife Lizzie Spender were in the charmed circle too. Back in the States, new friends of the 1980s and 1990s included Caroline Blackwood's daughter Evgenia Sands and her husband Julian Sands, Angelica Huston, Peter and Wendy Asher and the film director Pat O'Connor and his wife.[14] Though most of these people were a generation younger than Brian, all of them fulfilled his exacting requirements as far as social engagements were concerned. For all his amiability, he had a low threshold of boredom, and made no bones about separating himself from those whose company he found tedious or uninspiring. As an antidote to the ascetic life of Malibu ('We're like two monks,' Jean joked.[15] 'He's the contemplative one and I'm the one who cooks'), social occasions had to be savoured to the full, which presupposed plenty of gossip, wit, and an animated atmosphere.

At a certain point in his life, Brian Moore's son Michael – like his father before him – found himself married to the wrong woman, leaving him with no option but to initiate divorce proceedings. His second wife, whom he married a couple of years later (in 1986), was, like himself, a nurse; their son (Brian's only grandchild), Brendan Michael, was born in February 1987. These experiences of Michael's no doubt gave him a clearer understanding of what his father had gone through – though by this stage, indeed, the past and its emotional convulsions had been largely resolved. The newly formed family frequently stayed at Malibu – in increased comfort, after 1987, when a new wing was built on to the original 'shack on the Pacific'. Work on this extension began in April, and when it was completed, it turned the house into an even more stupendous dwelling place, brick and wood, light and space, huge open fires (for Malibu's unexpectedly chilly seasons), tropical blossoms on view through every window.

In the same year, 1987, the long-delayed film of *Judith Hearne* was finally set in motion, with Maggie Smith and Bob Hoskins in the leading roles. The director was Jack Clayton, and the script was credited to Peter Nelson, all the earlier scripts, including Brian Friel's, having been jettisoned. For some unaccountable reason,[16] the setting of this quintessential Belfast novel was moved to Dublin, and almost the entire cast of actors was imported from outside Ireland. Brian Moore was not at all happy with the result, and one can see why. While he had converted the bleakness of the 'Judith Hearne' story into a source of narrative energy, the film adaptation imposed a rather showy poignancy on top of it. Into the vacuum created by the change of locale rushes a measure of prettification never envisaged by the novelist. The first UK showing of *The Lonely Passion of Judith Hearne* took place in January 1989 (it was already running at the 68th Street Playhouse on Third Avenue in New York, where it netted some favourable responses) – by which time Brian was working on the novel that became *Lies of Silence*, a novel that constituted something of a *volte-face*.

Before that, however, came the prize-winning *The Colour of Blood* (1987), which treats the last four days in the life of a cardinal-turned-fugitive in Eastern Europe. The country in question, though unnamed, is clearly Poland; the book opens with a failed assassination attempt, followed by a kind of kidnapping, escape and pursuit. (The thriller elements of the novel are highly compressed.) His Eminence Cardinal Bem is obliged to hide in a potato field, sleep with down-and-outs under a bridge across the Volya River, and travel through the night in a refrigerated butcher's truck, wrapped in smelly blankets. A Colonel Poulnikov, the name appropriated from Brian Moore's Warsaw days, comes into the story. Certain details are highly evocative: 'The rich aroma of espresso coffee brought back a memory of those coffee shops that rose like small miracles of luxury in the ruined streets of the capital in the first post-war years.' Like its successor *Lies of Silence*, *The Colour of Blood* is an outcry (or at least, as much of an outcry as such a temperate, disabused novelist is capable of emitting) against extremism, with fanatical Catholicism presented as a destructive force. At the same time, the Cardinal himself stands for another kind of Catholicism: moderate and incorruptible, and not unaccommodating of theological uncertainties.

The Colour of Blood made the Booker shortlist but failed to win the prize.[17] It was the last of Brian Moore's novels to be published in England by the firm of Jonathan Cape. The new decade brought a new publisher, Bloomsbury. As had happened with Deutsch all those years earlier, Brian had become frustrated over what he judged to be the failure of Cape to promote his work to a satisfactory degree. His agent at the time was Anne McDermid of Curtis Brown and, through her, an outline of the novel that

Brian at twenty-two.
Courtesy Mrs Eibhlin Darbyshire.

Brian in Warsaw, 1946.
Courtesy Mrs Eibhlin Darbyshire.

Brian and Jackie Moore
on their wedding day,
Montreal, 1952. *Courtesy
Mrs Una Maguire.*

Eibhlin Moore, Michael Moore, Mrs Eileen Moore and Brian in the South of France, 1957. *Courtesy Mrs Eibhlin Darbyshire.*

At Cliftonville Avenue, Belfast, 1957. All the Moores, except Marie-Therese, summoned to their mother's deathbed. *Courtesy Mrs Una Maguire.*

Brian and Bill Weintraub at a Christmas party in Montreal, 1958.
Courtesy William Weintraub.

Brian, Jackie, unknown, and Stanley Price in London, 1961.
Courtesy Stanley Price.

Brian in borrowed robes. Oxford, 1961. *Photo: Stanley Price.*

Brian and Jean, *c.*1964. *Courtesy Mrs Una Maguire.*

Jean, *c.1962*. One of Brian's favourite photographs. *Courtesy Jean Moore.*

Brian and Jean in Malibu, 1965. *Photo: Stanley Price.*

Jean, Brian and Una, 1974. 'We all look like Nixon getting the bad news,' Brian has written on the back of this. *Courtesy Mrs Una Maguire.*

Brian with Seamus Heaney, *c.*1980. *Courtesy Jean Moore.*

Brian with three of his sisters: from left, Grainne, Eibhlin, Eilis, after being awarded an honorary degree by Queen's University, Belfast in 1987.

Brian with Nova Scotia house in the background, 1997. *Photo: P.C.*

became *Lies of Silence* made its way to the recently founded firm of Bloomsbury. Bloomsbury's editorial director, Liz Calder, who'd previously been with Cape and had met Brian and Jean in the early 1980s at a dinner party given by Tom Maschler, liked the idea and promptly made 'a handsome offer' for the book – an offer well in advance of anything a Brian Moore novel had generated before.[18] This was in September 1988. It was a moment of jubilation – and then a couple of weeks later came the announcement of the Hughes Prize in Dublin, with *The Colour of Blood* as joint winner. That November, the Moores were in London, Belfast and then London again (where Brian gave a reading at the Blackheath Halls), before returning to Malibu at the end of the month. By the start of 1989 Brian, back at his desk, was hard at work, and the first draft of the 'Dillon' novel was completed in June. The manuscript was with Bloomsbury by September; Liz Calder, who was already an admirer of Brian's work, found it totally engrossing, and set a publication date for the following April. Naturally keen to acquire a distinguished list for the budding company, she considered Brian Moore to be an invaluable acquisition, worth every penny of his large advance[19] – while he, at last, had a publisher who was happy to indulge his half-humorous yen for 'five-star treatment'. It was, in fact, an unusually felicitous professional relationship, which resulted in both parties quickly becoming great friends.

When *Lies of Silence* hit the bookshops in 1990, Brian Moore was taxed with having gone back on his resolve to steer clear of the Northern Irish Troubles as a theme for fiction. As Hermione Lee reminded him in an interview,[20] he'd disowned the subject many times previously, declaring that his particular store of Northern Irish material had already been mined, and adding that, in his opinion, it required a younger author, someone who'd lived through the whole upheaval, to get to grips effectively with the prevailing imbroglio. He, in Louis MacNeice's phrase, had succeeded in turning himself into 'one of your holiday visitors',[21] someone unfitted, by his long absence, to write about the Troubles directly. Which goes to show, he joked to Hermione Lee, that novelists shouldn't allow themselves to be interviewed, since they never can predict what their next project will be, what fictional subject will suggest itself so insistently that it can't be denied an outlet.

However – there is a sense in which Brian Moore has not, with *Lies of Silence*, attempted the 'Troubles' novel he'd judged an inappropriate undertaking for an expatriate. This book is indeed an extraordinary – indeed an exemplary – thriller, tightly constructed, beautifully judged in its dramatic effects, completely enthralling for the reader; but it has nothing of the atmosphere of the earlier Belfast novels, that inalienable sense of *milieu* and mores that sets off all kinds of narrative reverberations. Nor was it meant to have. Brian Moore often referred to the incident that formed the germ of the novel: he and Jean, staying in Belfast's Wellington Park Hotel near Queen's University, were rooted out of their bed in the middle of the night due to a bomb alert and found themselves in the street standing next to a group of elderly French tourists, bound for the Glens of Antrim, all of them completely bewildered as to the source of this annoyance being inflicted on them. What if it had been a bomb, Brian thought, and these innocent French tourists had lost their lives without having the slightest understanding of the cause of the atrocity? From that point on, the idea began to grow on him of ordinary people caught up in a terrorist transaction: it wasn't that he wanted to tackle the larger issue of republican disaffection or anything of that sort, but rather to consider the predicament of an apolitical protagonist coerced into participating in an outrage. The events of the story might have been located in any divided community in which terror tactics flourished; for Brian Moore, though, there wasn't any choice about the setting. It had to be Belfast, because Belfast was his home territory.

The setting is specific, but the novel adds up to an indictment of terrorism in the widest possible sense. Belfast may be read as 'a paradigm of any sort of terrorist threat',[22] while the core of the book is a moral dilemma of unimaginable magnitude. A youngish hotel manager, Michael Dillon, whose job has brought him home to Belfast though he'd rather be anywhere else in the world, falls into the hands of the Provisional IRA and is forced by them to drive a car containing a bomb to a conference of Canadian Orangemen being held at his own hotel (the Clarence/Wellington Park). The principal target is the Rev. Alun Pottinger, a Paisley look-alike. If Dillon takes any action to obstruct the terrorists' design, his wife Moira, who is being held hostage at their suburban home, will be executed; if he doesn't, many innocent bystanders will be blown to bits.[23] To complicate matters, Dillon had been planning to leave Moira anyway, and move to London with his mistress Andrea, a young Canadian reporter with the BBC. These events, and their outcome, are stage-managed by the author with stupendous showmanship. This, of all Brian Moore's novels, is the one that's hardest to put down, once you've started reading it; however, for reasons of which he was well aware, the response in Ireland was largely as he'd predicted. Some Irish critics felt that the thriller form demeaned a subject better approached by way of something sharper, more illuminating or more idiosyncratic; while others succumbed – however subtly or subliminally – to a kind of atavistic annoyance over the failure of a one-time Belfast Catholic (renegade or not) to present the tradition of republicanism in a more sympathetic light. Republicans in the novel are merely 'ignorant bully boys' with their guns and balaclavas, heirs, if of anything, of the nineteenth-century Ribbonmen, arsonists and cattle-mutilators, unconnected to any nobler republican ideology or aversion to injustice. In the terrible present, with its topsy-turvy values, the whole thing is debased. In place of the stagnation that scuppered Judith Hearne, a murderous backwardness is on the loose. *Lies of Silence* upholds the shaky and endangered middle ground; it speaks up *for* moderation and freedom from constraint, *against* all forms of bigotry and intimidation. But it can't be classed as a political novel: 'I'm not trying to make a great point,' Brian Moore said.[24] 'I'm just trying to make a small point – the point that in Ireland the extremists have taken over, on both sides, and the middle has completely fallen apart – and the great silent majority, the middle people, have got to rally themselves together and once again have a voice.'

One of the minor characters in *Lies of Silence* is a 'bad little priest', a Father Matt Connolly, who comes to Dillon as a spokesman for the IRA, conveying an unstated threat; Brian Moore's Jesuit friend Michael Paul Gallagher was dismayed by the inclusion of this creepy cleric in the novel, reading into it a reversion, on the part of the author, to the anti-Catholicism of his early years. He was dismayed, because this seemed to contradict his opinion that Brian had arrived at a more-or-less balanced view of the Church and its representatives. However, one of the points *Lies of Silence* makes is that religion in Northern Ireland, Catholic and Protestant, is deeply implicated in the lethal breakdown of social and moral restraints. Priests like Father Connolly – no less than Protestant ideologues – see to it that the sectarian viewpoint is perpetuated. As Cardinal Bem put it in *The Colour of Blood*: 'We still live under tyranny: the tyranny of an age when religious beliefs have become inextricably entwined with political hatreds.'

Lies of Silence had many admirers, including (once again) Graham Greene;[25] Greene's verdict on the novel, that he was 'very moved by it', was passed on to Brian by Greene's niece Louise Dennys of Knopf in Toronto. In the UK, the novel quickly went on to the *Sunday Times* 'Bestseller List'; and later in the year it gained its author a third nomination for the Booker Prize. (Once again, Brian Moore was fated not to come out as winner, being pipped at the post by A.S. Byatt with *Possession*.) But celebrity was now assured: Brian was photographed by Snowdon in Brompton Cemetery, whirled off on a publicity tour, subjected to many interviews, booked for readings and signing sessions, flown back and forth between England and America, invited as guest of honour to a champagne reception at Bloomsbury . . . all the paraphernalia of frenetic promotion. He relished all this, indeed, but at the same time succeeded in keeping an ironic distance from it. None of it went to his head.

In August 1990 he wrote to UCLA resigning from his position as Creative Writing Fellow: enough was enough. Once a week, for seventeen years, he'd been a patient overseer of the creativity of his class of twenty-year-olds, but the time had come to concentrate exclusively on his own concerns. (He continued to use the UCLA Library for research purposes.) He began rereading *Lies* in connection with a possible film version.[26] By the end of the year, he was working on a piece of fiction referred to in his notebook as the 'Una' story, which then became the 'Nora' story, before being put to one side while he got down to some serious reading for a different novel, one set in Haiti (a setting which drew inevitable comparisons with Graham Greene), called Ganae in the book, and based on the vicissitudes of a real-life president-in-exile, the black priest Jean-Bertrand Aristide. In the middle of all this, and on the advice of his doctor, he underwent a pulmonary test.

After all the years of preparing successive drafts of his novels on an electric typewriter, he finally gave in to persuasion from his son

Michael and – in March 1991 – acquired a computer and printer. Like many another diehard traditionalist, he immediately became an enthusiast for the new apparatus. He had to leave it behind, however, a month or so later, while he went to Dublin to receive an honorary degree from the National University of Ireland (no doubt he felt the presence of his uncle Eoin MacNeill looking over his shoulder). In Dublin, he had lunch at the President's residence, and later dined at the Shelbourne with his sister Peggy, and caught up with family gossip; then it was off to London to stay with Peter Crookston, and back home via New York[27] and Toronto (for the wedding of a nephew), where the bare bones of the Haiti/Ganae undertaking awaited him.

This tale of a poor black boy plucked out of a rural slum to become a priest and revolutionary leader, recounted by the man whose protégé he'd been (Father Paul Michel, he of the doubt-stricken mother) (see p. 152 above), proved as hard as anything else to knock into shape: it was abandoned altogether in October, only to be taken up again a week later, after a new way forward had suggested itself. The first six months of 1992 were entirely given over to the project, until, in July, came the triumphant exclamation: 'End! 66,828 words.' The rest of that month was spent in Nova Scotia – in Halifax, touring round the peninsula, before the book was dispatched to Liz Calder with the possible title, *The Other Life*. (It was Liz Calder who came up with the inspired amendment.) Bloomsbury, once again, were delighted with this novel, and their optimism in connection with it wasn't misplaced. When it was published the following year, it was a resounding success: 'It reverberates and haunts,' William Trevor wrote in the *New York Review of Books*,[28] 'its intensity lingering long after the book has come to an end. Brian Moore has written nothing as subtle, or as perfectly sustained.' It was comments like this that made the whole slog, the moments of frustration and despair, worthwhile. And after the hard work came the justifiable term of relaxation. Brian's seventy-first birthday was celebrated with a trip to Santa Barbara, up the Pacific coast, and an overnight stay at the Biltmore Hotel. At the end of September the Moores were in London; then Marseilles, Carcassonne and Perpignan, and London again, where Brian was interviewed by his friend Hermione Lee for the *Independent on Sunday*. Back home, he found the old 'Una' notes for a novel (rechristened 'Nora'), and worked throughout December to expand these into something fruitful. But this material proved intractable, and it was set aside yet again. Nothing came of it.

According to Brian Moore, the best times of his life occurred whenever he was deeply engaged with the ins and outs of the current fictional plot: getting to grips with a technical problem, or allowing the flow of the narrative to carry him along. 'I'm very happy when I'm writing. The time I'm *not* happy,' he added, was the period immediately following publication, the period when 'I'm waiting to be judged'. The boy who'd dreaded hearing his examination results had – perversely, in that sense – subjected himself to a similar recurrent ordeal throughout the greater part of his life. 'Every two years, another exam! That's how I look on reviews.' It's not a serious comment, indeed, but it does indicate a certain conformity with a pattern established early on – with the difference, of course, that the frustrated expectation of the distant past was now triumphantly reversed. Whatever else he had done with his life, Brian Moore had asserted to the fullest degree his capacity for success.

15

A SPECK ON THE WALL

'When we die there is nothing . . . There is no other life.'
No Other Life

IN AN INTERVIEW WITH Joe O'Connor in October 1995,[1] Brian Moore alluded to the house he and Jean had built near Port Medway, in Nova Scotia: 'It's beautiful. It looks out on a bay that looks just like Donegal. It's very wild there and empty. I love it for its emptiness. It's like Ireland probably once was.' And he added: 'Now that I'm so old it seems crazy to build another house, I know. Especially there. But I'm very happy I did it all the same.'

Over the course of several years, during their trips to Nova Scotia, the Moores had looked around for a suitable house to buy, but failed to find anything that fulfilled all their precise requirements (the main one being that it should overlook the sea). Jean, who'd set her sights on a traditional nineteenth-century dwelling, gradually came round to the idea of constructing something that would blend in with the landscape, using old building materials as far as possible, but also embodying a pleasing idea of newness with regard to domestic comfort, practicality and so forth. The result is something of an aesthetic triumph: gracious and spacious, designed to make the most of Nova Scotia's summer light, polished wooden floors throughout, exposed beams salvaged from demolished barns, with Jean's collection of antique patchwork quilts and the odd decoy duck contributing pungency. Just as Brian Moore's chosen homes were a world away from Belfast's unending discords, so the visual impact of each interior is at the opposite extreme from Victorian oppressiveness. And yet – as he said, the Nova Scotia house with its surround of pine trees, its marshy frontage and Atlantic outlook does, in certain lights, remind one of Donegal (well, leaving aside the porcupines in the undergrowth, the occasional bear and coyote not far away, the wild blueberries and other indigenous delicacies – and of course the local timber-framed buildings with their air of sedateness, the grass verges of gardens flush with the pavement, all – to Irish eyes – inescapably foreign). From this vantage point, Brian was always conscious that no land mass intervened between himself and the West Coast of Ireland: nothing but the vast North Atlantic Ocean. He liked the fact that both his principal home and his summer home faced the sea, and that both were secluded – the second more so than the first. The striking thing about this part of Nova Scotia, in fact, is the scarcity of people, even in the streets of the small fishing towns and villages. You can drive for hours and not see a soul. 'It's a misanthrope's paradise,' Brian joked.

The house was ready by 1995, and the Moores were in residence from June to September, setting a pattern for the next four years. The solitude was – as ever – enlivened by an inflow of visitors, many of whom experienced great difficulty in finding the hidden retreat. One or two[2] got lost altogether and had to put up for the first night in South Nova Scotia at a hotel. '*Don't* be tempted by a turn a mile back,' Brian warned those negotiating the twists and turns of the baffling approach road – but some were so tempted and paid for it in hair-tearing and blasphemy before getting on to the right track again. One of these was Michael Shelden, who'd come to interview Brian for the *Daily Telegraph*;[3] his reward for persevering and finally reaching his destination, he said, was 'a lavish feast of home-baked bread, green salad and fresh sea food', served by the immaculate Jean 'inside a screened porch overlooking the bay'. Earlier that summer, Sean and Cynthia Moore, and Una Maguire, had come for a visit; the three Moore siblings had a great time gossiping and reminiscing about their childhood in Clifton Street, Belfast, where 'big boy Brian' had played the family entertainer. Reunions between the three kindred spirits within the Moore family had been all too rare in the past, and they made the most of this one. (The first of the nine brothers and sisters 'to go' – Grainne – had died that spring.)

In 1993, a 'Bookmark' profile of Brian Moore was produced for BBC TV under the title, 'The Man from God Knows Where'. In the course of this programme, Brian's sister Eilis recalled the author, as a boy, reciting a poem of this title during the Christmas festivities at Clifton Street, organised by Aunt Maggie Moore; but she couldn't remember anything about the poem. In fact, the original 'Man from God-Knows-Where' was Thomas Russell, United Irishman and one-time Librarian of the Linen Hall Library in Belfast, who was executed at Downpatrick Jail in 1803 after a failed attempt to rally the North in support of Robert Emmet's Dublin uprising. The poem, which makes a splendid party-piece, is a stirring account of events in the North in 1795 and 1803. It was written by the wife of a Presbyterian solicitor from Lisburn, Co. Antrim, Florence M. Wilson, and first appeared in a collection called *The Coming of the Earls* (published in 1918). Brian was greatly amused by the BBC's appropriation of the title for their programme on himself, in which the narrator declares that, however much he is filmed and inter-viewed, Brian Moore nevertheless remains elusive. This 'elusive-ness', indeed, has to do with his playful ducking out of ponderous obligations: the obligation to be attached to a particular country, or credo, or style of writing. He told the interviewer that what enabled him to write about religious faith (to take that obvious example) was his detachment from it, describing himself as 'an observer, a speck on the wall – never a participant'.

The *Los Angeles Times*'s 'highest literary honour', the Robert Kirsch Award for a body of work by an author 'living in or writing on the American West', was added in 1994 to the list of prizes and tributes secured by Brian Moore in the course of his forty-odd years as an indispensable literary practitioner. Eventually – and despite his assiduous keeping of a low profile on the Pacific Coast – literary circles in the area were alerted to his presence, and professed themselves 'grateful' for it. He, no doubt, was grateful for their gratitude, but at the time it impinged only slightly on his con-sciousness, since the whole of his attention was concentrated on what proved to be his penultimate novel, *The Statement*: an examination, via the enhanced thriller form, of the complicity of Church and State in France in the protection and concealment of a Nazi war criminal.

The *Statement* is a work of fiction, but also – as Brian Moore said himself – something of a *roman-à-clef*, whose central character,

Pierre Brossard, is based on the real-life Paul Touvier, chief of the second section of the Lyons Region French *Milice* (a paramilitary police force organised by Vichy and run on Nazi lines). Touvier, after forty years on the run in France, sheltered and financially supported by various Catholic authorities, was finally tracked down and convicted of crimes against humanity: he died in a prison hospital in July 1996 at the age of eighty-one. The case, Brian Moore said, had caught his attention at the time of Touvier's arrest and trial in 1993. He wrote to his publicist at Bloomsbury:

> My interest in France's wartime record goes back to the time when as a very young man I landed with the British in the South of France in 1944 while the Germans were fleeing and saw the fate of collaborators in those first angry post-war years. A few months later I was present in Paris at the trial and sentencing of Pierre Laval, Vichy's foreign minister. It was the beginning of a lifelong fascination with French politics.[4]

What especially intrigued him about the Touvier case, he went on, was 'the astonishing involvement of the French Catholic clergy, at every level'. Imposing a fictional outline over the story allowed him scope to explore a few of the implications of Brossard's – or Touvier's – prolonged evasion of retribution, and to home in on the state of mind of his central character (as ever) at the point of crisis, when political imperatives are dictating a change of policy towards the murdering old racist fugitive. A couple of incompetent assassins are set on the trail of Brossard, supposedly at the instigation of a Jewish Commando group seeking justice for those 'Jewish victims of Dombey' executed in 1944 on the orders of the crypto-Nazi. But the plot, and the moral issues raised, are more complicated than this suggests. The novel 'has a sobriety and a seriousness of purpose which lift it well above the customary limits of the [thriller] genre', as John Gross wrote in the *New York Review of Books*.[5]

With the four novels preceding the final one, *The Magician's Wife* of 1997, Brian Moore seems to have come around at last to the 'journalistic' material he'd repudiated at the start of his career; however, by this stage, he'd perfected a method of fictional re-enactment adequate to the historical significance of the events in question. These are not 'documentary' novels, but full-blooded, compelling and illuminating works of the imagination. Their narrative excitements, which are plentiful, are held in equilibrium with an incisive economy of expression. Brian Moore, as well – as we've seen – had an interest in the rehabilitation of slightly suspect genres, recognising that his own strengths as a fiction writer lay in the area of traditional narration – though not traditional connotation. (When he tried his hand at an overtly experimental novel, *The Great Victorian Collection*, he brought it off, against the odds, precisely because of the tension between matter-of-fact telling and outlandish postulation.) When he came to write *The Magician's Wife*, he had on his hands, once again, a story encompassing many of his primary concerns: historical recreation, a political dimension, clash of ideologies, areas of betrayal, trickery and treachery, the feminine point of view. About a performer, an illusionist, entrusted with a political mission, and his increasingly disabused wife, the novel itself adds up to an intoxicating performance.

It grew out of an incident Brian Moore had come across while reading Flaubert's correspondence with George Sand. A famous magician, Jean-Eugène Robert-Houdin (whose name was later adopted in homage by Harry Houdini), was sent to Algeria in 1856 by the Arab Bureau set up by Napoleon III, with instructions to frighten the natives by showing off his supposedly 'magic' powers, and thereby discourage them, for the moment, from engaging in a 'holy war' against the European infidels (whose troops were in need of recuperation following the struggle in the Crimea). This extraordinary expedient seems to have paid off: Brian Moore tracked down another reference to it in the memoirs of Houdini; but, he says, 'It's not known what was its ultimate effect.'

The coincidence of Flaubert (whose novel *Madame Bovary* was issued in instalments in the *Revue de Paris* in the same year, 1856) and Algiers (Brian Moore's first port-of-call after escaping from Belfast), along with the possibilities suggested to the novelist by the bizarre pacifying tactic, proved irresistible. From Flaubert, too, he'd gained an awareness of that 'clairvoyance' or intuition singled out by the earlier author as essential to any effective recreation of the past. One of the most striking aspects of *The Magician's Wife*, indeed, is the enticing atmosphere in which the events of the plot are located: dark narrow lanes and whitewashed Moorish houses, rosewater and orange trees and faded pink silken robes. Somehow, for Emmeline Lambert, the magician's wife, her mission in Algiers – as an adjunct of her husband – must be weighed in the balance against the delicacy and integrity of the civilisation she's come face-to-face with, however fragmentarily.

Emmeline, though she's in the *Bovary* tradition, is no Doctor's Wife; and although adultery is on the cards at more than one moment, the book is so arranged that the emphasis falls elsewhere – essentially, on the moral dilemma awaiting the protagonist. Everything unfolds from Emmeline's vantage point, but at the same time – as Hermione Lee expressed it in a letter to Brian Moore[6] – the narrative 'opens out and keeps making you think about French history, class, colonisation, empire, treachery, manipulation . . . it's a very serious historical work and at the same time dazzlingly pleasurable'. And Joyce Carol Oates in the *TLS*[7] judged it to be 'a rich, absorbing and thoughtful meditation on the uses of "magic" and power, and the ways, sometimes with surprising effectiveness, individual human conscience can respond to such uses'. In spite of these and other accolades, *The Magician's Wife* did not get on to the Booker shortlist that year: though in many ways it seems a more suitable contender than any of the three previously listed Moore titles.

Brian Moore's amused aversion to the self-promotional *bonhomie* of the literary circuit didn't diminish during the last decade of his life, but – as ever – there were some exceptions to his rule of non-participation. He and Jean were in Toronto in October 1994, for example, attending the Harborfront International Festival of Authors, whose programme included an evening of tributes to himself; his old friend Bill Weintraub was among those enlisted to praise his achievements and his capacity for friendship, in a graceful (and funny) salutation. His prose, Bill said, '. . . besides being elegant, is wonderfully lucid and accessible. It's meant to be read, and not primarily to be studied. For this I think we can all be grateful, all of us with the possible exception of those persons who make their living from literary cryptanalysis.'

A George Moore Festival at Westport House enticed the Moores to Co. Mayo, where they made some new friends among the people assembled at the spot – the Belfast poet and academic Gerald Dawe, for instance, and Anthony Cronin, author of *Dead as Doornails*, a book about three exorbitant Irishmen (Brendan Behan, Patrick Kavanagh and Flann O'Brien) which had greatly impressed Brian when he first read it. They also renewed acquaintance with some old friends such as the novelist and playwright Thomas Kilroy, whose familiarity with Brian and his work dated back to New York, *c.* 1962, when he'd visited the Moores (Brian and Jackie) at their home in West 15th Street, and encountered 'an extremely angry man, utterly impatient with the Ireland he had left behind'.[8]

Also during the 1990s, the Moores added Australia to the list of foreign destinations they'd notched up over the years; they attended the Melbourne Literary Festival, had a week in Sydney, where Brian gave a couple of talks and readings, and managed a stopover in Singapore. Back in Britain – in Belfast to be precise, in 1997 – Brian was persuaded to give what a local newspaper called 'a rare reading' in the Linen Hall Library (from *The Magician's Wife*), which drew 'a packed audience'.[9] Brian Moore's growing acceptance in his native city had been signalled the previous year by a request, to which he acceded, that his name should be associated with a new literary competition: hence 'The Brian Moore Short Story Awards', set up under the auspices of the Creative Writers' Network and the *Belfast Telegraph*. It was quite an advance on the headlines of thirty years earlier, when the same newspaper had proclaimed, 'Novelist flays his native Belfast', *à propos* Brian's article in *Holiday* magazine,[10] in which a few of the city's short-comings were enumerated. Describing the droll greeting of one shipyard worker to another – 'Can ye stick it?' 'Aye' – he'd implied, humorously, that the inhabitants of Belfast did indeed have an awful lot to put up with. However, some of them did not take kindly to his observations – 'overplays his hand'; '[does] not love his native city'[11] – even though it was plain that he was criticising the place from a proprietorial perspective, which should have entitled him to speak his mind. But possibly because of the annoyance he'd aroused, subsequent flying visits to Belfast induced in him a slight nervousness, such as one might experience in the vicinity of an emphatic relative about whom one had made rude remarks in public. On an occasion in 1985, he was made even more nervous than usual by finding himself in the middle of a political demonstration. He was at the University Bookshop to sign copies of *Black Robe*, when protesters against the supergrass system invaded the premises. A newspaper photograph of the event shows Brian looking decidedly ill at ease, and his brother Seamus, who is also in the picture, looking impassive. Behind them are placards bearing such slogans as 'Smash the Paid Perjurer System'.

The National Film Board of Canada's 1986 film about Brian Moore includes a shot of the author being driven past his birthplace in Clifton Street; the house was still standing then, though derelict and boarded up. Alas, it soon fell victim to Belfast's terrible indifference to its Victorian architectural heritage; along with the greater part of that historic area, it was razed to the ground in 1995 to accommodate such essentials of modern living as the Westlink dual carriageway, a car-park and a lot of gimcrack housing. A vigorous campaign to save the house, organised by SDLP MP Dr Joe Hendron, Alliance coun-cillor Sean McBride and the writer Sam McAughtry, had come to nothing. They'd wanted No. 11, Clifton Street to be preserved as a tribute to the author. (A less realistic plan, to erect a statue of Brian Moore at Carlisle Circus on a plinth once occupied by the Presby-terian cleric 'Roaring' Hugh Hanna, before it was blown up by the IRA: this also, perhaps fortunately, failed to materialise – though it's intriguing to envisage the effect on Dr J.B. Moore of a monument to his son on the spot he walked past twice a day.)

By this stage, the Moore birthplace had degenerated into a refuge of glue-sniffers: its final incarnation. After the Second World War, its owners, the Church authorities, had refurbished it as a Home for Fallen Women, to be administered by the Sisters of Mercy and the Legion of Mary. Its inmates would have been mostly diseased or pregnant prostitutes, fallen into the hands of nuns. On one occa-sion, Seamus Moore, as a young doctor, was called to the house to attend to one of the Clifton Street fallen women. As he entered the room where she lay in bed, he came to a standstill, went into a kind of daze and stood contemplating the place with rapt attention. 'You seem very interested in this room, doctor,' the nurse in charge observed eventually. 'Indeed I am,' Seamus replied. 'I was born in this room.' Upon which the nurse reeled back in horror. 'My God!' she exclaimed. '*Who* was your mother?'[12]

*   *   *

A mild instinct for dandyism was among the characteristics separating Brian Moore from the majority of his Belfast contemporaries, and during the last thirty-odd years of his life he was able to indulge this trait to the full, ordering his suits (for example) from the Fulham tailor, Dimi Major, whose clients included the Duke of Norfolk, Lauren Bacall, Lord Weidenfeld, Mark Boxer and so on. (Major had trained with the famous Dougie Hayward, but charged only half the price of his mentor.) Brian liked to be correctly dressed. 'Oh God,' Jean would groan, humorously, after the fourth or fifth departure of her husband into the bedroom, 'he's gone to change his trousers *again*.' On one occasion, Peter Crookston, staying with the Moores in Malibu, had been running on the beach and returned to the house wearing rumpled jeans in time for a proposed shopping expedition to Rodeo Drive in Hollywood. Brian, in his Gucci shoes and immaculate blazer, hesitated before getting into the car. 'You're not going like that, are you?' he enquired, mildly but firmly. 'I really think you'd feel more comfortable if you changed into something else.' Back in the mid-1950s, Bill Weintraub had written to Brian describing his journalistic investigations into Savile Row in London without eliciting much response; but in later years Brian's literary celebrity had reinforced his sense of the importance of striking the right (understated) note in the image he presented. Classic English tailoring was the thing.

Throughout the '90s, whenever they were in London, the Moores would usually arrange to rent a large flat in a mansion block near the junction of Knightsbridge and Kensington Road, with a view of Hyde Park and the route taken, every morning, by ten mounted horsemen of the Household Cavalry. This was the regiment targeted by an IRA bomb in 1982, a fact which sometimes caused Brian to ponder the republican element in his family background, his own reasons for rejecting it, and the subsequent distortions overtaking the ideology promulgated by – among others – his uncle Eoin MacNeill. It was all there, a part of his inheritance. The older he got, he said, the more he came to realise that – Canadian citizenship notwithstanding – Ireland was his nation; 'ineluctably Irish', he described himself, deliberately employing the Joycean adverb, with a tinge of self-mockery. 'Joyce and I are the only people who've ever used that word, "ineluctably".'

*   *   *

Brian Moore once confided to Hermione Lee, in an interview, that he dreaded dying while he was in the middle of a novel – 'I think some other bastard will put an end to it, the way they do!'[13] In fact, his fear of leaving something uncompleted was not unfounded. He *did* die while he was deeply involved in what would have been his twenty-first novel, another historical undertaking, this time based on Rimbaud's life in Africa. It was an enthralling subject, again requiring a good deal of research which would be put aside once the imaginative faculty came into play. Reading in connection with the project had been under way since the start of 1998, and by early July he was ready to begin the first draft. He and Jean had just arrived in Nova Scotia, where they planned to stay until the end of September. Brian got down to the book with his usual concentration and carried on working until he could do no more – when he was more than halfway through.[14] For the whole of that year he'd known he was dying from an incurable disease, pulmonary fibrosis. Pride, and a natural disinclination to present himself as an object of sympathy or morbid speculation, led him to keep this knowledge to himself, with very few exceptions. Only those closest to him, his wife Jean, of course, his son Michael and his brother Sean, knew the true state of affairs. Others, noticing his increasing breathlessness, put it down to just another routine affliction of old age (he turned seventy-seven on 25 August).

It was a year of doctors, tests, hospital appointments, more tests, medication, different medication. Through it all, as his brother Sean wrote in a posthumous tribute, he remained 'courageous, upbeat, optimistic, and as usual good company with much perceptive and witty conversation'. That August, Sean and Cynthia Moore had visited Brian and Jean at Port Medway, and the four spent a high-spirited day 'sightseeing' in the decorative town of Lunenburg. Early in September, Brian was in Halifax at the CBC Headquarters to be interviewed 'down the line' by Hermione Lee in London (it proved to be his final, very shaky, interview); this went out the following month on BBC Radio 3. In it, he reiterated his wish to 'disappear' into his books; he wanted the books to be remembered, not the author. He located the apex of human happiness, for him, in going into his study, forgetting himself and everyone else for the time being, settling down to work, getting the narrative to flow along – 'That is joy,'[15] he said. It was his final broadcast word: 'That is joy.'

A week after the Halifax interview, he was in hospital for more tests. He and Jean returned to Malibu on 17 September; a month later, they spent three days in Seattle. Back home, Brian was provided with a new oxygen adjuster, which effected a small improvement, for the moment. Sean and Cynthia came for a visit in December, and a repeat of the summer expedition took place, this time to Santa Barbara, up the coast. But Brian's condition was worsening: he could only walk a short distance before having to sit down to recover. He sat in the middle of Santa Barbara and looked around him at the palm trees, the vibrant colours, the quasi-Mexican architecture of the rebuilt town (rebuilt in the 1920s after an earthquake). It was his last opportunity to relish these things, and others. On New Year's Eve, Brian and Jean, and their guests, were invited to a celebration in Malibu at the home of Wendy and Peter Asher. On leaving the car, Brian suffered an attack of breathlessness and had a taxing walk to the house. Once inside, however, he seemed to throw off all signs of ill-health; he was in amazing form (Jean recalled) and everyone was dazzled by his humour, conversation and anecdotes. A number of women present commented on the handsomeness of his appearance. He enjoyed himself immensely. The next day came a sad parting from Sean and Cynthia when they left for Montreal. For many years Brian had been in the habit of going for a run (lately, this had become a walk) before breakfast, to make a good start to the day. The last entry in his diary, on 31 December 1998, reads simply, 'No walk.' The end was creeping up on him.

He didn't want to die. Many people, when they reach a certain stage of ill-health and curtailment of their normal activities, give up, bow down to the inevitable, turn their face to the wall. Some may have the hope of something better to come. But for Brian Moore, the view of the Indian Chomina in *Black Robe* coincided with his own view: ' "You have no sense, Nicanis," ' Chomina tells the Jesuit, Laforgue. ' "No man should welcome death . . . Look around you. The sun, the forest, the animals. This is all we have . . . This world is a cruel place but it is the sunlight. And I grieve now, for I am leaving it." '

The new year came and went. On 10 January, Brian became ill

during the night, seemed to recover for a bit, but then got worse again. Jean rang for an ambulance, while holding him in her arms and trying to revive him. Paramedics came but it was too late. An ambulance took him and Jean to hospital, where he was pronounced dead. Half a lifetime of delight, companionship and shared enthusiasms was at an end.

There was no deathbed reversion to the Catholic faith. That particular form of belief, a closed book to Brian even in his church-ridden youth, remained a closed book. However, at the instigation of his relatives, a Requiem Mass was held for him in Belfast, in the very church – St Patrick's in Donegall Street – where his enforced attendance in childhood had caused him so much resentment and boredom. A kind of wheel of infelicity had come full circle. It is likely that those emotions, resentment and boredom, would have overtaken Brian Moore yet again had he been present as a speck on the wall at that occasion. A Father McKenna, who addressed the congregation,[16] appeared to be under the impression that the subject of his comments had written twenty-seven novels, that he'd emigrated to Canada in the 1930s as a young writer driven out of Belfast by 'the confines of religion', and never again set foot in the place. If he had revisited Belfast, Father McKenna went on, as he had planned to do in 1999, 'he would have found that it had changed a hell of a lot since the 1930s'. Perhaps; but he might have found it had changed somewhat less egregiously since his previous visit in 1997.

The Requiem Mass at St Patrick's was just an acknowledgement of a part of Brian Moore's past, not an attempt to reclaim him for Catholicism. It enabled those members of his family who'd remained in the Church to take leave of him in their own way. The officiating priest got it wrong again when he drew an analogy between Brian and his character Judith Hearne. 'Judith's refrain, "Oh Lord I do not believe, help me in my disbelief," could have been Brian's,' Father McKenna said. This observation is, in fact, as wide of the mark[17] as that of the *Daily Telegraph* obituarist who claimed that the novelist's 'whole career . . . had been moulded by an unsuccessful flight from religion'.[18]

Brian Moore's famous 'disappearing act', his utterly dispassionate approach to the art of fiction-writing, allowed scope for critics and readers to bring their own ideas to bear on his preoccupations.

He might have declared, with Elizabeth Bowen, 'I am dead against art's being self-expression'[19] – but supposed self-revelation was foisted on him nevertheless. He used to joke that the adoption of a female persona (to take that example) allowed him to write about himself without being taxed with autobiography – but it was just a joke. As with every other worthwhile novelist, his own life, along with reading, research, observation and so on, provided material, while an inventive faculty did the rest. And once he'd got started on his spellbinding course, he followed it, with the dedication of the true artist, right to the end.

It is foolhardy to make an assumption about the probable opinion of someone no longer available to confirm or deny it; nevertheless, I believe that Brian Moore would have relished, more than the Requiem Mass, the memorial celebration held for him in London, at Leighton House in Kensington, in the autumn of 1999. This secular occasion, organised by his publisher Liz Calder, together with his friends Hermione Lee and Julian Barnes, drew in a lot of people from various directions, including many who'd figured prominently in his life at one period or another. Three of his sisters were there, his brother Sean from Montreal, his son Michael and grandson Brendan, twelve years old at the time and the youngest person present. Alice Trillin was there from New York; Jim Norton, who starred in the adaptation of *The Temptation of Eileen Hughes*; film directors Bruce Beresford and Pat O'Connor. From Ireland came such old and valued friends as Seamus and Marie Heaney, and Brian and Anne Friel. Newer friends, such as Wendy and Peter Asher, were present among the invited guests. The Frenches were there; Tom Rosenthal, Georgina Howell and her mother Gwen Howell, Peter Crookston . . . All in all, it was a packed and distinguished gathering.

The graceful tribute to his brother by Sean Moore,[20] which he read in London, was first delivered at an earlier memorial gathering in Montreal, a city you might rate second only to Belfast in fashioning the Brian Moore persona. (Bill Weintraub was also among those present on that occasion, reminiscing vividly about Brian's journalistic past and regretting the closure of a friendship that had lasted for more than fifty years.)

Sean made his audience laugh by describing how, because of his physical similarity to his brother, he would often be accosted by someone at a cocktail party or literary gathering, demanding to be told what he himself considered his best work. 'I always resisted the temptation to reply, *Injury Mechanisms in Athersclerosis*,' Sean declared drily. He went on to quote from the story, 'A Vocation', the bit about the child's world expanding outwards from Clifton Street – but only an infinitesimal distance – and the sense of sin instilled in every kindergarten Catholic. The unspoken correlative here is the immensity of the ground traversed by the novelist, his eventual arrival at a position of moral commitment uncontained by any formal creed. Sean Moore ended by reading an early Philip Larkin poem, 'Going',[21] which expresses something of universal anxieties about disenchantment and mortality:

> There is an evening coming in
> Across the fields, one never seen before,
> That lights no lamps.
>
> Silken it seems at a distance, yet
> When it is drawn up over the knees and breast
> It brings no comfort.
>
> Where has the tree gone, that locked
> Earth to the sky? What is under my hands,
> That I cannot feel?
>
> What loads my hands down?

On one of their leisurely tours of the West of Ireland, the Moores stumbled across a tiny graveyard in romantic Connemara facing the Atlantic Ocean – the most unpretentious of places, it seemed, with its random stone crosses and five phlegmatic cows. Picking his way among the gravestones, peering at inscriptions, Brian was surprised to light on a name he recognised. Bulmer Hobson. This name had often cropped up in conversation at Clifton Street. A Belfast Quaker, one-time vice-president of Sinn Fein and founder-editor of the periodical *Irish Freedom*, he was the person from whom, in 1916, Eoin MacNeill had learned of the impending Easter Rising (which he immediately took steps to avert). Being

a Quaker and opponent of violent measures, in any cause whatsoever, Bulmer Hobson had somehow come to exemplify, not only in
the minds of Brian Moore's father and uncle, but in Brian's mind
too, a kind of political integrity and personal steadfastness which
were very attractive. And, 'That his body lay here, in this small
Connemara field facing the ocean, under a simple marker, was
somehow emblematic of his life.'[22] It was a moment of repose, and
also, for Brian Moore, a kind of coming-to-terms with atavistic
undercurrents he'd long repudiated – notions of homeland, local
attachment, instinctive allegiances.

It was only a mood, brought on by the peacefulness of the
overgrown, unfrequented West of Ireland cemetery, but it lasted
long enough to crystallise into a tentative plan for the future; and it
affected Jean as well. Some time later, the two fell into a conversation about death, and funeral arrangements, and where, ideally,
they'd like their ashes to end up. 'Here's a piece of paper,' Brian
said. 'You write down what you'd like to happen, and I'll do the
same, and then each of us will read what the other has written.'
Amazingly, their choices of final resting-place were identical: the
little Bulmer Hobson graveyard on the Connemara coast. At the
time of writing, Brian Moore's ashes have not yet made it to this
beatific spot, but, when they do, it will make a fitting place of
interment for the voluntary exile, cosmopolitan and equivocal
Northern Irishman: facing westwards, with windswept grasses,
cows grazing, distant headlands, the tang of turf smoke, and fierce
Atlantic breakers for ever crashing on the shore.

NOTES

Introduction

1. 'The Lonely Passion of Brian Moore'. National Film Board of Canada, 1985.
2. Elizabeth Bowen, *Pictures and Conversations*. Jonathan Cape, London, 1975.
3. Terry Eagleton, 'Lapsing'. *London Review of Books*, 8 April 1993.
4. Seamus Heaney to P.C.
5. John Gregory Dunne, quoted in the *Los Angeles Times*, 13 January 1999.
6. B.M. to Michael Paul Gallagher, 10 July 1971. Calgary 31.29.1.
7. Michael Moore to P.C.
8. Hermione Lee, *Virginia Woolf*. Chatto & Windus, London, 1996.
9. Virginia Woolf to Vita Sackville-West, 1938. *Collected Letters*, Vol VI (Six Vols). Hogarth Press, London, 1975–80.
10. B.M. to Christopher Murray, 11 May 1988.
11. B.M. warned me that I would find it difficult to persuade his wife to talk about herself.
12. Some readers may be impatient to reach the years of B.M.'s actual lifetime, but I make no apology for recounting in some detail those ancestral circumstances which seem to me to be crucial to a proper understanding of the subsequent story.

1. Old Ballymena

1. The opening poem in the sequence, 'Clearances', in *The Haw Lantern*. Faber, London, 1987.
2. I am indebted to Seamus Heaney for this information.
3. J.W. Good, *Ulster and Ireland*. Maunsel, Dublin and London, 1919.
4. Rev. Henry Cooke, quoted in J.L. Porter, *The Life and Times of the Rev. Henry Cooke*, 1871.
5. The proportion of Catholics to non-Catholics in the town was in the region of one to five.
6. According to his great-great-granddaughter Eibhlin Tierney, he built Bryan Street and part of Market Square; but there is no mention of either in the Ordnance Survey records of the 1830s. Bryan Street seems

to have been called Crawford Street after it was constructed in 1812, with the name being changed some time between 1834 and 1842.

7. Burned down in 1919 and replaced by the present town hall in 1929.

8. Samuel McSkimin, *Annals of Ulster* MDCCCXLIX.

9. A letter written by John O'Rawe in Charleston, South Carolina, in 1809, to his parents in Ballymena, describes a nightmarish voyage, with the passengers first struck with the flux ('one child died of it') and then shipwrecked off the coast of Bermuda. 'We now,' he reports, 'had to go through difficulties on land almost as distressing as the dangers we had encountered at sea' – with six of the passengers immediately being 'pressed and put on board British ships of war among which was John Boyd's two eldest sons and Robert Gibson from near Crebilly. I would of shared the same fate as those poor fellows had I been along with them as they went to St Georges the principal town on the island and I went to a country part of it.' Penniless (the captain sold all the ship's cargo and made off for New York with the proceeds), still in danger of being pressed and reduced almost to a skeleton by the flux, John O'Rawe managed to get himself on board another ship sailing for America, was nearly shipwrecked again ('but that good and merciful God which had brought us through all our former dangers now saved us at this dreadful moment'), but finally made it to Charleston, where – eventually – he 'got into an eligible situation . . . in a large grocery and liquor store'. Before this, though, he nearly died of a fever, after which, while recovering, he 'teached for 1 year' in Newberry. He mentions an Alexander O'Hara of Belfast who reached Charleston via Africa bringing with him four Negroes whom he sold for 1,200 dollars – as well as passing on news about various Ballymena people settled in the place ('I seen George Savage some time ago in this city. I saw him pass several times in the street but did not speak to him. He had a ragged shabby appearance'). Some of those he mentions, e.g. William Bones and William John Swan, are likely – judging by the surnames that appear in the historical records – to be ex-United Irishmen, like himself. PRONI 36/3/2.

10. The names Bryan (or Brian) and Bernard seem to have been inter-changeable among B.M.'s ancestors.

11. All these places are in the vicinity of Ballymena.

12. Eoin MacNeill, in a document found among the MacNeill Papers, recalls having 'twice carried a coffin up the loanin' to Skerry graveyard.

13. Kitty O'Rawe married James McAuley, a Ballymena hotel keeper who seems to have made himself pretty unpopular; the story goes that even his wife got fed up with his meanness and general disagreeableness in the end and flung her wedding ring into the fire. James was one of four brothers known in the neighbourhood as 'the soul-saver, the body-saver, the knave and the slave'. The body-saver was Dr Charles McAuley whose daughter Rosetta became the mother of Eoin MacNeill.

14. See Jonathan Bardon, *A History of Ulster*. Blackstaff, Belfast, 1992.
15. John Hewitt, 'The Scar'. In *Collected Poems*, Blackstaff, Belfast, 1991.
16. Letter from Eoin MacNeill's daughter Eibhlin Tierney to Paddy O'Hara, 1982.
17. *Ordnance Survey Memoirs*, 1830s.
18. 'My Ain Native Toun', in *Select Works of David Herbison*. Belfast, 1883.
19. These might have included the Rev. P. Baker's *The Devout Communicant* (1832), such pamphlets as *Catholic Piety* and *Grounds of the Catholic Doctrine*, and *The Catholic's Manual* by J.B. Bossuet (1832).
20. Mary O'Rawe married the owner of a hotel in Antrim Town. James and Ellen Moore's daughter Mary (Minnie) remembered visiting this hotel, with its enormous kitchen lined with dark wooden cupboards; the poor, she said, were always certain of getting something to eat here. Judges of the Assizes were also, traditionally, accommodated in the hotel – and, during the uprising of 1798, the cellar was a storehouse for guns and ammunition. Eibhlin Tierney, who relayed this information to Paddy O'Hara in a letter of 1982, comments sardonically, 'It must have been a pretty busy place coping with the Judges of the Assizes upstairs, the poor being fed for free in the kitchen, and rebel guns in the cellars.'
21. The range of Christian names appears to have been rather limited in Co. Antrim during the nineteenth century.
22. A group of Moravians, or United Brethren, had settled at Gracehill in 1745, and soon established 'an expensive boarding-school for young ladies'. This was later joined by a boarding-school for young gentlemen, and a day school for children of the district.
23. Mrs Gaskell (1810–65). Sketches of a small town.
24. Dr Mulholland's daughter Rosa (1841–1921), later Lady Gilbert, became a popular late-Victorian novelist, author of such works as *The Wild Birds of Killeevy* (1883) and *Father Tim* (1910). One of her themes, the rise of a Catholic gentry in Victorian Ireland, reflects the real-life experience of some of B.M.'s ancestors. Donegall Street, where she lived as a girl, is a continuation of Clifton Street, where he was born in 1921, the year she died.
25. Dr J.B. Moore, as he became, was known as Brian in the family (he was 'Uncle Brian' to his MacNeill nephews and nieces); I shall call him James B., to distinguish him from his father James, and his son Brian.
26. The Irish Republican Brotherhood, or Fenian Brotherhood, founded in Dublin in 1858 by James Stephens, a veteran of the 'Young Ireland' uprising of 1848, advocated physical force in the drive to attain its end, i.e. the establishment of an Irish republic. The Fenian revolution which was supposed to erupt in March 1867 didn't in fact amount to much; it was defeated almost before it started by the activities of informers, a tremendous fall of snow and the tactics of the constabulary (subse-

quently rewarded by being given the title 'Royal Irish'). Nevertheless, Fenianism struck deep into the psyche of revolutionary Ireland, and showed a way forward for the architects of 1916.

27. The Ribbonmen, successors of the Whiteboys, were a band of Catholic malcontents whose repertoire included arson, cattle-maiming and other agrarian misdeeds. The novelist William Carleton (1794–1869) places the Ribbon Movement alongside the Orange Order and among 'the accursed systems' plaguing the North in his day.

28. *A History of Ulster*, op. cit.

29. He grew up to refer to 'the intensely Protestant and bigoted atmosphere of [his native] mid-Antrim town' – of which he'd had personal experience from the word go.

30. One of the nine glens of Antrim.

31. He received an acknowledgement from Queen Victoria for his services – but when neighbours, getting wind of this, called to see the Royal Letter, they were told he had put it on the fire. I don't know if Catholicism or carelessness was responsible for this.

32. She was adamant that it was coffee, not tea.

33. Very little is known about the Presbyterian side of the family, from whom James Moore seems to have cut himself off. Many years later, a daughter of his sister Mrs Ferguson entered the Mater Hospital in Belfast where she was attended by Dr J.B. Moore – James's son and her first cousin – but it's possible that neither was aware of the other's identity.

34. Letter from Eibhlin Tierney to Paddy O'Hara, 1982.

35. It's said that he hoped to go into partnership with Alexander O'Rourke, but O'Rourke wasn't willing to go along with this.

36. Equivalent to £84,000 today.

37. Its founder was Dr Crolly, then Archbishop of Down and Connor.

38. St Patrick's College, Carlow, a Lay College attached to Maynooth, a college at Navan, St Jarlath's College, Tuam, and the Jesuit Foundation at Clongowes Wood were the others.

39. St Malachy's was among the earliest schools to adopt this system, and, in the first Intermediate Examination held in 1880, it was placed seventh in order of merit.

40. Michael Tierney, *Eoin MacNeill: Scholar and Man of Action 1867–1945*. Clarendon Press, Oxford, 1980.

41. According to a report in the *Belfast News Letter*.

42. *Eoin MacNeill*, op. cit.

43. Eibhlin Tierney's phrase.

44. Clearly, humdrum Ballymena wasn't without its eccentricities.

45. Literally, the hill, or height, of the sun.

46. Taken by the photographic firm of Irwin's in Ballymena.

47. Alexander Street in Ballymena gained this title by virtue of its insalubriousness.

48. Though it leaves a lot of questions unanswered – for instance, what McNally's relatives were thinking of is a mystery; and there must surely have been more to the incident in the Paris Opera than the bare bones that passed into family history.

49. It's true that Minnie Moore went on to make medical history, about twelve years later, by becoming the first person in Ireland to undergo, successfully, an operation for a perforated gastric ulcer. The man who performed the operation was Dr Patrick Joseph O'Hara, a friend of James B. Moore's and, in fact, an uncle of one of his future sons-in-law. The kitchen table which did service as an operating table is still in the possession of the O'Hara family.

50. R.N.D. Wilson, 'Elegy in a Presbyterian Burying Ground'. *The Dublin Magazine*, April–June 1950.

2. The Great Exam Passer

1. Testimonial to J.B. Moore from S. O'Sullivan, M.D., M.Ch., F.R.C.S.I. (1892).

2. Testimonial to J.B. Moore from Henry Corby, B.A., M.D., M.Ch., F.O.S.L. (1892).

3. Testimonial to J.B. Moore from Henry E. Clarke, F.F.P.S., M.R.C.S. (1892).

4. Ibid.

5. Testimonial to J.B. Moore from John Lindsay Steven, M.D. (1892).

6. Apart from his application in 1902 for a post as Medical Officer to the Royal Irish Constabulary, which was unsuccessful despite his glowing recommendations.

7. *Eoin MacNeill*, op. cit.

8. Robert Lloyd Praeger, *The Way That I Went*. Methuen, London, 1937. MacNeill, possibly influenced by this old friend, took an interest in botany throughout his life.

9. Quoted by Sean Mac Réamoinn, in his Introduction to *The Pleasures of Gaelic Poetry*. Allen Lane, London, 1982.

10. Eoin MacNeill is known to have been a member of the Ardrigh circle, and it's inconceivable that he didn't take his friend James B. Moore to gatherings there.

11. MacNeill's annual income had gone up to £300 – about £14,500 in today's terms.

12. Michael J. F. McCarthy, *Priests and People in Ireland*. Simpkin, Marshall, Hamilton & Kent, London, 1902.

13. *Fergus* is basically a comic novel, in which ghosts from the past, not all of them dead, rise up to confront the hero in his Californian living room.

14. 'An Frainnc', in *An Claidheamh Soluis* (The Sword of Light), 30 September 1899.

15. Where Francis O'Rawe had run his apothecary's shop, and where the earliest St Malachy's pupils had received their schooling.

16. Louis MacNeice, *Autumn Journal*, Section XVI. Faber, London, 1938.

17. Rev. W.M. O'Hanlon, *Walks Among the Poor of Belfast*. Belfast, 1852.

18. These evictions were the result of a bitter dispute between the landlord, a Mr Adair (who had started off his overlordship of the district with good enough intentions), and his tenants, whom he accused of poisoning his sheep – though the evidence suggested that these had died from natural causes. Adair's estate manager was subsequently found dead on Derry Veagh mountain – *not* from natural causes. Things got worse, until in the end Adair served eviction notices on the whole community – with the result that police and troops spent three days dragging people out of their homes and razing the little buildings to the ground. The affair attracted such widespread attention that the government of Victoria promised free passages to all evicted tenants who cared to avail themselves of the offer. Many did, and it was these whom Father McFadden accompanied part of the way to Australia.

19. The same thing recurs, indeed, with the young Moores and their uncles and aunts who are pushed back a whole generation.

20. It's possible that this brother was a 'spoiled priest'. Eileen McFadden sometimes wondered what had become of him in later years, joking that he might have ended up as a bootlegger (this was the Prohibition era).

21. A death notice in a local paper refers to him as 'Mr Patrick McFadden, JP, of Duntally Lodge'.

22. Later Mrs Maguire. Her son Michael stayed for a while with Brian Moore in Montreal in the 1950s.

23. The Knights of St Columbanus is a middle-class Catholic organisation comparable to the Freemasons.

24. Which, in a sense, acted as an inspiration for pro-Home Rulers.

25. F.X. Martin, 'MacNeill and the Irish Volunteers', in F.X. Martin and F.J. Byrne (eds), *The Scholar Revolutionary*. Irish University Press, Dublin, 1973.

26. He was doubly unfortunate, in that he was later involved in the Boundary Commission and got himself known as the man who gave away the six Northern counties.

27. Note written by Eoin MacNeill, 9 May 1916. MacNeill Papers.

28. In the event, he served just over a year in prison in England, being released with the other Irish felons in June 1917.

29. MacNeill Papers. He quite enjoyed this work, and became good at it. 'There were possibly several hearth-rugs woven by my hands that since then have been under the feet of various government officials in England when they were warming the backs of their legs at the office fire,' he went on.

30. Pronounced 'Evleen'. This is an Irish form of Eileen. Four of the Moore children bore the same Christian names as their cousins the MacNeills. The naming of children still seemed to be set in a traditional mould.
31. 'Brian is the first member of the family I remember as a baby.' Letter from Eibhlin Darbyshire to P.C.
32. Dorothy Macardle, *The Irish Republic*. Victor Gollancz, London, 1937.
33. Ibid.
34. John Hewitt, *Kites in Spring*. Blackstaff, Belfast, 1980.
35. *The Irish Republic*, op. cit.
36. *Eoin MacNeill*, op. cit.
37. It's indicative both of the confusions of the time, and of Brian Moore's indifference to the ins and outs of Irish politics, that he has claimed his cousin Brian MacNeill was killed in the Troubles, 'shot by de Valera's people, because he was on the other side'. He was, of course, fighting on the same side as de Valera, the republican side.

3. A House of Children

1. Eibhlin Darbyshire to P.C.
2. His older brother Seamus had gone straight into the preparatory school attached to St Malachy's College; but, although there was only eighteen months between them, it was decided to send Brian to a different school.
3. Unlike his brother Seamus who can recall their grandmother Ellen O'Rawe (d. 1924), who intrigued him by having been born as long ago as 1836, 'before Victoria came to the throne'.
4. Culminating in the Act of 1908, with the establishment by Royal Charter of the National University (Dublin, Cork and Galway). Queen's in Belfast became a university in its own right.
5. When it came to the naming of characters, especially Irish characters, Brian Moore appropriated many names belonging to family connections and acquaintances.
6. A seaside resort on the north coast.
7. Seamus Moore to P.C.
8. Dr James B. Moore, who was 'Brian' to his sisters.
9. Eibhlin Darbyshire to P.C.
10. This was long before the days of political correctness. Two kinds of Catholic prejudice are indicated here: first, the association of tight-fistedness with Jewishness – and Brian Moore had a slightly Jewish look about him – and second the assumption that the black people of Africa were in need of conversion and 'civilising' by Catholic missionaries, into whose coffers the contents of the appallingly named 'Black Baby Fund' went.
11. B.M., 'A Vocation'. *Tamarack Review*, Autumn 1956: 18–22.

12. B.M., 'Going Home'. *Independent on Sunday*, 7 February 1999.
13. B.M., 'Bloody Ulster', *Atlantic Monthly*, September 1970.
14. Ibid.
15. Sam Hanna Bell, *Erin's Orange Lily*. Dobson, London, 1956.
16. *Kites in Spring*, op. cit.
17. Mrs Peggy Igoe to P.C.
18. She was born in 1863.
19. B.M. gave this aunt's name as both Annie and Martha. It is possible that he conflated two Donegal relatives.
20. B.M., 'Donegal', *Thirty-Two Counties*. Secker & Warburg, London, 1989.
21. He tended to associate this with a knowledge of Irish, but it seems clear that Eileen Moore was not a native speaker. Irish-speaking districts weren't far from the area where she grew up – at Gortahork, for example, the Bloody Foreland and throughout the Rosses – but outside these dwindling communities, the language even of subsistence farmers was English.
22. 'Donegal', op. cit.
23. He was a son of Mary O'Rawe and the one-time grocer's clerk James McAllister.
24. B.M. specified this number.
25. She was made very welcome there, as were all the children's schoolfriends. Mrs Aimie Stammers to P.C.
26. Colonel Niall MacNeill, 'the head of the Irish Ordnance Survey', according to Brian Moore, lived in the Ordnance Survey headquarters, 'a beautiful old mansion in Phoenix Park where they did all the maps'.
27. B.M., 'St Malachy's Alumnus'. *TLS*, 31 July 1981.
28. It wasn't declared a republic until 1949.
29. Gush, flattery.

4. St Malachy's Alumnus

1. The title of B.M.'s *TLS* review of Michael Tierney's biography of Eoin MacNeill, op. cit.
2. B.M. in interview with Tom Adair. *Linen Hall Review*, Winter 1985.
3. 'Going Home', op. cit.
4. The two eldest girls, Eibhlin and Grainne, started off like Brian at a kindergarten run by Mercy Sisters, but soon transferred to Newington.
5. Eibhlin Darbyshire to P.C.
6. Whose children were, of course, all fluent Irish-speakers.
7. In later life, Brian regretted not being able to speak Irish.
8. Seamus Moore to P.C.
9. Eilis Moore (Sister Anne) to P.C.
10. For example, Cardinal McRory, Dr Mageean and Dr Mulhern, Bishop of Dromore.

11. 'The Centenary Celebrations – Our Day' by Cahal Daly, Senior A Class, St Malachy's College. *The Collegian*, 1933.

12. 'Brian was different from the rest of the family – always did his own thing.' Niall Dempsey to P.C.

13. In later life, he became a good table-tennis player, and enjoyed watching motor racing and horse racing. Like his father though, he was indifferent to other games, such as football.

14. There is evidence from his contemporaries to suggest that he's painting too black a picture here.

15. Niall Dempsey to P.C.

16. Rory Casement to P.C.

17. Like many people associated with Brian at this time, he later became a successful doctor.

18. In Thomas Kinsella and John Montague (eds), *The Dolmen Miscellany of Irish Writing*. Dolmen Press, Dublin, 1962.

19. Calgary 31.1.5.24a.

20. The writer must have seen the American reviews, since it wasn't published in England until the following year.

21. Reported in a letter from Seamus Moore to B.M., 11 March 1957. Calgary 31.1.5.7a.

22. In fact, as any reasonably attentive reader will understand, it's the novel's central character who hasn't outgrown adolescence.

23. Other reports bear out this view. The Ballymena solicitor and local historian Jack McCann (1916–93), for example, recalled in an article: 'My parents decided that I was not applying myself to my studies and they sent me to board in St Malachy's College, Belfast. As a result none of our eight children has gone to boarding-school. Belfast's Crumlin Road Prison overlooked the College's playing fields and I was soon to learn that it was rod-of-iron rule for the inmates of both institutions.' 'Childhood in Ballymena'. *Further Articles on Ballymena and District*, Mid-Antrim Historical Group, 1991.

24. B.M. in Antonia Fraser (ed), *The Pleasure of Reading*. Bloomsbury, London, 1992.

25. Michael McLaverty, *Call My Brother Back*. Longmans & Co, London, 1939.

26. Ibid.

27. McLaverty's novels after this date are pervaded by a terrible Catholic piety and triteness.

28. 'People were always trying to hide their poverty and they were exposing it. They always came after twelve o'clock Mass and the world and their wives saw them.' Anne Boyle, quoted in Ronnie Munck and Bill Rolston, *Belfast in the Thirties*. Blackstaff, Belfast, 1987.

29. 'Going Home', op. cit.

30. *The Feast of Lupercal*.

31. *The Emperor of Ice Cream*.

32. For example, the Outdoor Relief Riots of October 1932.
33. It was recreated in *Fergus*.
34. Seamus Moore to P.C.
35. Boys' weekly papers published by the Amalgamated Press.
36. Seamus Moore to P.C.
37. Jeanne Flood, *Brian Moore*, Irish Writers' Series. Bucknell University Press, Lewisburg, 1974.
38. Niall Dempsey to P.C.
39. *Call My Brother Back*, op. cit.
40. Rory Casement to P.C.

5. Bombs Over Belfast

1. Officer Training Corps.
2. There was no conscription in Northern Ireland.
3. This move, however, was not in keeping with his family's social position. Many ARP recruits came from the ranks of the unemployed, were complete no-hopers or in some sense unfitted for the responsibilities of ordinary professional life. His family must have felt keenly that it was a come-down for Brian to volunteer for such a lowly position.
4. Actually, his second cousin. Tom Graham's mother Kate McAllister was a cousin of Dr Moore's.
5. Virginia Woolf, 15 January 1941. Anne Olivier Bell and Andrew McNeillie (eds), *The Diary of Virginia Woolf*. Hogarth Press, London, 1977–84.
6. *The Pleasure of Reading*, op. cit.
7. This attitude is documented in Brian Barton's *The Blitz: Belfast in the War Years*. Blackstaff, Belfast, 1989, especially pp. 52–3.
8. Owned by Davy McLean.
9. If the two met at all at this period, it would have been only in passing – and in fact, once B.M. left Belfast, they didn't come face to face again for many years, and indeed only had one further encounter, when Niall Dempsey was practising as a doctor in Manchester and attended one of his old friend's book launches there.
10. B.M. remembered going into a bar with Teddy Millington, and seeing the actors Micheal MacLíammoír and Hilton Edwards, both of them wearing make-up; such things, he claimed laughingly, helped to broaden his outlook.
11. Terence Pim's father, incidentally, was a very peculiar and excruciatingly awful writer named Herbert Moore Pim, who deserves to be remembered for one pronouncement, *c.* 1916, when he referred to Belfast's Smithfield Market as 'a storehouse of splendours, for the loss of which nothing could compensate this city of success'. Smithfield was burned to the ground in 1974.

12. Eibhlin had had a year at Queen's University taking the general degree course, but transferred to the Civil Service when she failed to get through her first-year examinations. She had, subsequently, a long and distinguished career and was awarded an OBE in 1979.
13. Eilis Moore (Sister Anne) to P.C.
14. Michael Tierney had married Eoin MacNeill's eldest daughter Eibhlin.
15. See *The Blitz: Belfast in the War Years*, op. cit.
16. Ibid.
17. I'm indebted to Patrick Hicks for pointing this out.
18. Eilis McDowell to P.C. Eilis McDowell was the youngest daughter of Eoin MacNeill.
19. *Irish News*, 2 March 1942.
20. 'The Lonely Passion of Brian Moore', op. cit.
21. It is, in part, a description of the framed photograph of Dr Moore which Brian kept hanging on his study wall.
22. 'The Writer as Exile'. A talk delivered at York University, November 1976. *Canadian Journal of Irish Studies*, 2.2 (1976) 12.
23. Ibid.

6. Goodbye to All That

1. Interview with Hallvard Dahlie, *Tamarack Review*, Winter 1968.
2. These people, who'd been ship owners, or employed in shipping during peacetime, were exempted from conscription.
3. The city had been taken by the Fifth Army in October 1943.
4. Mussolini had fallen from power the previous July, thereby opening the way for an Allied invasion of Italy.
5. This was something of a strategic error. The Allied troops who landed at Anzio, far from helping the main Allied force to break through the German lines, actually had to be bailed out by the same force as they found themselves trapped in the beach-head.
6. *Black Lamb and Grey Falcon* (1941) by Rebecca West was an account of Yugoslav life and politics in the immediate pre-war era.
7. B.M., 'Roman Holiday'. Unpublished story, *c.* 1945.
8. The Moores had moved to this address in Belfast after the bombing of their Clifton Street house and their brief wartime sojourn at Camden Street.
9. Thanks to his bilingualism he was used as an interpreter and moved from camp to camp, and was not ill-treated.
10. It was one of the reasons why he remained a non-driver for such a long time. He didn't pass the driving test until the 1970s.
11. Even before he left Belfast he'd been something of a Francophile, partly due to his Aunt Maggie's influence. He told Hallvard Dahlie, op. cit., that he had a 'French cast of mind'.

12. B.M., Introduction to Ann Vachon (ed), *Poland 1946: the Photographs and Letters of John Vachon*. Washington DC, Smithsonian, xiii–xvii.
13. 'St Malachy's Alumnus', op. cit.
14. It was reported to him years later that she had married a Swiss doctor and gone to live in Switzerland.
15. 'That was very painful, very difficult for me,' B.M. said. 'And I'm sure painful for her, because we were – we were very good friends.'
16. Her father was Professor of Economics at the University of Saskatchewan.
17. Introduction to *Poland 1946*, op. cit.
18. See R. Ford, *UNRRA in Europe, 1945–47*. UNRRA European Regional Office, London, 1947.
19. Introduction to *Poland 1946*, op. cit.
20. In her version of events, rival groups of Jewish citizens would try to ensure that others, not they, were transported to the death-camps; and, she claimed, there was even a Jewish police force working in cahoots with the Nazis. According to B.M., a 'sanitised version' of these claims formed the basis of John Hersey's novel *The Wall*.
21. His desire to learn the Russian language was tied up with his continuing socialist beliefs, though, as it happened, these were being undermined by certain contradictions he became aware of: for example, his moderate socialism seemed more of a threat to his Communist acquaintances than an out-and-out reactionary stance would have been.
22. He retained a strong, but not a detailed, recollection of this particular occasion in Stockholm.
23. She was capable, for example, of ordering an elaborate and expensive meal in a restaurant, and then, on a whim, refusing to eat a bite of it.
24. An uncompleted novel from the 1950s has a protagonist, clearly based on B.M., who returns to his family in Belfast after the war, and tries to persuade his sister to leave home with him.
25. He actually put in an application for employment to two oil companies, but – as he said – luckily he was passed over, and so escaped having to sign up for a five-year sojourn in the Middle East, and goodness knows what kind of a life after that.
26. 'The Writer as Exile', op. cit.

7. A City Unique in the World

1. 'The Writer as Exile', op. cit.
2. B.M., *Canada*. Time Inc., New York, 1963.
3. It's noticeable that he didn't mention the supposed articles for the Irish *Sunday Independent*.
4. His novel *Black Robe* drew on his memories of this bush camp.
5. B.M., 'A Fresh Look at Montreal'. *Holiday* magazine, September 1959.

6. Of course, in this article, B.M. was trying to entertain and please his readers, not necessarily to give a true account of his arrival in Montreal. At other times he has claimed that he and Art Bulmer went straight to Toronto when they left the construction camp, and that Montreal came later.

7. In the *Holiday* article, he makes her Scottish.

8. Brian Cahill, quoted in William Weintraub, *City Unique: Montreal Days and Nights in the 1940s and 50s*. McClelland & Stewart, Toronto, 1996.

9. Ibid.

10. Ibid.

11. William Weintraub to P.C.

12. He was fired for insubordination, after it became known that he'd called the editor of the *Montreal Gazette* 'a pig'.

13. William Weintraub, *Getting Started*. McClelland & Stewart, Toronto, 2001.

14. This is how he put it to friends who included Bill Weintraub and – later – the publisher Diana Athill.

15. Mavis Gallant was writing from Paris to Bill Weintraub, who was then in Geneva; she seems to have moved the date of the wedding forward by a couple of weeks. Quoted in *Getting Started*, op. cit.

16. *Getting Started*, op. cit.

17. Ibid.

18. B.M. used his ex-father-in-law, Frank Scully, as the model for the father in *I Am Mary Dunne*.

19. See *Getting Started*, op. cit.

20. Ibid.

21. Unlike those deluded individuals who have only to read an apparantly unlaboured piece of fiction to think they can equal it themselves, B.M. was perfectly correct in his literary assumptions.

22. B.M. to W.W., April 1951.

23. *This Gun for Gloria*. Gold Medal Books, New York, 1956.

24. 'Gold Medal' was a detective/adventure subsidiary of Fawcett who became B.M.'s American publishers with his third – pseudonymous – commercial thriller.

25. B.M. suffered all his life over the question of whether he was 'Brian' pronounced in the ordinary way, or the Irish 'Bree-an', as he was known by his family. 'Bree-an' eventually took over completely – though many Belfast people consider it pretentious – but during the middle part of his life he was often called simply Brian by friends such as Mordecai Richler.

26. The editor-in-chief of the Fawcett World Library at this time was Fred Kerner.

27. The first draft of the Judith Hearne story exists in a notebook dating from this year, under the title 'Sunday Visitor'.

28. B.M., 'Sunday Visitor'.
29. Borrowed from the parents of his friend Alex Cherney. The rent was shared between the Moores and a number of Montreal friends.
30. 'The Writer as Exile', op. cit.
31. *Judith Hearne*.
32. Montreal had become an important centre of medical research in the years following the Second World War.
33. The much later 'metaphysical thriller', *Cold Heaven*, draws heavily on the experience; and on a considerably more mundane level the penultimate potboiler, *Intent to Kill*, uses the hospital setting to striking effect.
34. For example, 'It's almost as though fate had cast me in the perfect role of the outsider without my even being aware of it. It starts with this [though I am a Catholic] I have a Protestant name . . .' Quoted in Hallvard Dahlie, *Brian Moore*. Copp Clark, Toronto, 1969.
35. This was the heading applied to a series in *Holiday* magazine for which B.M. was interviewed in 1958.

8. Creative Montrealers

1. Mordecai Richler.
2. By Caesarean section. Jacqueline Moore was advised not to have any more children.
3. He waited until he was over forty to write his *Bildungsroman, The Emperor of Ice Cream*.
4. There is a novel by Patrick Hamilton, *The Slaves of Solitude* (1947), which evokes a kind of boarding-house life not dissimilar to Miss Hearne's, and has a heroine similarly misled; however, there's a touch of frumpishness about Hamilton's prose, and in fact the two novels proceed along entirely different lines. It's unlikely that B.M. would have read the Hamilton novel.
5. B.M., 'Old Father, Old Artificer'. *Irish University Review* 12:1 (1982), 13–14.
6. Actually, B.M. was never a natural inheritor of the modernist mantle; his talents lay more in the line of straightforward storytelling, with an edge. However, Joyce loomed so large at the time in the field of Irish letters, that an understandable 'anxiety of influence' was a factor in the literary approach of any would-be Irish novelist worth his salt.
7. 'The Writer as Exile', op. cit.
8. Richard T. Bray, 'A Conversation with Brian Moore'. *The Critic*, XXXV: 1, Fall 1976, 46.
9. Eilis McDowell to P.C.
10. Including his sister Una, who wrote to him, 'I must hand it to you . . . if Bernard is yourself, you sure had courage.'
11. John Vachon, for instance, pointed out to him that the landlady, Mrs

Rice, was far too old to be having periods, or even pretending to have them; and this detail does not appear in the published work.

12. Wing, who was disabled – 'a big man – he looked wonderful sitting behind his desk, but then he would go off to lunch on crutches' – became B.M.'s agent with his third thriller, and the two always remained on cordial terms.

13. 'Fitz' – i.e. Gerald Fitzgerald, the *Gazette* columnist who introduced B.M. to Harry Larkin.

14. The incident later contributed to the plot of *An Answer From Limbo*.

15. B.M. to W.W., March 1954.

16. Diana Athill of André Deutsch remembers him declaring firmly, 'I am very fond of my wife,' the first time they met.

17. B.M. to W.W., 18 May 1954.

18. Putnam & Sons Ltd to Willis Kingsley Wing, May 1954.

19. Michael Horniman to B.M., May 1954.

20. Best known for his autobiographical work, *Cider with Rosie* (1958).

21. As reported by Diana Athill in a letter to Mordecai Richler, June 1954.

22. Ibid.

23. B.M. to André Deutsch, 16 June 1954. Calgary 31.1.1.

24. There were twelve rejections in all.

25. Seymour Lawrence had earlier rejected a couple of B.M.'s stories, but expressed an interest in seeing any full-length work he might go on to write.

26. Willis Kingsley Wing to B.M., 25 September 1955. Calgary 31.1.1.86.

27. B.M. to W.W. – who was once again living and working abroad – 25 September 1955.

28. This was the phrase used by John Leggett of Houghton Mifflin in turning down the novel.

29. Calgary 31.1.3.

30. Archbishop McQuaid, the ruler of Catholic Dublin between 1940 and 1973, told Michael Tierney: 'I know that boy's connected to your family. It's ridiculous that he would write this sort of book.' Quoted in Julia Carlson, *Banned in Ireland*. Routledge, London, 1990.

31. 'A very bad critic, by the way,' B.M. said; he told Bill Weintraub he thought there must be something wrong with the book if that 'crap artist' liked it.

32. B.M. installed his character in the house in Camden Street, Belfast, which his family had occupied after the 1941 Blitz had damaged their Clifton Street home.

33. B.M. to W.W., 21 November 1955.

34. Mordecai Richler to P.C.

35. B.M. to W.W., 8 April 1956.

36. Sean Moore to P.C.

37. Sean Moore went on to enjoy a distinguished medical career, becoming a Professor of Pathology at McGill.

38. Michael Moore to P.C.
39. B.M. to Mordecai Richler, 21 July 1954. Calgary 36.9.19.
40. W.W. to B.M., 1955.
41. Mordecai Richler to P.C.

9. Litry Gossip

1. B.M. to W.W., 19 February 1956.
2. W.W. to B.M., 1956.
3. Calgary 31.1.5.18.
4. B.M. to Una Maguire, November 1957.
5. Graham Greene to B.M., January 1966. Calgary 31.2.4.17.
6. This probably refers to the first meeting between the two novelists in Montreal when Greene was halfway through *Judith Hearne* and told B.M. that he liked it very much. B.M. reciprocated by stating how much he liked *The Heart of the Matter*, whereupon the older novelist groaned, 'Oh God, it's quite my unfavourite book.' A 'hell of a lot of doubles' were imbibed on this occasion.
7. B.M. to W.W., 3 March 1956.
8. Ibid.
9. Ibid.
10. B.M. to W.W., March 1956.
11. B.M. to W.W., 7 September 1956. Bill Weintraub was well aware that Brian actually carried out meticulous research for his thrillers, surrounding himself with street maps, directories and reference books to bolster the sense of authenticity in relation to places he didn't know well.
12. B.M to W.W., January 1957.
13. Seymour Lawrence to B.M., 19 September 1956. Calgary 31.1.4.7a.
14. Mordecai Richler to B.M., 28 December 1956. Calgary 31.1.4.39.
15. Ibid.
16. Diana Athill to B.M., 14 January 1957. Calgary 31.1.4.43.
17. B.M. to Diana Athill, 10 February 1957. Calgary 31.1.4.49.
18. B.M. to Seymour Lawrence, 31 October 1956. Calgary 31.1.4.22a.
19. Forrest Reid (1875–1947). When this Belfast author mentions the city in his novels, it's with a certain amount of statutory revulsion, complete with standard epithets: 'greasy pavements', 'mean drab houses', 'unattractive shops'.
20. B.M. to Hallvard Dahlie, op. cit. It was also to Hallvard Dahlie that B.M. first quoted the remark relayed to him, about 'biting the hand that birched him'.
21. B.M. to Seymour Lawrence, 31 October 1956. Calgary 31.1.4.22a.
22. 'The Lonely Passion of Brian Moore', op. cit.
23. B.M. to W.W. Quoted in *Getting Started*, op. cit.
24. Ibid.

25. Ibid.
26. B.M. to W.W., 2 January 1957.
27. Ibid.
28. Diana Athill to P.C.
29. Paid for by B.M., who also sent regular sums of money to his mother in Belfast.
30. Sean Moore to P.C.
31. Eilis Moore (Sister Anne) to P.C.
32. 'The Lonely Passion of Brian Moore', op. cit.
33. B.M., letter to Richard Parker. Calgary 49.4.85.2e.
34. This was a way of repaying the debt occasioned when Mordecai Richler had recommended *Judith Hearne* to Deutsch.
35. Diana Athill to B.M., 1958.

10. 'An Alien Among Aliens During My New York Time'

1. Derek Mahon, 'America Deserta'. In *The Yellow Book* (1997).
2. Jacqueline Moore to William Weintraub, October 1959.
3. See Interview with Hallvard Dahlie, *Tamarack Review*, op. cit.
4. Jack Ludwig, 'A Mirror of Moore'. *Canadian Literature*, 7, Winter 1961.
5. B.M. to W.W., December 1959.
6. He gradually got back to drinking the odd whisky, which he would have along with a glass of milk. The milk kept the ulcer happy, he joked, while the whisky kept him happy.
7. B.M. to W.W., February 1960.
8. B.M. to W.W., January 1960.
9. Stanley Price to P.C.
10. B.M. recommended to his friend that he should spend at least an hour a day on creative writing, and backed up this advice with an increasingly laconic series of postcards, the last of which read simply, 'ONE HOUR.' Partly as a result of this, William Weintraub's novel *Why Rock the Boat?* was published in 1961.
11. He was apt to be cross if his advice wasn't taken.
12. Stanley Price is the author of a number of satirical novels published in the 1960s and 1970s, including *Me For Posterity*; he is also a West End playwright and documentary filmmaker.
13. Stanley Price to P.C.
14. See Maurice Harmon, *Sean O'Faolain – A Life*. Constable, London, 1994.
15. 'When the soul of a man is born in this country, there are nets flung at it to keep it back from flight. You talk to me of nationality, language, religion. I shall try to fly by these nets.' James Joyce, *Portrait of the Artist as a Young Man*. London, 1916.
16. Stanley Price to P.C.

17. Twenty, if you count the documentary novel *The Revolution Script*.
18. The thought, not unreasonably, had occurred to Mordecai Richler that Max Bronstein was a caricature of himself; but B.M., though he might have taken more care to avoid offending his friend, had no real target in mind when he created this character. A letter to B.M. from Mordecai Richler (Calgary 31.2.2.4b) refers to an occasion when Jackie Moore 'got upset' about this matter, and Mordecai assures B.M. that he can see only one point of resemblance between himself and Max – the fact that he'd had a novel published first. While praising *Limbo* ('full of admiration . . . solid . . . at times moving') he goes on to say he finds the Tierney character 'so disagreeable, such a bastard, so self-absorbed' that it's impossible to feel any sympathy for him or his predicament – which may be a way of retaliating, under the guise of discussing a work of fiction, for any supposed slight.
19. He falls off a slide in a playground and cuts his head. A similar accident had befallen Michael Moore in October 1959, when he fell off a swing and had to have his head X-rayed.
20. 'Limbo is the modern condition,' he noted. Calgary 31.17.2.
21. B.M. to W.W., 11 August 1960.
22. Ibid.
23. 'The People of Belfast', which didn't go down too well in that city, was eventually published by *Holiday* magazine in February 1964.
24. B.M. to W.W., 25 September 1961.
25. He'd been educated at Downside, spoke with a strikingly upper-class accent, and was – according to B.M. – 'something of a star-chaser, but in the nicest possible way'. One of his protégées was the young Edna O'Brien, whom B.M. met around this time.
26. B.M. to W.W., 25 September 1961.
27. B.M. to W.W., October 1961.
28. Karl Miller, *Rebecca's Vest*. Hamish Hamilton, London, 1993.
29. B.M. to W.W., October 1961.
30. Brian Inglis (1916–91), born in Malahide, Co. Dublin, was an author and journalist, first with the *Irish Times* and later with the London *Spectator*. His autobiography, *West Briton*, was published in 1966.
31. *Spectator*, September 1961.
32. Author of the remarkable *Balkan* and *Levant* trilogies (1960–80). Her reputation blossomed for a time after 1987 when the BBC dramatised all six novels under the title *Fortunes of War* – but by then, unfortunately, she was dead. Though she was born in Portsmouth, Olivia Manning had family connections with Bangor in Northern Ireland, and this may have exacerbated her – imagined – rivalry with B.M. He was adamant that she 'absolutely hated' him, a fact he referred to in a ruefully amused tone.
33. Ronald Bryden at the time was principal drama critic for the *Observer*.
34. Another photograph of B.M. taken by Stanley Price appeared on the

back flap of the dust-jacket for the Deutsch edition of *An Answer From Limbo*.

35. 'An intensely boring piece of nonsense,' B.M. described it.
36. Doris Lessing, *Walking in the Shade*. HarperCollins, London, 1997.
37. B.M. to W.W., 14 February 1962.
38. B.M. to W.W., 27 April 1962.
39. Stanley Price to P.C.
40. Ibid.

11. Brian's Jean

1. B.M. to W.W., 30 November 1962.
2. Including Margaret Atwood and Mordecai Richler.
3. B.M. to W.W., 30 November 1962.
4. The book begins with a description of a similar flight.
5. B.M. to W.W., March 1964.
6. B.M. to Rory Fitzpatrick. Calgary 31.2.3.
7. With the broadcaster Roisin McAuley. BBC Northern Ireland, 1998.
8. B.M. to W.W., 16 September 1963.
9. Sir John Heggate had sent Elizabeth Bowen copies of *Judith Hearne* and *Lupercal*, and she records the 'tremendous pleasure' they gave her. Calgary 31.1.13.2.
10. The papers were signed on 10 July 1964.
11. The new publishers had no rights in connection with previous novels, and the old publisher had no incentive to keep them in print.
12. 'I was the motivating force,' B.M. said. 'I'd told myself, this is my life; and here is my one chance to do something to change it for the better. So I did.'
13. Diana Athill to P.C.
14. Diana Athill, *Stet*. Granta, London, 2000.
15. Ibid.
16. Diana Athill to P.C.
17. *Stet*, op. cit.
18. Jean Moore to P.C.
19. Including Sean Moore in Montreal – who, however, was not receptive to criticisms of his brother.
20. B.M. to W.W., 16 December 1964.
21. Guy Burgess and Donald Maclean, 'the missing diplomats', were Soviet agents who defected to Moscow in May 1951.
22. B.M. to W.W., 17 April 1965.
23. Ibid.
24. Ibid.
25. Ibid.
26. B.M. to W.W., 24 June 1965.
27. B.M. to W.W., 20 March 1965.

28. B.M. to W.W., 17 March 1967.
29. Ibid.
30. *Getting Started*, op. cit.
31. Ibid.
32. *Stet*, op. cit.
33. B.M. to W.W., 17 April 1968.
34. Diana Athill to B.M., 3 June 1968. Calgary 31.2.6.1.
35. B.M. to W.W., 9 December 1967.
36. B.M. to Una Maguire, 1 February 1968.
37. Michael Shelden, 'Life Without the Lions'. *Daily Telegraph*, 13 December 1997.
38. B.M. to Una Maguire, 14 June 1969.
39. B.M. to Una Maguire, 18 November 1967.
40. B.M. to W.W., 5 December 1967.

12. Quiet Days in Malibu

1. This title is borrowed from Joan Didion's essay in *The White Album*. Simon & Schuster, New York, 1979.
2. B.M. to W.W., 23 April 1970.
3. B.M. to W.W., February 1969.
4. A letter from Peter Crookston in November 1967 refers to 'scary reports' in Los Angeles newspapers, and expresses the hope that the Moores' house has not been seriously affected by the current brush fires – which it wasn't. Calgary 31.4.5.8a.
5. *The White Album*, op. cit.
6. See Robert Sullivan, *A Matter of Faith: The Fiction of Brian Moore*. Greenwood Press, Westport, Connecticut, 1996, pp. 110–17.
7. Christopher Ricks, *New Statesman*, 18 February 1966.
8. B.M. to W.W., 26 February 1966.
9. B.M. to Philip French, 13 February 1966.
10. B.M. to W.W. [undated] 1969.
11. B.M. to W.W., 26 November 1967.
12. Ibid.
13. B.M. to Una Maguire, 18 November 1967.
14. This study, brief but perceptive, claimed B.M. as a Canadian writer – his, the author said, is 'one of the truly distinctive voices in Canadian fiction' – even though he was only 'a bird of passage'. *Brian Moore*, op. cit.
15. Evelyn Waugh, *The Ordeal of Gilbert Pinfold*. Chapman & Hall, London, 1952.
16. The Wallace Stevens epigraph to the novel refers to the 'outlandish' as 'another day/of the week, queerer than Sunday . . .'
17. B.M. was waiting for his American agent Perry Knowlton (Willis Kingsley Wing's successor) to break the news to Viking that he was changing publishers.

18. B.M. to W.W., 11 February 1970.
19. Susan Hill, *New Statesman*, 28 March 1971.
20. B.M. to W.W., 28 October 1970.
21. For example, Jo O'Donoghue, in *Brian Moore: A Critical Study*. Gill & Macmillan, Dublin, 1990.
22. Calgary 31.3.1.83d.
23. B.M. to Perry Knowlton, 12 January 1971. Calgary 31.3.1.1a.
24. See *A Matter of Faith*, op. cit., p. 31.
25. *Fergus*.
26. 'Bloody Ulster', op. cit.
27. B.M. to Una Maguire, 3 February 1972.
28. B.M. to W.W., 27 August 1969.
29. 'Bloody Ulster', op. cit.
30. The *Sunday Times*, for example, ran a number of excerpts around the time of publication.
31. B.M. to W.W., 21 May 1970.
32. Huston was no longer available by the time the film came to be made.
33. *Bookseller*, 10 November 1972.
34. B.M. to W.W., November 1973.
35. A version of this verdict, by the Dublin *Sunday Press* critic (February 1972), was conveyed to Brian in a letter from the Jesuit priest Father Michael Paul Gallagher, with whom he had become friendly.
36. B.M. to W.W., 7 June 1971.
37. Ibid.

13. Alarms and Excursions

1. B.M. to W.W., 28 September 1970.
2. B.M. to W.W., 26 January 1971.
3. Seamus Heaney to B.M., 30 October 1980. Calgary 49.4.22.
4. Louis MacNeice, 'The Strand', *Collected Poems*. Faber, London, 1948.
5. They'd been in contact since 1962, when Montague published B.M.'s 'Preliminary Pages for a Work of Revenge' in the *Dolmen Miscellany of Irish Writing*, op. cit.
6. B.M. to Brian Friel, 10 October 1971. Calgary 31.1.2.84a.
7. B.M. to Morton Leavy, 30 July 1972. Calgary 31.3.2.10a.
8. B.M. to Tom Maschler, 24 July 1972. Calgary 31.5.4a.
9. The friendship even survived M.P. Gallagher's annoyance over the unsympathetic depiction of the priest in *Lies of Silence*, though this put it under some strain.
10. B.M. to W.W., September 1972.
11. B.M. to Una Maguire, 7 January 1973.
12. A remark that has often been misattributed.
13. B.M. to W.W., 18 February 1973.
14. Ibid.

15. B.M. to W.W., 20 March 1973.
16. Charles J. Hitch, President of UCLA, in his letter of 15 July 1974, inviting B.M. to take up the post.
17. B.M. to W.W., September 1973.
18. B.M. to W.W., November 1973.
19. B.M. to W.W., October 1974.
20. In the late 1990s, he spent a couple of summers 'house-sitting' for the Moores while they were in Nova Scotia.
21. Scott Bradfield to P.C.
22. Ibid.
23. B.M. to W.W., 26 November 1974.
24. B.M. to W.W., September 1973.
25. When her doctor broke the news to Jacqueline Moore that she had a tumour in her stomach, she immediately pressed him for details. What size was it, she wanted to know. With some reluctance, he came up with a comparison: about the size of a grapefruit. But that wasn't sufficient: 'Do you mean the sort of grapefruit where you get two for a dollar, or four for a dollar?' she persisted. This anecdote was recounted by her old friend Stanley Price as an instance of her resilience and unquenchable spirit.
26. During the last few months of her life he kept in touch with her by telephone.
27. She was cremated and her ashes scattered on the sea by her husband Frank Russell.
28. The fact that Michael Moore had turned out so well reflected considerable credit on his mother, Jacqueline Moore.
29. B.M. to W.W., 1973.
30. *Irish University Review*. Brian Moore Issue. Vol. 18 No. 1. Spring 1988.
31. Seamus Deane, 'The Real Thing: Brian Moore in Disneyland', ibid.
32. Philip French, 'Dream Machinery'. *Times Literary Supplement*, 17 October 1975.
33. B.M. to W.W., 16 June 1976.
34. The title was suggested by Aaron Asher.
35. Edna Longley, 'Brian Moore's Women'. *Fortnight*, Christmas 1981.
36. Michael Moore to B.M., 1 November 1976. Calgary 49.4.68.1.
37. B.M. to W.W., 17 May 1974.
38. V.S. Pritchett, *Midnight Oil*. Chatto & Windus, London, 1971.
39. B.M. to Una Maguire, 23 December 1975.
40. B.M. to W.W., 22 May 1976.
41. B.M. to W.W., May 1975.
42. B.M. to W.W., 9 November 1975.
43. B.M. to Una Maguire, 7 February 1975.
44. B.M. to W.W., 12 August 1976.
45. Ibid.

46. Hermione Lee, 'Nomadic Life of Brian'. *Independent on Sunday*, 14 February 1993.
47. Sean O'Faolain to Jean Moore, 17 August 1977. Calgary 49.4.78.
48. Seamus Deane to B.M., 25 November 1977. Calgary 49.3.57.
49. Diana Athill to B.M., 2 September 1977. Calgary 49.3.12.1.
50. The first mention of this story occurs in June 1976.
51. James Clarence Mangan, 'The Nameless One'. B.M.'s literary ancestor, James Joyce, read a paper on Mangan to the Dublin University Literary and Historical Society in 1902.
52. Roy Foster, 'More *Maudit* than Most'. *Times Literary Supplement*, 16 November 1979.
53. Christopher Ricks, 'A Novel Without a Hero'. *London Review of Books*, 6 December 1979.
54. Tom Rosenthal to B.M., 28 November 1979.

14. A Sixty-year-old Smiling Public Man

1. B.M. had adapted this for the stage himself. It was fairly successful, enjoying a three-week run.
2. *The Temptation of Eileen Hughes*. BBC2, Easter Sunday, 1988.
3. Christopher Murray, Introduction. *Irish University Review*. Brian Moore Issue, op. cit.
4. Sixty-five-year-old, actually. The presentation took place on 7 July 1987.
5. One of the signatories of the 1916 Proclamation. His poem, 'I See His Blood Upon the Rose', would have been known to B.M., as to all Catholic schoolchildren.
6. Michael Wood, 'God's Role in the Novel'. *The Times*, 30 October 1983.
7. There's a minuscule part in the novel for a Dr Bernard Mara, whose name directs us back to Brian Moore in a previous incarnation.
8. Doubleday published *Lies of Silence* and *No Other Life*, but considerably reduced the advance offered for B.M.'s next novel when these failed to sell as well as they'd hoped. So he went back to Dutton – but remained on very friendly terms with Nan Talese, whom he greatly admired.
9. 'Nomadic Life of Brian', op. cit.
10. 'Black Robes' was the name the Indians applied to the Jesuit missionaries.
11. B.M., Author's Note to *Black Robe*.
12. Tom Maschler, in 'The Lonely Passion of Brian Moore', op. cit.
13. Graham Greene, *Ways of Escape*. Lester & Orpen Dennys, Toronto, 1980.
14. At one point Pat O'Connor was going to direct a film of *The Mangan Inheritance*, but for various technical reasons this project was not realised.

15. Quoted in 'Nomadic Life of Brian', op. cit.
16. Rumour had it that the cast and crew were reluctant to expose themselves to the dangers of war-torn Belfast.
17. It was won by Penelope Lively's *Moon Tiger*.
18. £130,000 for British rights alone.
19. Liz Calder found it touching that B.M. was constantly in a state of anxiety lest Bloomsbury should fail to recoup its advance.
20. Hermione Lee, 'Third Ear'. BBC Radio 3, 24 April 1990.
21. 'I shall acquire an attitude not yours,' MacNeice had written in his poem 'Valediction', 'And become as one of your holiday visitors.'
22. 'Third Ear', op. cit.
23. Dillon's dilemma is akin to the one experienced by Benedict Kiely's protagonist in *Proxopera* (1977), another out-and-out condemnation of terrorist expedients.
24. 'Third Ear', op. cit.
25. When Graham Greene died a year later, B.M. was asked to contribute obituary pieces to the *Guardian*, the *Independent* and the *Sunday Review*.
26. This didn't come to anything, but an earlier novel, *Cold Heaven*, was filmed, not very satisfactorily, by Nicholas Roeg and released in 1992, without B.M.'s co-operation as scriptwriter.
27. When they were in New York, the Moores would often borrow the Greenwich Village 'state-of-the-art mansion' (as the author and journalist Penny Perrick described it) belonging to their friends Calvin and Alice Trillin.
28. William Trevor, 'Lives of the Saints'. *New York Review of Books*, 21 October 1993.

15. A Speck on the Wall

1. Joe O'Connor, *Sunday Tribune Magazine*, 1 October 1995.
2. Including Hermione Lee and her husband John Barnard.
3. 'Life Without the Lions', op. cit.
4. B.M., fax to Florence Whyte, 18 July 1995.
5. John Gross, 'Marked Man'. *New York Review of Books*, 3 October 1996.
6. Hermione Lee to B.M., 26 August 1997.
7. Joyce Carol Oates, 'A Longing for Home'. *TLS*, 12 September 1997.
8. Thomas Kilroy, 'Belfast Was Moore's Moscow of the Mind'. *Sunday Times Magazine*, 17 January 1999.
9. *Irish News*, 12 January 1999.
10. 'The People of Belfast', op. cit.
11. 'An Ulsterman's Diary'. *Belfast Telegraph*, 30 January 1964.
12. Seamus Moore to P.C.

13. 'Nomadic Life of Brian', op. cit.
14. An entry in his work notebook for December 1998 reads: 'R. to 170' – that is, 170 pages of the Rimbaud novel had been written.
15. Hermione Lee, Interview with B.M. BBC Radio 3, October 1998.
16. Reported in the *Irish News*, 25 January 1999.
17. There is more truth in the view of Thomas Kilroy that B.M. 'writes about the Church because it serves his essentially secular purpose'. 'Belfast Was Moore's Moscow of the Mind', op. cit.
18. *Daily Telegraph*, 12 January 1999.
19. Elizabeth Bowen, Preface to *Selected Stories of Elizabeth Bowen*. Vintage Books, Inc, New York, 1959.
20. Sean Moore died in June 2001.
21. Philip Larkin, 'Going', *The Less Deceived*. Faber, London, 1955.
22. B.M., 'Going Home', op. cit. This short article, originally written some years previously for *Granta* magazine, got into print in the end as B.M.'s final word on the piece of ground he envisaged as his final resting place.

INDEX

A NOTE ON THE AUTHOR

Patricia Craig is an acclaimed anthologist and critic, whose works include the *Oxford Books of Detective Stories, Modern Women's Stories, Travel Stories* and *Ireland: The Belfast Anthology*; *Elizabeth Bowen* (in the Penguin 'Lives of Modern Women' Series); and (with Mary Cadogan) *You're a Brick, Angela! A New Look at Girls' Fiction 1839–1975*. A regular contributor to the *TLS* and the *Independent*, she was born in Belfast, lived in London for many years, and now lives in Antrim, Northern Ireland.

A NOTE ON THE TYPE

The text of this book is set in Linotype Sabon, named after the type founder, Jacques Sabon. It was designed by Jan Tschichold and jointly developed by Linotype, Monotype and Stempel, in response to a need for a typeface to be available in identical form for mechanical hot metal composition and hand composition using foundry type.

Tschichold based his design for Sabon roman on a fount engraved by Garamond, and Sabon italic on a fount by Granjon. It was first used in 1966 and has proved an enduring modern classic.